LA PETITE PHILOSOPHIE

Anglo-Norman Text Society
No. 1

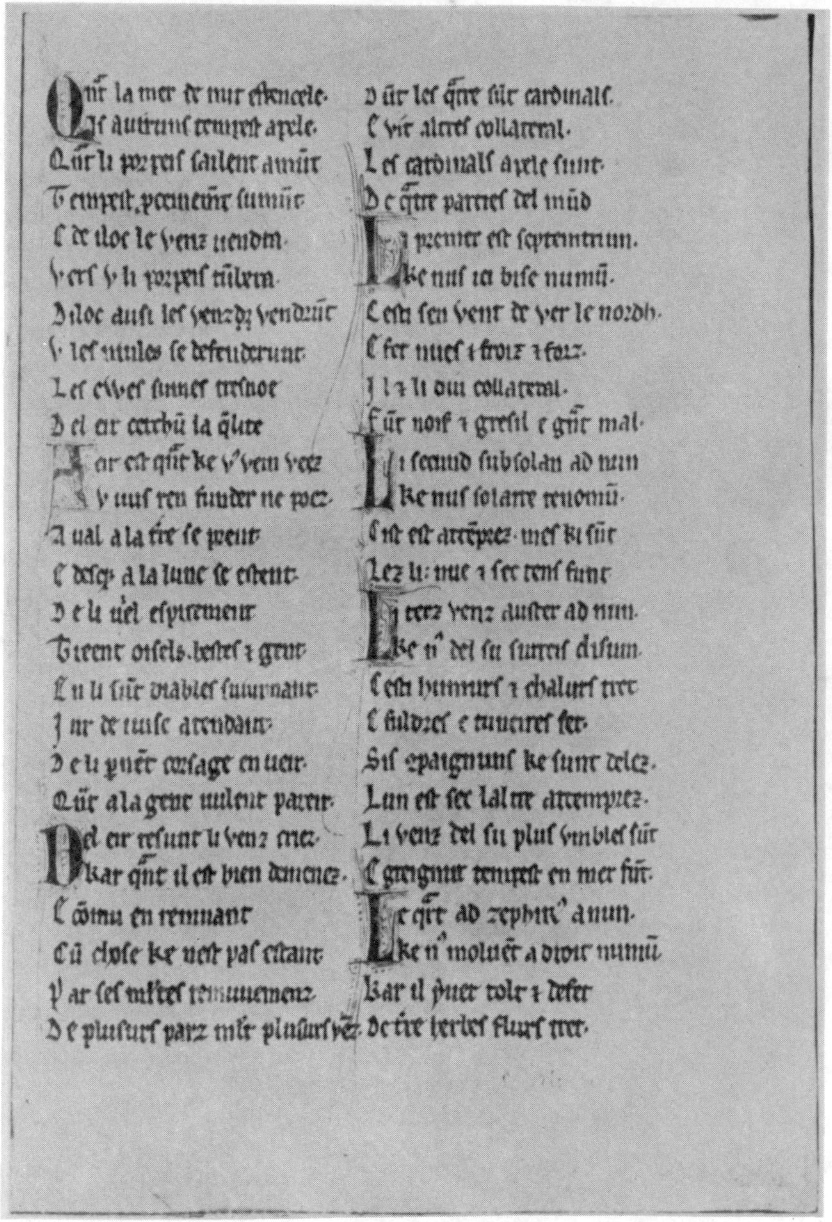

MS. Brit. Mus. Add. 45103, fol. 201r//MS. *P*, ll. 1655-1706.

Frontispiece

ANGLO-NORMAN TEXTS — I

La Petite Philosophie

AN ANGLO-NORMAN POEM OF THE THIRTEENTH CENTURY

TEXT WITH INTRODUCTION,
NOTES AND GLOSSARY

Edited by

WILLIAM HILLIARD TRETHEWEY, Ph.D.

Assistant Professor of French
Victoria College, University of Toronto
Toronto, Canada

OXFORD

Published for the ANGLO-NORMAN TEXT SOCIETY
by BASIL BLACKWELL

1939

JOHNSON REPRINT CORPORATION   JOHNSON REPRINT COMPANY LTD.
111 Fifth Avenue, New York, N.Y, 10003   Berkeley Square House, London, W.1

TO MY WIFE

DELLA MAY TRETHEWEY

First reprinting, 1967, Johnson Reprint Corporation
Printed in the United States of America

PREFACE

THE *Petite Philosophie* is a didactic poem written in England during the early thirteenth century. It belongs to that body of informative literature characteristic of the full maturity of mediaeval culture in England and France. The purpose of this literature was to render accessible to those who could not read Latin, the mass of information hitherto available in that language only. In large measure it consisted of translations, adaptations, and compilations made from Latin sources. For a literature which aimed at the dissemination of knowledge the encyclopaedic form naturally commended itself. The popularity of this type in mediaeval Latin writing needs no illustration. In French verse an excellent example of the compendium of practical information is afforded by the *Image du monde* of Gautier de Metz: in England, Pierre de Peckham composed his *Lumiere as Lais* to serve as a manual of instruction for the laity. The *Petite Philosophie*, though less imposing in bulk, is nevertheless of the same kith and kin, namely, a verse adaptation of a Latin original, the twelfth century *Imago mundi*, and a summary of those facts about geography, natural science and cosmography, with which an educated member of the thirteenth century society was supposed to be familiar.

The existence of the *Petite Philosophie* was first pointed out by Paul Meyer in *Romania* of 1879 in an article on the French manuscripts at Cambridge. In this and later articles he described five manuscripts at Oxford and Cambridge which contained this work in complete or fragmentary form. Meanwhile Koch had identified another fragment in a Vatican manuscript. Meyer indicated the source and nature of the poem, and published excerpts from the manuscripts. In his article in *Romania* of 1900 he remarked, '*La Petite Philosophie* mériterait d'être étudiée de près.' Despite Meyer's estimate, the *Petite Philosophie* has remained unedited, though not entirely unnoticed. Gode-

i

froy, for instance, made full use of Meyer's excerpts in his *Dictionnaire*, and likewise Tanquerey in his study on the Anglo-Norman verb. More recently Ch.–V. Langlois expressed his regret at not being able to include an analysis of this poem in his study on mediaeval French life and culture, inasmuch as no manuscript of it was available in France.

In March 1929 an additional manuscript of the *Petite Philosophie* came to light. It was offered for sale in London, and purchased by Boies Penrose II, Esq., of Nettlecombe, Combe, Somerset, England. The attention of Mr. Penrose had been drawn to the manuscript by Professor John Manly of the University of Chicago, at that time in England engaged in Chaucer research. After acquiring the manuscript Mr. Penrose generously accorded to Professor Manly permission to photostat it, and thus to make its contents available for study. During 1937 this manuscript was purchased from Mr. Penrose by Lord Wakefield, who presented it to the British Museum Library, where it is now catalogued as Additional Manuscript 45103.

This edition of the *Petite Philosophie* was undertaken in the autumn of 1932 at the suggestion of the late Professor T. Atkinson Jenkins of the University of Chicago, and submitted in December 1935 to the Department of Romance Languages and Literatures of that University as a doctoral dissertation. I wish to take this opportunity to express my appreciation of the counsel and inspiration I received from Professor Jenkins during his final year at Chicago, and even after his retirement from active work. I deeply regret that his untimely death left me to complete the task without his direction. It is also a pleasure to acknowledge my debt to Professor William A. Nitze, Head of the Department of Romance Languages in the same University, for his guidance and assistance, and to Professor John Manly of Chicago for permission to use his photostats and description of the manuscript.

Early in 1938 the *Petite Philosophie* was accepted for publication by the Anglo-Norman Text Society. To this end the manuscript of the dissertation has been revised and put into suitable form. I wish to express my gratitude to the Editorial Board of the society for making possible the publication of this edition, and especially to Professors M. K. Pope of Manchester University and A. Ewert of Oxford University, to whom I am heavily indebted for advice in the revision of the manuscript. Finally it is a pleasure to acknowledge the constant assistance throughout of my wife to whom this edition is dedicated and without whose many hours of labour it would still be far from completed.

W.H.T.

Victoria College,
    Toronto, Canada.

TABLE OF CONTENTS

INTRODUCTION

I. TITLE

THE title, *La Petite Philosophie*, is given in the rubrics of MSS *C* (*ici comence la petite philosophie*), and *V* (*ci comce la petite philosophie*). In line 246 the author himself gives the title in the form *La philosophie petite* (*PRCG*), or *Philosophie la petite* (*DV*). The position of the adjective is explained by the rhyme, the scribes knowing the poem as *La Petite Philosophie*. This title suggested to Paul Meyer that the work was based on the *De philosophia mundi libri quatuor* of William of Conches, commonly attributed to Honorius Augustodunensis,[1] and which has sometimes been entitled *Philosophia minor*.[2] Meyer soon discovered, however, that the real source was the *Imago mundi*, likewise erroneously attributed to Honorius.[3] Whether or not the author of *La Petite Philosophie* had in mind the *Philosophia minor*, his title is the exact equivalent of the Latin, both in form and in meaning. This use of *philosophia* differs sharply from the usual more or less restricted and technical sense of the word today. The term *philosophia* embraced in the Middle Ages all the liberal arts and sciences, and served as a synonym for advanced learning in general.[4] *Philosophia minor*, or *petite philosophie*, would therefore mean an elementary survey of general knowledge, a sort of manual of instruction reduced to

[1] See Paul Meyer on page 255 of his second article on 'Les Manuscrits français de Cambridge,' entitled 'Bibliothèque de l'Université,' *Romania* XV (1886) 236 ff.

[2] Published under this title by Migne in the volume containing Honorius' works, *Patrologia Latina* CLXXII 39 ff. Hauréau has proved, however, in his article in the *Nouvelle biographie générale* XXII 667, that the real author was William of Conches. This work has also been attributed to Bede under the title *Elementorum philosophiae libri quatuor;* see the *Opera dubia et spuria* of Bede *Pat. Lat.* XC, 1127 ff.

[3] See below under 'Source,' p. liii, n. 2.

[4] Philosophy is defined by William of Conches as follows: 'Philosophia est eorum quae sunt et non videntur et eorum quae sunt et videntur vera comprehensio' (Migne *Pat. Lat.* CLXXII 43). This definition is striking in its inclusiveness.

handy size, and written as far as possible in non-technical language, in order that it might be understood by those unprepared for the reading of more detailed and technical treatises.[1]

2. MANUSCRIPTS

P. British Museum Add. MS. 45103. This MS was presented to the library during 1937 by Lord Wakefield who acquired it from Boies Penrose II, Esq., of Nettlecombe, Combe, Somerset. Mr. Penrose purchased it in London in 1929 at the Lambarde sale, which family had possessed the MS continuously since 1582. In that year it was given to William Lambarde by Stephen Theobald of Seal near Seven Oaks as shown by the following entry at the top of fol. 1, 'Guilielmo Lambardo dedit Stephanus Taobauld 1582.' In 1929 Mr. J. P. Gilson, then Keeper of the Manuscripts in the Museum, identified the MS as one having been in the Library of Christ Church at Canterbury in the year 1508 by the fact that it figures in a list of books sent to the bindery in that year.[2] In an article published in the London *Times* of December 28th, 1937, Mr. R. Flower, Deputy Keeper of Manuscripts, has shown that our MS was in all probability among those bequeathed to Christ Church in 1331 by Prior Eastry, and further that it is identical in format, lay-out, and in handwriting for the most part, with a MS of Sir Robert Cotton's collection which contained a copy of a chronicle of Christ Church and which is known to been written in that monastery in 1275. Thus it is beyond doubt that the Wakefield MS was also written at Canterbury in or very shortly after 1275.

---

[1] The word *petit* is frequent in Anglo-Norman titles, for instance the *Petit Plet* of Chardri (J. Koch *Chardry's Josaphaz, Set Dormanz und Petit Plet* Heilbronn, 1879); the *Petit sermun* sometimes found in the MSS of William of Waddington's *Manuel des péchés* (cf. Paul Meyer in *Romania* XXIX [1900] p. 5); an abridgment of Wace's *Brut* entitled *Le Petit Brut* (cf. J. Vising *Anglo-Norman Language and Literature* [London, 1923] p. 74); and finally the *Petite sume des set pechés morteus* (cf. F.J. Tanquerey *L'Évolution du verbe en anglo-français* [Paris, 1915] p. xvi.

[2] See Montague Rhodes James *Ancient Libraries of Canterbury and Dover* (Cambridge, 1903). On page 152 begins a list of books repaired in 1508. Entry No. 161, p. 158, reads '*Historia Troianorum et Grecorum*, 2nd fol. *dendum eum.*' This entry refers to our MS, folio 2 of which begins as indicated.

The MS is of vellum, illuminated throughout with finely executed coloured initials, consists of 220 folios plus two paper fly-leaves, arranged in gatherings of twelve, except nos. 11 and 14 which have 11, and 16 which has 6, 14 3/4 × 10 1/4 inches, written in a large clear book-hand in double columns of twenty-five or twenty-six lines each, except for one selection, the *Prophecies of Merlin*, which, being in Alexandrines, is written in single columns. Apparently it was written by three scribes trained in the same school and probably working together.

The contents and arrangement of the MS are as follows: (1) *Historia troianorum et grecorum*, foll. 1–10^r (10^v, 11 and 12 are blank), a copy of Dares Phrygius unique in phraseology and arrangement.[1] (2) Wace's *Brut*,[2] foll. 13–166^r (166^v is blank),[3] except 86–97^r (97^v is blank), which represent an inserted gathering and contain (3) the *Prophecies of Merlin*. This version is in Alexandrines, and seems unknown to modern writers on the *Prophecies*.[4] It is apparently related to an Anglo-Norman twelve-syllable version mentioned by Michel, of which he knew two MSS, one in Lincoln Cathedral, MS A I, 8, and the other MS Harley 1605.[5] (4) *Les Estatuz du Roi Edward*, the Statutes of Westminster of 1275, foll. 167–183^r (183^v and 184 are blank). The three gatherings which follow (17–19 of the MS, foll. 185–220) are in one hand and constitute

[1] The standard version has been edited by Ferdinand Meister *Daretis Phrygius De excidio Troiae historia* (Lipsiae, 1873).

[2] Edited by Le Roux de Lincy *Le Roman de Brut*, 2 vols. (Rouen, 1836). A new edition utilizing MS P is in course of publication by Professor Ivor Arnold of Leeds for the *Société des anciens textes français*, vol. I of which has appeared this year.

[3] In the foliation at present in the MS (the official foliation has not yet been made) there are two errors in this section: (a) After fol. 15 a folio has been passed over. (b) After fol. 155 the foliation jumps to 160. The foliation as given above is corrected by + 1 from 16–155 and by – 3 after 155. Thus the foliation now in the MS for the *Petite Philosophie* is 188–215 instead of 185–212 as given in this edition.

[4] Miss Paton does not mention this version in her study: Lucy Allen Paton *The Prophecies of Merlin* ('Modern Language Monographs' I; New York and London, 1926–27).

[5] See F. Michel et T. Wright *Galfredi de Monemuta vita Merlini* (Paris, 1837) p. lxiv. On the Harley MS see H. L. D. Ward *Catalogue of Romances* I, 272 ff.

a scribal unit as shown by catchwords on 196 and 208. Here the items, four in all, are not separated by blank pages or written in separate gatherings, as is the case in the rest of the MS. The *Petite Philosophie* comes first, occupying foll. 185ʳ to 212ʳ, col. 2, l. 4. It is immediately followed by *Les Quatre filles Deu* which runs to fol. 214ᵛ, col. 2, l. 20.[1] Following this is a fragment of an Anglo-Norman poem on the *Apocalypse* which is apparently unique. It runs to the end of col. 1 of fol. 215ʳ. The final item is the *Resurrection Play* which runs to the end of the MS.[2]

The *Petite Philosophie* begins without title or rubric as in the edition and ends at l. 2819. There are 2704 lines of text counting 2533, of which the latter part is wanting. Of these 5, ll. 266 and 677–80, appear twice in the MS, leaving 2699 lines represented in the edition. Lines 265–6 are inserted in P after 246, fol. 187ʳ, col. 2, l. 12, the second being in a different hand. In the proper position l. 266 alone is written.[3] At the top of fol. 192ᵛ, col. 1, the scribe re-copied six lines, 675–80, already written in exactly the same position on fol. 191. Evidently he was copying his original folio by folio and, forgetting to turn the page just completed, began to copy a second time what he had already written. He erased the first pair of lines and then crossed out the remaining four, placing over the beginning of the first a *va* and a *cat* (*vacat*) over the end of the fourth. Five lines, 376 and 2477–80, are wanting in P and have been supplied from the other MSS. On the other hand P contains no lines not found in at least one other MS. Also the couplet 2483–4, fol. 208ᵛ, col. 2, is represented by a single line in P,

---

[1] This poem has been published by Francisque Michel *Libri psalmorum versio antiqua gallica* (Oxford, 1860) pp. 364 ff. There is also a version incorporated in the *Chasteau d'Amour* of Robert Grosseteste, see edition by J. Murray (Paris, 1918) pp. 71 ff. See also the study by Hope Traver *The Four Daughters of God* ('Bryn Mawr Monographs' VI; Philadelphia, 1907); Gröber's *Grundriss* II, 1, 690; and A. Längfors *Notices et Extraits des Manuscrits* XLII (1933) pp. 172 ff.

[2] See Flower's article in the London *Times* referred to above, p. vi. The only other version of this work known has been published for the *CFMA* by J. G. Wright, *La Résurrection du Sauveur* (Paris, 1931).

[3] See note to ll. 265–6.

the reduction resulting from internal haplography.[1] The error, however, was not made by the scribe of P who noticed a rhyme was wanting and left a blank line in his MS, thus proving that the error was already in his original. R has the couplet correct, which proves that P and R are not copies of the same MS. After l. 1924, fol. 203^v, col. 1, two lines are left blank, the first of which represents the erasure of 1929 which can still be deciphered. Since R at this point incorrectly inserts ll. 1929–30 and repeats them in the correct position, P has merely avoided a repetition in his original.[2] A lacuna of 114 lines begins in P at l. 2031, fol. 204^v, col. 1, l. 16, and extends to l. 2144 at the end of col. 1, fol. 205^v, the intervening space being left blank. The scribe left space for exactly 114 lines, which shows that the length of the lacuna was indicated in his original. Since both P and R lack the passage in question the loss goes back necessarily to their common original, which was not the immediate source of P. P and R end at l. 2819, thus lacking 101 lines of text at the end of the poem. Since l. 2819 offers a plausible ending for the long sermon which concludes the poem, neither P nor R appears to have suspected the loss. There are 675 lines of text from the end of the lacuna, l. 2144, to the end of MS P at l. 2819, which would represent approximately six folios in the MS which lost the folio causing the lacuna if that MS contained approximately 114 lines per folio. It thus appears that this MS lost the outer sheet of a gathering of four sheets or eight folios, thus causing the disappearance of the two passages in question. Lines 597–600 are displaced in P, being found after l. 628, and similarly ll. 1067–8 are misplaced after l. 1072.[3] Finally ll. 839–40 are transposed in order.[4]

R. Oxford, Bodleian, Rawlinson Poetry 241, formerly Rawlinson Miscellaneous 473, foll. 211, col. 1 to 246, col. 1.[5]

[1] Cf. note to ll. 2483–4. For the relationship of P and R see below, pp. xvii ff.
[2] See note to ll. 1929–30.
[3] See notes to these lines.
[4] See notes to these lines.
[5] See Falconer Madan *A Summary Catalogue of Western Manuscripts in the Bodleian Library at Oxford* III (Oxford, 1895), 338, No. 14732.

This MS was received by the Bodleian after the death of Richard Rawlinson in 1755. Previously it had been No. 110 in the library of Sir Thomas Tempest, baronet, but I have not been able to discover where he acquired it. The MS contains a valuable collection of thirteenth century Anglo-Norman poems mostly of a religious nature. It was described by E. Stengel (*ZFSL* XIV [1892] 127 ff.), but a fuller description with copious extracts has since been given by Paul Meyer (*Romania* XXIX [1900] 1 ff.). Meyer transcribed 221 lines from the beginning of the *Petite Philosophie* and 10 from the end. Since then two selections from the MS have been published: *La Plainte d'Amour*,[1] and *Les Proverbes de bon enseignement de Nicole Bozon*.[2] The MS is of parchment, written in English cursive, three hands, in double columns of thirty-eight lines each, and dated by Meyer and Stengel as early fourteenth century. This date has recently been disputed by Professor S. Harrison Thomson who places it *ca.* 1275,[3] but this date is almost certainly too early. It is more probably late thirteenth century. The *Petite Philosophie* begins and ends as in *P*. There are 2684 lines of text, of which ll. 265 and 1929–30 occur twice,[4] ll. 2728–9 have been· written as three, and the spurious line *Ieo vous dirrai mon auys* is added after l. 1962. The same lacunae, displacements and transposition of lines occur as in MS *P* above, except that the first lacuna begins at l. 2027 instead of 2031. *R* also transposes ll. 51–52, 265–6, 379–80 and 1081–2, and lacks in all 22 lines as follows: 465–70, 606, 900, 902–8, 995, 1141, 1413–4, 2219, 2600 and 2799.

    C. Cambridge, Library of St. John's College, MS I. 11. foll. 127ʳ, col. 1 to 144ʳ, col 2: according to an old foliation, foll.

---

[1] Edited by Johan Vising (Göteborg, 1905).
[2] Edited by A. Chr. Thorn (Lund and Leipzig, 1921).
[3] See S. Harrison Thomson 'The Significance of the Criteria of Latin Paleography in the Study of Anglo-Norman Documents' *Romanic Review* XXIX (1938) 112 ff. On p. 113 Professor Thomson, referring to our MS, states that it can be 'dated with complete confidence *ca.* 1275.'
[4] See notes to these lines.

152^r to 169^t.[1] The MS is of vellum and contains 2 + 156 folios (24 folios have been lost from the beginning of the MS). It was donated to St. John's by Thomas Baker (d. 1740); previously it had been No. 3473 in the library of Sir Thomas Wagstaff according to Bernard's *Catalogue*. At one time this MS had belonged to Syon Monastery, in the catalogue of which it had the number K. 28. It was the gift of John Bracebridge, a London priest who joined the community shortly after its foundation in 1414.[2] The MS is in two parts, originally distinct. Part I contains a version of the *Otia imperialia* of Gervase of Tilbury, and the *Chronicle* of Martinus Polonus. Part II contains the *Petite Philosophie*, a French translation of the *Recapitulatio Terrae Sancte et descriptio ejusdem*, and a *Recapitulatio Romae et descriptio ejusdem*. The *Petite Philosophie* begins *Li sages ki iadis esteient*, corresponding to line 167 of this edition, and runs to the end. Over the first line is the rubric *Ici comence la petite philosophie*. The text is in double columns of forty lines each, and the caption titles of the *Imago mundi* appear in Latin or in French in the body of the text or in the left-hand margin. The MS is in one hand throughout; is carefully executed; and is dated by Meyer and James as late thirteenth century. Its language and orthography are relatively uniform. Sometimes the MS shows attempts at emendation, for instance the lines comparing the universe to an egg, 259–268, have been recast. The scribe of C was copying an original containing passages already corrupt, which he endeavoured to correct as best he could. Of the 2720 lines of text in the MS six

[1] On this MS see the following: Montague Rhodes James *A Descriptive Catalogue of the Manuscripts in the Library of St. John's College Cambridge* (Cambridge 1913), p. 249, No. 219: the Rev. Morgan Cowie 'A Descriptive Catalogue of the Manuscripts and Scarce Books in the Library of St. John's College, Cambridge (1842–43),' *Publications of the Cambridge Antiquarian Society* (Cambridge, 1846–62 I, Nos. 6 and 8; Part II, p. 89: Mary Bateson *Catalogue of the Library of Syon Monastery Isleworth* (Cambridge, 1897) pp. xv, xviii, and 83: Edward Bernard *Catalogi librorum manuscriptorum Angliae et Hiberniae in unum collecti* (Oxoniae, 1697) II, 1, p. 85: Paul Meyer *Romania* VIII (1879) 336 ff. Meyer's excellent description includes a transcript of 184 ll. from the beginning of the *Petite Philosophie* and 33 from the end.

[2] See on this monastery the *Monasticon Anglicanum*, VI 540–41.

are found only in C,[1] three of these serving to replace lost lines, and four are repetitions, ll. 1817–9 having been copied a second time immediately after they were first written, and l. 2904 occurring first after 2898. There are 44 lines missing,[2] and the following couplets are inverted in order, 356–7, 995–6, 1279–80, 1389–90 and 2723–4. Lines 721–8 are displaced, following 734, and ll. 1283–4 follow l. 1266.[3]

D. Cambridge, University Library, Dd x. 31, foll. 128^v col. 1 to 146^v, col. 2.[4] This MS came to the University Library from the collection of Bishop Moore (d. 1714), whose library was bought by George I and presented to Cambridge. It was No. 824 of Moore's collection according to Bernard's *Catalogue* (II, 399). The list of contents there given indicates that the MS was complete in 1697, as four items not now found in the MS were listed after the *Petite Philosophie*, but Halliwell's description shows that in 1841 the MS was in its present condition. Paul Meyer gave a careful description of the MS in *Romania* XV (1886) 241 ff. He transcribed 192 lines from the beginning of the *Petite Philosophie*, and 126 from the end. The MS is of parchment, in double columns of 30 lines each, and dates from the end of the thirteenth century. The first part of the MS contains Latin works, (1) a *Historia regum Britanniae*, incomplete at the beginning and with a continuation to 1265; (2) a *Chronicle* of emperors and popes ending 1221; (3) the *De excidio Troiae historia* of Dares Phrygius. The last three gatherings contain French verse in a slightly different hand. This part alone was numbered when Meyer described the MS, but there is now a modern foliation, 1–147. Preceding our poem in the MS are short French lyric verses published by Meyer in his article on the MS. The *Petite Philosophie* begins without

[1] For these lines see the notes to the edition, pp. 99, 100.
[2] For these lines see the notes to the edition, pp. 99, 100.
[3] See notes to these lines.
[4] See *A Catalogue of the Manuscripts Preserved in the Library of the University of Cambridge, Edited for the Syndics of the University Press* I (Cambridge, 1856), 427, No. 590. See also J. D. Halliwell *The Manuscript Rarities of the University of Cambridge* (London, 1841) p. 77.

title or rubric *Ky uout suuer del mapemund*, the first forty lines constituting a prologue not found elsewhere,[1] line 41 corresponding to line 167 of the edition. The MS is incomplete, breaking off at l. 2546, *Kar il auentist par sun peche*, but the presence of the catchword *nent ist* proves that this is merely the end of a gathering and that the MS was probably complete originally. It contains, apart from the prologue, 2179 lines of text, of which six are spurious.[2] Beside the 374 lines wanting at the end, there are 207 lines missing in the part of the text covered by the MS.[2] *D* is much inferior to *P*, *R*, and *C*. Though written in a meticulously even hand, it contains many corrupt and unintelligible lines. It appears that the scribe of *D* was more conscientious than careless, and that his text represents a faithful copy of a poor original.

V. Rome, Vatican Library, MS Regina 1659, foll. 98ᵛ, col. 1 to 100ʳ, col. 1, l. 39. This MS formerly belonged to Queen Christina of Sweden, who, according to Gaston Paris, probably acquired it from the collection of Paul Pethau (d. 1614). The history of this MS is given in detail by Gaston Paris.[3] It is of parchment, containing 100 folios, in two parts, originally separate MSS, and both executed in England. Part I, foll. 1–90, thirteenth century, contains the *Estoire*, and a short poem in Provençal on the death of King Richard I. Part II, foll. 91–100, is in double columns, 60–63 lines per column for the *Petite Philosophie*, and contains Chardri's *Petit Plet*, followed by the fragment of our poem: it is dated by Paris as end of thirteenth

---

[1] For the prologue see the 'Appendix,' pp. 97, 98. Meyer misnumbered these lines to 36 instead of 40 (see his transcription *Romania* XV [1886] 256), and then proceeded to enter his incorrect numbering of *D* opposite the corresponding lines in MS *G*.

[2] For these lines see the notes to the edition, pp. 99, 100.

[3] See the introduction to his edition of the *Estoire de la guerre sainte, histoire en vers de la troisième croisade par Ambroise* ('Collection de documents inédits sur l'histoire de France', Paris 1897). See also Ernest Langlois *Notices et extraits des manuscrits* XXXIII, Part II; John Koch *Chardry's Josaphaz, Set Dormanz und Petit Plet* (Heilbronn, 1879) p. viii; Adelbert Keller *Romvart* (Mannheim and Paris, 1844) p. 411. Keller transcribed the last thirteen lines of the *Petite Philosophie* believing them to be part of the *Petit Plet*, in which error he was followed by Langlois.

century, by Langlois and Koch as of the fourteenth century. The *Petite Philosophie* begins (*L*)*es sages que iadis esteient* (l. 167 of this edition) and ends abruptly in the midst of a column *Dunt le peyuere trestut nersist* (l. 581). Over the first column is the incipit *Ci cõmce la petite philosophie.* There are 414 lines of text, of which one, *Sachez de fi si Deu me uaulz*, following 449 is found in *D* and *V* only. Only 2 lines, 215–6, are missing and the couplet 229–30 is inverted in order. This MS is closely related to *D* above. Though written in a less careful hand it is a better MS, often giving the correct reading when *D* is corrupt.

G. Cambridge, University Library, Gg. vi. 28, folio 15ᵛ, col. 1 to 51ᵛ, col. 2, l. 4. This MS is described in the *University Catalogue*, III (1858) 230, No. 590, but does not figure in Halliwell's *Catalogue*, which ends with class F. It belonged, as did *D*, to Bishop Moore's collection, and is probably No. 118 in Bernard's *Catalogue* (II, 364). The MS is a small quarto volume in parchment, of 113 leaves, in single columns of 32 lines each, except folio 51, which has two columns per page. A leaf is lacking at the beginning of the MS, and it is also defective at the end. The hand is an English cursive of the first quarter of the fourteenth century.[1] The first item in the MS is an incomplete copy of *Le Char d'Orgueil* of Nicole Bozon,[2] which is followed by Hue of Tabarie's *L'Ordre de chevalerie*.[3] Then comes the *Petite Philosophie*, followed by an *Itinéraire à Jérusalem*, the *Rapport du patriarche de Jérusalem à Innocent III sur l'état des Sarrazins*, a *Description de la terre sainte*, and lastly an incomplete version in prose of the *Roman des Sept Sages*. Paul Meyer des-

---

[1] Meyer, in *Romania* XV (1886) 343, dated the MS as about 1300. The *University Catalogue* gives early fifteenth century, which is probably an error. Meyer advanced his date to the first half of the fourteenth century, in the preface to his edition of the *Contes moralisés de Nicole Bozon* (Paris, 1889) p. xxx, which date is accepted by Vising in his *Anglo-Norman Language and Literature* p. 94. The MS is probably not later than 1325.

[2] Published by Johan Vising *Deux poèmes de Nicholas Bozon, le char d'Orgueil et la lettre de l'Empereur Orgueil* (Göteborg, 1919).

[3] Published by Roy Temple House *L'Ordene de chevalerie, an Old French Poem, Text with Introduction and Notes* (University of Chicago Dissertation, Chicago, 1918).

cribed this MS in the same article as that in which he described D,[1] giving variants from G with the passages of the
Petite Philosophie transcribed from D. The text of G begins
without title or rubric, *Li sage Iens iadis esteynt*, l. 167 of this
edition, and runs to the end of the poem. It contains 2363
lines, of which 13 are found in G alone, and two others in B
and G.[2] The MS lacks 406 lines of the edition,[2] incorrectly
places ll. 721–4 after 734[3] and l. 1667 after 1670, and transposes
the following couplets, 631–2, 780–1, 1323–4, 1899–1900,
2221–2, 2223–4, 2642–3 and 2670–1. There are two lacunae
corresponding to ll. 1611–1662, and to ll. 2003–2054, both of
52 lines, which makes it evident that two folios have disappeared from a MS in the tradition of G. The first lacuna begins
in the midst of the passage dealing with the element water and
continues up to the opening lines on air. The second lacuna
extends from the beginning of the passage on celestial measurements into the first part of a sermon of over 200 lines. These
lacunae have caused the re-arrangement of the material coming
between and after them. The order in the poem of the passages
which preceded and followed the second lacuna has been
reversed, ll. 2055–2242 having been moved back to line 1610
and appended to the material on water, ll. 1663–2002 having
been moved forward in their place. This change in order is
explained by the fact that the passage immediately preceding
the second lacuna deals with the planets and celestial music,
and that beginning at l. 2243, following the sermon mentioned
above, treats of the sky. The similarity of subject matter made it
easy to fit these passages together. But when this was done the
only place left for the displaced lines was between the passages
on water and air. Since there was no possibility of making
smooth transitions at these points, no attempt was made to do
so. The crude seams thus left occur in G in the midst of pages

[1] *Romania* XV (1886) 343 ff. See his article for bibliography on the latter items
of the MS.
[2] For these lines see notes to the edition, pp. 99, 100.
[3] See note to ll. 721–8.

xvi LA PETITE PHILOSOPHIE

in a gathering which is intact, this proving that *G* itself has survived without disarrangement or loss of folios.

In the rest of the poem the passages on geography, as a result of the frequent occurrence of names unfamiliar to the scribes, have shrunk considerably. Some forty lines have been lost in the portion dealing with Asia and Europe (cf. ll. 725–758, and 791–806). The heaviest loss occurs between ll. 1201–1360, in the description of Africa and the islands of the Mediterranean where ninety-one lines have dropped out. Another twenty-eight lines concerning stars are lost between 2409–2446. Finally forty-nine lines are omitted between ll. 2817–2887, in the long sermon concluding the poem. These with the lacunae account for 312 of *G*'s lost lines. Elsewhere the MS is relatively good, and runs complete for long passages.

B. Oxford, Bodleian, Douce 210, folios 13ʳ, col. 1 to 15ʳ, col. 2, l. 7: a fragmentary MS containing 454 lines from the end of the poem. The MS is of parchment, 2 + 61 folios, badly damaged and incomplete. It is written in double columns of about 50 lines each, in English cursive of the early fourteenth century. The MS is No. 21784 in Madan's *Summary Catalogue* (IV, 556), and also appears in the catalogue of Douce's collection published by Coxe.[1] Paul Meyer described it in detail in *Bulletin de la société des anciens textes français* (1880) pp. 46 ff., and transcribed the first 44 lines and the last 33 lines of the text. In the fly-leaf is a note by Francis Douce 'Bought at Lord Donegal's Sale,' but there is no mention of the MS in the catalogue of the sale. There are sixteen items in all in the MS, of which the most interesting are (1) *Le Roman de Fortune* by Simund de Freine.[2] (2) *Le Roman des Romans.*[3] (3) The

---

[1] H. D. Coxe *Catalogue of the Printed Books and Manuscripts Bequeathed by Francis Douce, Esq., to the Bodleian Library at Oxford* (Oxford, 1840). See the 'Catalogue of Manuscripts,' p. 34, No. CCX.

[2] Also known as *Le Roman de Philosophie*, and published under this title by John E. Matzke in *Les Oeuvres de Simund de Freine* (Paris, 1909).

[3] This text has been twice published, see F. J. Tanquerey *Deux poèmes moraux anglo-français*: *Le roman des romans et le sermon en vers* (Paris, 1922); Irville C. Lecompte *Le Roman des romans* (Princeton, 1923).

Lettre de l'Empereur Orgueil.[1] The text begins at l. 2466, *Qe a tot dis ount ioye graunt*, and runs to the end. Folio 13ʳ is badly stained but still legible, and the lower outside corners have been torn away slightly damaging the outer columns of text. The MS omits ll. 2468, 2713, and 2740, and inserts the following couplet after l. 2572, *E sey vendu par son peche Ceo est la monnaie al maufee* (cf. MS *G*). The couplet 2723–4 is inverted in order as in *C*.

3. CLASSIFICATION OF MANUSCRIPTS

The classification of the manuscripts of the *Petite Philosophie* is much facilitated by the fact that the poem is based on a Latin original, agreement with which provides an excellent criterion for distinguishing good from corrupt readings. Readings which reproduce exactly the content of the Latin text must represent in substance what the author wrote, and are necessarily to be preferred to those which differ from the Latin in meaning. This criterion would become unreliable only in the event of one or more of our MSS having been emended by collation with a MS of the *Imago mundi*. Apparently no such collation has been made, inasmuch as all the MSS contain a number of common errors which could hardly have been overlooked by a scribe who had undertaken to emend his OF text. The following cases are typical: (1) In l. 520 the OF states that the Tygris and Euphrates rivers rise in the *Caucasus* mountains, whereas the Latin text reads 'de monte *Barchoatro* funduntur.'[2] (2) In l. 994 the OF, referring to the western limit of Germany reads 'Vers *ocean* en Ren se fine,' against the Latin 'versus *occasum* Rheno . . . fluvio terminatur.' (3) In l. 1763 the OF states that the dew falls 'Par le *chaut* de la nut,' whereas the Latin text reads correctly '*rigore* noctis.' Including corrupt forms of proper names common to all the MSS there are about 20 such cases. Conjectural explanations of these errors might be attempted.

[1] Cf. above, p. xiv, n. 2. For the remaining items see Meyer's article.
[2] See note to this line.

The author may have used a faulty Latin MS: he may have misunderstood his source, or thought it incorrect and deviated deliberately from it: all our MSS may derive from one OF MS which was not the original and already contained errors. In any case the existence of these errors in the text of the *Petite Philosophie* shows that none of its MSS has been emended by collation with a Latin MS. Agreement with the Latin can therefore be used as a test to determine the grouping of the MSS. On this basis the MSS of the *Petite Philosophie* fall into two groups, *PR* and *CDVGB*.[1] These groups we shall designate as *x* and *y* respectively. Evidence to support this grouping is much too abundant to cite in detail. Some cases of common error in *y* are (1) line 534, where *y* gives the course of the Indus river as toward *Indie* instead of toward the *midi*. (2) Line 998, in which the Latin states that the name Alemania is derived from Lake Lemanus; *x* reads *lai* against *roi* in *y*. (3) Line 1573, where *y* erroneously states that *Dolcor* nourishes the moon instead of *Duce ewe*. (4) Lines 669–70, 1019–20 and 1428–9, based on the Latin, are preserved in *x* but wanting in *y*.

There are in all nearly 50 such cases, not counting those where a line is wanting in a MS of *y*.[2] Conversely the group *x* is occasionally in error against *y* and the Latin as in the following cases: (1) Line 707, where, speaking of the reptiles in the Ganges, *x* refers to their *testes* instead of *braz* (Lat. *brachia*). (2) Line 778, which states that Jethro was priest in the land of Madian; *x* reads *Jerico*. (3) Line 1786, according to which eternal calm (*serenum*) exists above the moon; *y* reads correctly *clarté* but *x* reads *chaud*.[3] Besides these cases it has already been pointed out above under 'Manuscripts' that *P* and *R* have a prologue not in *y* and also have common lacunae and dis-

---

[1] The fragment *B* contains only the end of the poem for which there is no Latin equivalent, but it clearly belongs to group *y*. Its relation to the other MSS will be studied below, p. xxii, in the discussion of group *y*.

[2] Cases of opposition between *x* and *y* are indicated in the variants of almost every page of text.

[3] For other cases see the emendations in the text.

placement of lines. The group y lacks the prologue and has one common displacement of lines.[1]

The evidence against the x and y grouping has little weight. When x agrees with one or more manuscripts of y, and likewise when y agrees with either P or R, the readings offered are regularly correct. But both P and R occasionally agree with one or more manuscripts of y in a reading which seems doubtful. On examination these cases all prove to be of the sort where the possibility of independent agreement exists. For instance, in l. 560 PRD read *Ke il ne poent issir ne passer*. *CVG* omit the *Ke il* which is unnecessary and is undoubtedly an expansion. In any case the insertion or omission could have been made independantly and cannot be admitted as evidence to prove relationship.

P and R divide occasionally to give groupings different from that accepted for x and y above. The most important cases are (1) line 377 giving the measure of the earth's circumference, in which RDV give a hybrid reading as a result of confusion between the two Latin forms of the computation.[2] (2) RDG lack l. 2219. Lines 2218 and 2219 both begin with *Ki* and occur in a series of monorhymes. The omission may therefore be independent. (3) In l. 746 PG qualify *Mesopotamie* as *la late* whereas RCD read *la cité*. The unusual form *late*, a Latinism for *lee* to provide a rhyme with *Eufrate* (l. 745), evidently puzzled the scribes who made the substitution of *cité*. As the word *cité* occurs repeatedly in this part of the poem it would suggest itself easily to the copyists.[3]

Since there are relatively few such cases, and since they show no consistent grouping, they cannot be taken to invalidate the x and y grouping established above.

Group x.—The tradition of the x group is clearly better than that of y. Except for the long lacunae P and R possess together

[1] See note to lines 721–8.
[2] See the explanation given in the note to this line. Cf. also the note to ll. 2011–3.
[3] Cf. note to this line.

every line which can be established for the original text, whereas *y* lacks at least six.[1] Secondly, the common errors of *y* against the Latin are roughly four times more numerous than those of *x*. Finally MS *P* is much superior to *C*, the best MS of *y*. Within *x* no hesitation is possible, *P* being decidedly more reliable than R and to judge from its forms and orthography, almost certainly an earlier MS. For instance the form *lui* for the definite article is freely used in R but does not occur in *P*. We may also mention in R the extensive use of *y* for *i*, *vyent* for *vient*, and the almost constant use of *aun* for *an* which is rare in *P*. From the foregoing it follows that *P* is the best MS of the *Petite Philosophie* and should be chosen as the basis of an edition.

Group y.—This group includes the five MSS *CDGVB*. An examination of errors and omissions shows that no MS of the five is a copy of any other. *DV* form a sub-group, and their common ancestor was related to *G*. The archetype of these three, *DVG*, was in its turn related to *B*, while *C* stands by itself.[2] Evidence will now be offered to substantiate these relationships, beginning with that of *DV*. Characteristic cases to establish this sub-group are (1) after l. 449 *DV* add the line *Sachez de fi si Deu me vaille (uaulz V)*. This line was inserted in the archetype of *DV* to avoid the rhyme *solalz:chalz* 449, which the scribe evidently considered incorrect. After 450 *D* has a second line, *Dunt nus en sumes plus baud* which provides a rhyme for *chaud* 450. *V* omits this line, leaving the couplet incomplete. (2) *DV* replace l. 416, *Cinq cercles altresi freit* found in *PRCG* and in the Latin, by the line *Ces chalurs ausi remirret (remuereit V)*, which reading is manifestly corrupt. (3) *DV* invert in order ll. 229–30, omit to mention snow and dew, and give the rhyme *aubegele:brisile*.[3] The omission of snow and dew

---

[1] Cf. above p. xviii. The couplets 215–6 and 1629–30, wanting in *y* (G has a lacuna in the second case), and for which there is no Latin, may represent additions in *x*.

[2] Cf. the stemma given below, p. xxvi.

[3] See note to these lines.

from the list of projected topics is an error, as they are discussed in the poem ll. 1755 and following.

In all there are fifteen cases of agreement in common error for *DV*, besides numerous cases of common deviation from the readings of the other MSS. The relationship of *DV* is evident in almost every line.

Contrary evidence is limited, the most important cases being (1) l. 174, which is wanting in *CD* but present in *PRVG*. This line occurs in a series of rhymes in -*erent* (pf. 6), in which the couplets are not clearly marked. The omission, though surprising, might conceivably have occurred independently. (2) In l. 251 *V* reads *Aturt a mai*, *D Escut a mai*, *G Escoute a moy*, *C Escote ore*, and *PR E aturt oie*. It appears that the original reading, which was doubtless *Aturt oie*, stood in the archetype of *y*.[1] In *C* the corruption of *oie* to *ore* led to the substitution of *Escote* for *Aturt*. In the archetype of *DVG* the reading had become *Aturt a mai*, which phrase was emended independently by *D* and *G*.

The evidence of these cases, neither of which is convincing, cannot counterbalance the constant agreement of *DV* as shown above.

D vs. G.—Since *V* is a fragment, and closely related to *D*, we shall disregard it in studying the relationship of *DG*. Evidence to establish this relationship is abundant. Disregarding those cases where omissions in the two MSS merely overlap and do not coincide exactly (there are seven such cases) five cases of common omission occur as follows: ll. 1005–6, 1117–8, 1333–4, 2177–8, and 2249–50. Likewise cases of common error are frequent. Examples are (1) line 877 where the phrase *mes Nil surunde* reads in *DG mes ele surunde*. (2) Line 1225 where *DG* read *habiterent* for *abatirent*. (3) Line 1990 where *DG* read *la lune* for *l'alme*. (4) Line 2471 where *DG* omit *loinz*. These cases are relatively numerous and are supported by frequent agreement in minor variations. Along with the

---

[1] Cf. the stemma, p. xxvi below.

common omissions noted above they constitute a weight of evidence which is convincing.

DG vs. B.—The fragment *B* clearly belongs to *y* whose readings it supports consistently when *x* and *y* show variation. It also has the end of the poem complete as in *C* and *G*. Apparently it was an excellent MS before mutilation, usually offering correct readings with *C*, but never agreeing with it in common error.[1] *B* lacks the part of the poem found in *V*, and it is concurrent with *D* for only 81 lines, ll. 2466–2546. In this passage *DG* are several times found in error against *BCPR*. In l. 2509 *DG* read, *Sanz labur* (*G trauailer*) *est gouernor*, against *BCPR*, *Sanz labour est al gouerner*. Likewise in l. 2510 *DG* read *est oueror* instead of *a tut ovrer*. In l. 2471 mentioned above *B* reads with *PRC* against *DG*, and in l. 2508 *DG* have the future *ert* for *est* in *PRCB*. In all 12 cases occur where *DG* have common readings different from *PRCB* and apparently inferior. Consequently *B* must stand outside rather than within the group *DVG*. However after *D* breaks off, *B* agrees with *G* in a number of incorrect readings. Both MSS insert a couplet after 2572, not found elsewhere, and which constitutes an awkward expansion.[2] In l. 2681 *GB* read *bountez* against *PRC beutez*, in l. 2684 *poez* against *purrez* and in l. 2739 *grant* for *quant*. These cases are not numerous, there are only eight in all, but they all give the same grouping and the readings of *GB* are consistently inferior. Thus since *B* stands outside the group *DVG*, the cases of agreement in error with *G* show that *B* is related to the archetype of *DVG*, as indicated in the stemma.

However the tradition for *y* is much less clear than the above cases might indicate. Up to this point the evidence seems convincing, but difficulties arise when we attempt to establish the precise relationship of *C* to the other MSS. Setting aside the fragment *B*, which does not agree in error with *C*, and considering *D* and *V* as one MS, we have three MSS *CDG* to study.

[1] *CB* transpose ll. 2723–4, but since *G*, the only other MS of *y* running at this point, omits ll. 2724–5, the inversion of *CB* is probably a *y* variant.

[2] See above under 'Manuscripts' and also in the notes, pp. 99, 100.

The possible combinations are therefore *DG*, established above, *CG* and *CD*. If the conclusion reached regarding *DG* is correct, we should not expect to find *CD* agreeing in error or in frequent common variation against *G*, nor *CG* combining similarly against *D*. In studying the filiation of a group of MSS written by scribes familiar with the same scribal and literary tradition care must be taken not to accept as evidence for relationship common readings which could result from similar habits of thought and expression on the part of the scribes. It is only when MSS show repeated agreement in cases where such an explanation is difficult or impossible that we can assume relationship as established. Agreement in minor cases may serve as corroborative evidence, but has by itself little weight. The following examples from *y* may serve as illustrations: (1) In l. 1043 *CD* replaces the reading *Elen fiz Hector* by *Eleine fille Hector*. This change proves nothing beyond the fact that two scribes, who knew nothing of Helenus but were familiar with Helen of Troy from the *Roman de Troie*, made what they considered an obvious correction of their originals. (2) Both *C* and *G* lack ll. 2409–12 which are found in *PRD*. The omission is simply a case of haplography due to the fact that ll. 2408 and 2412 both end in the same word *franceis*. All the omission proves is that two scribes made the error of dropping their eyes to the second word and thus unintentionally omitting the lines.

Thus cautioned we may now proceed to examine the evidence in favour of the grouping *CG*. Numerous cases of agreement in unique readings occur, but on examination they prove unconvincing. Four cases of common omissions occur. One of these has already been discussed above.[1] In two other cases, ll. 1624–5 and 2437–8, *G* has a long lacuna, whereas *C* lacks a couplet only. The remaining case is ll. 951–2. *G* also drops ll. 950 and 953 at this point, and *C*'s omission can be explained because ll. 950 and 952 both end in *apelee*. The cases

---

[1] Lines 2409–12; see above.

of common variants are of the following sort: line 980 reads as follows in *P, Dit de Thanai roi del pais. CG* omit the name which is found in *PRD*, but corruption and omission of these proper names is too common to have any significance. Again in l. 1674 *CG* read *as homes* instead of *a la gent* of *PRD*. Such a substitution proves nothing. Since there are no cases which force us to postulate a common ancestor for *CG* within *y*, we may conclude that such relationship did not exist.

Evidence for the relationship of *C* to *D* is more difficult to interpret. There are four cases of common omissions. The first is l. 174,[1] which omission must be independent since the missing line occurs in *V*, the MS most closely related to *D. C* lacks ll. 1472 and 1474. At this point *D* lacks ll. 1471–6. Since the omissions do not coincide exactly they have little weight. *C* and *D* both lack ll. 1145–6, which are present in *G*, but quite corrupt. The corruption may go back to the archetype of *y* which could explain the independent disappearance of the couplet in *C* and *D*. The fourth case is the omission in *CD* of the couplet 969–70. This loss is most difficult to accept as independent inasmuch as the lines refer to Saint Clement, and references to the lives of saints are not likely to be overlooked by the scribes. The cases of common variants have less significance. In addition to the example cited above,[2] we may cite l. 1544, which reads in *P, Li marinail loinz en la mer. RG* support *P*, but *CD* read, *ki vont par la* (not in *D*) *mer*. The alteration does not change the sense materially, and may represent the substitution of a current phrase for the original. Another characteristic case is the rhyme *jors: cors* 1875 of *CD* against *jurnees: estrees* of *PGR*. Since the loss of a syllable was of no consequence to the scribes' sense of meter such a change has little weight as the meaning is not altered. Additional cases of similar nature may be seen in ll. 1153, 1309–10, and 2245.[3]

Taken alone, the common variants of *CD* against *PRG* do

---

[1] See above, p. xxi.
[2] Line 1043, see p. xxiii above.
[3] See the variants to these lines.

not, therefore, constitute conclusive proof of close relationship between these two MSS. But these variants assume increased significance when supported by one case of common omission for which no plausible explanation exists and a second for which only a conjectural explanation can be offered. As shown above, the evidence for the relationship of *DG* is excellent, therefore *G* should not frequently offer correct readings with *PR* against *CD*. Nevertheless the evidence at hand will not permit any other grouping of the MSS of *y* than that suggested above. To explain the cases where *G* agrees with *PR* against *CD* we are consequently reduced to the hypothesis of a contamination into *G* from *x* or another unknown source outside *y*. Since *G* contains lacunae and re-arrangement of material this contamination must have existed already in his base MS. If this hypothesis be admitted, it follows that the common variants of *CD* descend to them from the archetype of *y* and therefore merely indicate their family relationship.

This explanation receives support from within *G* itself. There exist in this MS certain alterations in readings made by the scribe which suggest the possibility that he was choosing between more than one available reading. In l. 1111, *De Capua est la cité* (PRD) *dite*, *G* wrote *cité*, crossed it out and wrote in *terre*, the reading of *C*. In line 405, *Le chaud se ameine a la froidure*, *G* wrote *meigne*, compare *meine* in *DV*, expunctuated it and wrote in *medle*, which corresponds to *meille* in *C*. In l. 327 *G* wrote *cule* (PRCD), expunctuated it and wrote *turne* in the margin. In 334 *se lie* the reading of *D* has been altered to *s'alie* which agrees with *PR*. In 654 *cum*, the reading of *D* has been expunctuated and *de* inserted, which agrees with *CPR*. It is not possible to determine precisely the conditions which produced such alterations, but it seems to be at least possible that *G* was copying a MS containing marginal corrections or variants. To go further than this would be to indulge in vain speculation.

The conclusions reached in the foregoing examination of

the manuscript tradition of the *Petite Philosophie* may be represented by the following stemma.

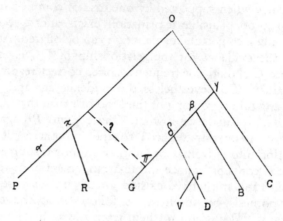

4. LANGUAGE

A. *Phonology.*—The evidence offered by the rhymes of the *Petite Philosophie* reveals the following phonological characteristics.

1. *e* < tonic free *a* rhymes with *e* < *ie* from any source, *perent* (< *parent*):*querent* 927, *mer*:*adverser* 843, *besturnez*:*piez* 603; with the imperfect indicative of *estre*, *deviserent*:*erent* 173,[1] and with *e* in loan words from Latin, whatever the original quantity, *signifer*:*cler* 1907, *Galilee*:*numee* 833.[2]

tale > *tel*, *tel*:*cel* (< *caelu*) 2189, but also *tal*, *mal*:*tal* 2097, the form *mal* being assured by the rhyme *collateral*:*mal* 1689.

The suffix -*ale* > -*al* regularly in learned words, *austral*:*estal* 453, *Ytal*:*comunal* 1087, etc. The popular development appears to be -*el*, *ciel*:*uel* (< *aequale*) 2303, and within the line *viel* (< *vitale*) 1669 P, but compare *equinoccial*:*paringal* 439, and *parigal*:*equinoxial* 2385. This hesitation, found also in Norman,

---

[1] Cf. E. G. R. Waters *The Anglo-Norman Voyage of St. Brendan* (Oxford, 1928) p. cxxxvi.

[2] Cf. Waters *ibid.* The text also offers examples of Latin *e* treated as open, cf. *Ysmael*:*bel* 855, and *arbest*(< *arbaston*):*tempest* 1071.

is common in Anglo-Norman.[1] It is especially to be noted in *Gui de Warewic*,[2] in Chardri's poems,[3] and in *Le Chateau d'Amour*.[4] Forms in -*al* occur also in south-western French.[5]

Of interest here is the rhyme *vol* (verb. subs. < *voler*):*asol* 2305, in which *asol* is for *essol* by substitution of prefix (*P* alone has *a*-). Starting from the form **axale* (*REW* 840) we get *aissiel*, which in Anglo-Norman, by reduction of *ai* to *ę*,[6] *ie* to *e*[7] and the opening of *ę* before *l*,[8] would give the form *essęl*, the reading found in MS *G*. The passage of -*ęl* to -*ǫl* has not yet been satisfactorily explained. Menger believed that it resulted from the development of the glide vowel *ǫ* between *ę* and *l* (cf. *iceols* in the *Cambridge Psalter*) instead of the more usual *a*, and the reduction of -*ęǫl* to -*ǫl*,[9] but this theory demands further investigation. A second example of this phenomenon is furnished in our text by the rhyme *fous:avels* 2525,[10] which indicates that the vocalization of *l* before consonant[11] did not affect the development of -*ǫl* < -*ęl*.

If our deduction concerning the form *essęl* is correct, *e* < tonic free *a* has opened before *l*, which suggests that the vowel in the rhymes *tel:cel* and *ciel:uel* cited above is also open. This in turn would entail accepting the rhyme *ciel:camel* in paragraph 3 as open. The vowel of the rhyme *cels* (< *caelos*):*Deus* in the same paragraph is apparently close, but this latter case is not strictly parallel in that it involves a vocalizing *l*. However in

[1] Cf. L. E. Menger *The Anglo-Norman Dialect* (New York, 1904) p. 48, and Waters *op. cit.* p. cxxxvii.

[2] See A. Ewert *Gui de Warewic* (Paris 1932-3) I, pp. xix f.

[3] J. Koch *Chardry's Josaphaz, Set Dormanz und Petit Plet* (Heilbronn, 1879) p. xxv.

[4] J. Murray *Le Chateau d'Amour de Robert Grosseteste* (Paris, 1918), p. 45.

[5] Cf. M. K. Pope *From Latin to Modern French* (Manchester, 1934) sec. 502.

[6] See paragraph 4.

[7] See paragraph 3.

[8] Cf. Pope *op. cit.* sec. 1146.

[9] For a discussion of this development with examples see Menger *op. cit.* pp. 59 f.; A. Stimming *Der anglonormannische Boeve de Haumtone* (Halle, 1899) p. 175, and H. Suchier *Voyelles toniques du vieux français* (Paris, 1906) sec. 59b.

[10] See the discussion of this rhyme below in paragraph 14.

[11] See below, paragraph 16.

paragraph 2 *e* < tonic *ĭ* checked has opened before a vocalizing *l* in the rhyme *cels* (< *ecce ĭllos*)*:beals*, and *solalz:chalz*. It appears possible therefore that *e* of any sort has opened before *l* in our text,[1] but this deduction rests on the evidence of the one rhyme *vol:asol*, in which the stages of development are still obscure.

Elsewhere there is no evidence to indicate that *e* < tonic free *a* is open. In view of the frequency of this vowel in rhyme, absence of rhymes in open *e* except before *l* is significant, and may be accepted as establishing its value as close.

2. **e** < tonic **ĭ** checked is open in the following rhymes, *governe:cerne* (< *circinat*) 2477, *cels* (< *ecce ĭllos*)*:beals* 403, *espiremenz:dedenz* (< *de ĭntus*) 1495, *destre:senestre* 2349, *bele: meissele* 677, and *estencele:apele* 1655. OF *ĕ* opened to *ę* during the twelfth century, first before *r* + consonant.[2] Already in the *Brendan cerne* has an open *e*, *-ęls:-ęls*, *ęn:ęn*,[3] and Gaimar and Fantosme rhyme similarly.[4] The open *e* of *senestre* results from the analogy of *destre*,[5] and of *meissele* and *estencele* from the substitution of the suffix *-ĕlla* for *-ĭlla*.[6]

The rhyme *solalz:chalz* 449 (*solauz:chauz*) is to be explained by depalatalization of *l*-mouillé before final consonant, *-el'z* (< *-ĭculus*) giving *-ęlz*,[7] the opening of *e* before *l*, the development of the glide vowel *a* before a vocalizing *l* and the reduction of *-ęauz* to *-auz*.[8]

Elsewhere the *e* in question rhymes only with itself, *secheresce: blesce* 345, *ignelesce:peresce* 1799, etc. From the foregoing it

---

[1] Suchier (*op. cit.* sec. 17 f.) believed this to be true in Anglo-Norman.

[2] See M. K. Pope *op. cit.* sec. 575 and 1145–6; and J. Vising 'Die *e* Laute im Reime der A. N. Dichter des xii[ten] Jahrhunderts' *Zeitschrift für französische Sprache und Literatur* XXXIX (1912) 1–17.

[3] See Waters *op. cit.* pp. cxli f., and cxliv; and J. Vising *Etude sur le dialecte anglo-normand du xiie siècle* (Upsala 1882) p. 67.

[4] Cf. Vising *op. cit.* pp. 80 and 92.

[5] See Schwan-Behrens *Grammaire de l'ancien français* (4th ed.; Leipzig, 1932) sec. 11[1].

[6] Cf. Suchier *op. cit.* sec. 15b.

[7] Cf. Waters *Brendan* p. cliv.

[8] See Suchier *op. cit.* sec. 60; Menger *op. cit.* pp. 54 and 58 f.; M. K. Pope *Etude sur la langue de Frère Angier* (Paris, 1903) p. 9.

follows that the open value of this *e* is established only when it is followed by *r*, *l*, or nasal consonant.

3. The diphthong *ié*, whatever its provenience, is reduced to **e**, and rhymes freely with *e* < tonic free *a*, *piez:armez* 693, *mer:fier* 557, *manere:clere* 329, *mester:tresnoer* 639, and *esteilé*: *moité* 2307.[1] It rhymes also with *e* in words borrowed from Latin, *ciel* (< *caelu*):*camel* (< *camelu*) 2035, *cels* (< *caelos*): *Deus* 2473, *Grece:pece* (<*pettia*) 1079, and *Boece*[2] (< *Betica*):*pece* 1167. Except for the rhyme *ciel:camel*, discussed above in paragraph 1, these rhymes points to a close value for *e* < *ie*,[3] since *e* < tonic free *a* has been accepted as close in paragraph 1 above, and *Grece* and *Boece*, being Latin loan words, may have close vowels,[4] which value is supported by the Modern English pronunciation of *Greece* and *piece*. Lastly *Deu(s)* assonances in OF with *e* < tonic free *a*.[5] Since no example of rhyme with *ę* occurs except possibly before *l*, *e* < *ie* is doubtless close for our author in all other cases.

4. The OF diphthongs **ai** and **ei** rhyme freely together, (a) before *st*, *nest:crest* 1549, *crest:lest* (< *laxat*) 1559; (b) before a final consonant, *defeit:soit* (< *sĭt*) 1175, *exploit:fet* (<*facit*) 535, *veir:eir* (< *aeru*) 1399, *estoit* (impf. of *estre*):*tret* (< *trahit*) 1311; (c) final in a syllable, *toneire:escleire* 227, *veire:refere* 305, *froide: plede* 339, *pleise:curteise* 75; (d) once in final position, *fei:mustrai* 407; (e) before *l* or a depalatalized *l*-mouillé, *apuail:fedail* 369, *solail:fail* 1867. The text offers no rhymes combining *ai* or *ei* forms with *ę*. Nevertheless the phonetic value of the above rhymes of types *a*, *b* and *c* is probably *ę*. Vising points out that

---

[1] Cf. also paragraph 1 above.

[2] The diagraph *oe* may have resulted from confusion of Betica with Boeotia, cf. the text ll. 1047 and 1053. Menger (*op. cit.* p. 52) claims that *oe* may be written for any *e* in Anglo-Norman, but there are no other cases in MS *P*.

[3] On the value of this *e* see Menger *op. cit.* p. 56.

[4] See above, p. xxvi, n. 2.

[5] See Gaston Paris *La Vie de Saint Alexis* (3rd ed.; Paris, 1925) laisses xviii, xxiv, etc., and T. A. Jenkins *La Chanson de Roland* (New York, 1924) p. ci. Note also that *Deu(s)* suffers reduction in Anglo-Norman as well as on the Continent to *De(s)*, which rhymes with *e* < tonic free *a*, cf. Ewert *op. cit.* I, p. xix; and Stimming *op. cit.* p. x.

in Fantosme and Chardri *ai:ę* freely but that *ei:ę* rarely, and that neither poet rhymes *ai* with *ei* except before *-re*. He concludes that *ai* reduces to *ę* earlier than did *ei* and that these two rhyme consequently only on the basis of *ę*.[1] The *ę* value of rhymes combining these diphthongs seems to be established by the fact that texts in which they are frequent regularly combine them both with *ę*, e.g. Simund de Freine,[2] *Gui de Warewic*,[3] the *Chateau d'Amour*,[4] *Boeve de Haumtone*[5] and the *Sermon en Vers*.[6] Thus the rhymes in question in our text presumably have the value of *ę*.

This conclusion is supported by consideration of the rhyme *apuail:fedail* 369, in which *apuail* represents the stem *apu* (< *apui* = *apoi*,[7] cf. *apoiier* < VL *apodiare*, *REW* 550) + the suffix *-alium*, which would reduce in Anglo-Norman through *-al'* and *-ail*[8] to *-ęl*,[9] which value is established by the variant *apuel:bel* of *DV*. In its turn *fedail* represents *fedęl* < *fedeil* < *fidēle* (the adjective being apparently oblique). Here again the *ę* value of the rhyme seems reasonably certain.

Nevertheless there is reason to hesitate regarding the phonetic value of the rhyme *solail:fail* 1867. The Modern English forms *travel* and *counsel* bear witness of the reduction of *-al'* and *-el'* forms through *-ail* and *-eil* to *-ęl*. But this reduction has not affected numerous other words such as *assail*, *avail*, *bail*, *mail*, *fail*, etc. Not only do *ę* rhymes for such words

[1] See Vising *Etude* pp. 75 and 93. Suchier (*op. cit.* sec. 30b) expresses the opinion that *ei* became *ai* thus permitting a rhyme; and O. H. Prior (*Cambridge Anglo-Norman Texts* [Cambridge, 1924] pp. 4 f.) concludes that *ai* was raised to *ei* and that both were then levelled to close *e*.

[2] See J. E. Matzke *Les Oeuvres de Simund de Freine* (Paris, 1909), pp. xxiv–xxvi.

[3] Cf. Ewert *op. cit.* I, p. xx.

[4] Cf. Murray *op. cit.* p. 46.

[5] Cf. Stimming *op. cit.* p. viii.

[6] See F. J. Tanquerey *Deux poèmes moraux anglo-français: le roman des romans et le sermon en vers* (Paris, 1922) pp. 32 f.

[7] For the equivalence of *oi* and *ui* and the reduction of the latter to *u* see below, paragraph 11.

[8] Depalatalization of *l*-mouillé is widespread in Anglo-Norman and had begun as early as the *Brendan*, cf. Waters *op. cit.* p. lxiii; Stimming *op. cit.* p. 212 f.; and Menger *op. cit.* p. 88.

[9] On this reduction cf. M. K. Pope *From Latin to Modern French* sec. 1182.

seem non-existent but it is of interest to note that the orthography is uniformly -*ail* in contrast to types *a*, *b* and *c* where *ai, ei, e* and even *oi* (this latter owing to Continental influence) are found. This distinction in orthography observed by the scribes can hardly be accidental and suggests that the phonetic value differs in the two cases. The whole problem of *ai* and *ei* rhymes demands further investigation.

The phonetic value of *ai:ei* in final position is also uncertain but it is usually considered a diphthong.[1] This rhyme is found first in Chardri and Freine,[2] and appears regularly in texts of the first half of the thirteenth century.[3]

The product of -*aria* occurs once in rhyme in a Latin loan word, *Samarie:afeire* 829, also that of -*arius*, *Sagitrarie:fere* 2395. The orthography of the MSS is regularly -*arie*, but since the tonic vowels of *afeire* and *fere* seem to be ẹ, -*arie* must represent a phonetic -*ẹre*.

5. The *Petite Philosophie* does not rhyme infinitives in -*eir* < -*ēre* with those in -*er* <-*are*, all the rhymes occurring for -*eir* verbs being pure.[4] This is surprising since such rhymes appear as early as Chardri and Freine and are found in most texts of the early thirteenth century.[5]

6. Final atonic *e* may disappear, (a) when in hiatus after tonic *e*, *cité:assemblee* 939, *cité:fundé* (f.) 727, 1269 (possibly lack of agreement of past participle in these cases), etc.; (b) after *st*, *est:tempest* 1431, 1753, *tempeste:vest(e)* (< *vestit*) 1781, *arbest* (< *arbaston):tempest* 1071, probably also *Horest:est* 1067 (RC add *e* to *Horest*); (c) after *r*, *creature:honur(e)* 2201, *colur:verdur* 1731, *toneire:escleir(e)* 227, *froidur(e):atemprure* 405, *froidur(e):nature* 1635, *sustenirs:empirs* 2503[6]; (d) after *rt*,

---

[1] Cf. Stimming *op. cit.* p. viii; Pope *op. cit.* sec. 1157; and Menger *op. cit.* p. 45.

[2] See Koch *op. cit.* p. xxvii; and Matzke *op. cit.* p. xxiii.

[3] Cf. notes 3 to 6 on p. xxx.

[4] The rhyme *chair:aoverir* 1511 is an apparent exception only as *chair* was a frequent Anglo-Norman form of this infinitive.

[5] On this rhyme see especially F. J. Tanquerey *L'Evolution du verbe en anglo-français* (Paris, 1915) pp. 390 ff.

[6] See note to l. 2504.

pert(e):deserte 2053. The scribes sometimes restored a rhyme for the eye by adding an unetymological *e* as in *veste* and *honure*.

Loss of final atonic *e* has been studied in detail by Suchier.[1] During the second half of the twelfth century feminine *e* in hiatus after the tonic vowel began to lose phonetic value. Likewise it began to fall after certain final consonants. Suchier lists examples from Fantosme of fall after *st*, *nt* and *r*, compare the cases established by rhyme for our text.[2] Further examples occur in Chardri and are quite frequent in *Gui de Warewic*.[3] Thus the practice of our text is well established by the early thirteenth century.

7. *ĕ* + yod 〉 *i*, *ist:verdist* 545, *enmi:alsi* 2253, *dit:delit* 1121. For *intĕgra* we have *entere:maniere* 219.

For the product of *-eria* the following rhymes are found, *deboneire:matire* 289, *matire:afeire* 313, *matire:empire* 285, and *sustenirs:empirs* 2503.[4] This latter rhyme establishes the form *empire* which in turn establishes *matire* in l. 285. *Empire* occurs regularly in Anglo-Norman texts and has survived in Modern English. On the other hand there existed in Anglo-Norman alongside *matire* the form *mateire*, probably based directly on the Latin *materia*, compare the rhyme *veire:mateire* 1679 of the *Brendan* and the orthographies *mateire* and *materie* found in our MSS. This form explains the first two rhymes above, which represent therefore *-aire:-eire* with the value of *-ęre*.[5]

8. The rhyme *anᶜ:enᶜ* occurs twice, *essample:ample* 283, and

---

[1] H. Suchier *Ueber die Matthaeus Paris zugeschriebene Vie de Seint Auban* (Halle, 1876) pp. 5–6 and 36 ff. Cf. also Stimming *op. cit.* p. 1; Menger *op. cit.* pp. 63 f.; and Tanquerey *op. cit.* p. 772.

[2] There is reason to believe that fall occurs within the line after certain other consonants, cf. note to l. 224.

[3] Koch *op. cit.* p. xxxii; and Ewert *op. cit.* I, p. xxi.

[4] Cf. p. xxxi, n. 6.

[5] An alternative explanation is to consider the form *matęre* as a reduction of *matere* < *matiere*, but this reduction is not established for our text except possibly before *l*, cf. above, paragraph 1, and the evidence at hand does not favour this interpretation.

curant:talant 625, but compare *lungement:talent* 2171. These two words, *essample* and *talent*, figure in the list established by Suchier,[1] which rhyme with either *an* or *en* forms. Elsewhere the rhymes of our text are pure.

9. **ain** and **ein** rhyme freely, *pleine* (< *plēna*):*humeine* 649, *serain:endemain* 2313, *feint:remaint* 475, *esteint:seint* (< *sanctu*) 2597, *suveraine:estraine* (<*strēna*) 1845, *peine:funtaine* 1641, *miluein:plein* 399.[2]

ein rhymes once with *en*, *prendre:rendre (reindre)* 165.[3]

10. **ien.** In the rhyme *reprent:tient* 1471, *reprent* stands probably for *reprient*,[4] and in *tent:reprent* 1473, *tent* may be from *tendit*. Pure rhymes such as *ren:bien* 1973 are relatively frequent. *Nient* rhymes only with -*ent* words, *susprent:nient* 673, *prent:nient* 1385, *nient:cumprent* 2251, but it is uncertain, owing to the varying syllable count, whether *nient* is monosyllablic, disyllabic, or variable.[5]

Learned words in -*ien* invariably rhyme with -*en* words, the ending -*ien* in these cases being probably disyllabic, *orient:occident* 1479, *orient:gent* 1255, *sentence:sapience* 171, *conscience:tence* 2065, but note *Indien:bien* 539. Similarly treated are words in -*ian*, *Madian:an* 777; -*ean*, *occean:pan* 481; -*iun*, *creaciun:truvum* 271, *distinctiun:envirun* 467; and -*eun*, *draguns:leuns* 527.

11. ǒ + yod> **u i** and rhymes with *ui* < *ū* + yod, *nuist*(< *nǒcet*): *luist* (<*lūcet*) 1553, *lust:nust* 1183, and *relut:nut* 1869 (with loss of *s* before cons., apparently scribal). Within the line we have *ennui* 1308.

The rhyme *cult:bult* (< *bǔllit*) 1455 and 1621 represents a reduction of *cuilt:built*, in which *cuilt* is probably by analogy

---

[1] See H. Suchier *Reimpredigt* (Halle, 1879) pp. 69 f.; cf. also Menger *op. cit.* p. 54.
[2] For the form *miluein* see note to l. 351.
[3] The rhyme *miens:tens* occurs in Gaimar *Estorie des Engleis* l. 1811. For the infinitive *reindre* see Pope *op. cit.* sec. 936 (ii), Cf. also *parreindre* in l. 2208 of the text.
[4] See note to l. 1471.
[5] On this word see E. Walberg *Le Bestiaire de Philippe de Thaün* (Lund, 1900) pp. li f.

with the infinitive *cuillir*. The phonetic value of the rhyme is not assured, but since *l* before consonant vocalizes,[1] and since reduction of *ui* to *u* is probably true for the author, we can conjecture a rhyme **kut:but**. It is not certain whether this *ui* can be equated with those discussed above, the only other rhyme occurring being *cunoisse:anguisse* 2179.

Reduction of *ui* to *u* is not established by rhyme since the rhymes *use:aguse* 2357 and *pertuz:veluz* 631 indicate rather that palatal *s* did not resolve into *is* but depalatalized to dental *s* as in Western French.[2] However, since this reduction is usual in Anglo-Norman texts of the thirteenth century, it is altogether probable that it was familiar to our author.[3] Reduction to **wi** is established after *c*(**k**) by the rhymes *defit:quit* (< *cöquit*) 1617 and *petit:quit* (< *cöquit*) 2061.[4]

The *ui* of *cestui* and *lui* rhymes with *i* and is reduced to *i* in spelling at least by the scribes: *cestui:si* 909, *ci:cesti* 1423, *enemi:li* 2559. The diphthong must have been ascending in this case. Such rhymes began to appear in the twelfth century.[5]

The diphthong resulting from *au* + yod does not occur in rhyme. Its orthography is regularly *oi*, compare ll. 784, 1543, 2088, 2739, etc.

One rhyme combines the product of -*ūniu* with that of -*ŭniu*, *juin:essoin* 1379.[6]

12. For tonic free **o** our text offers but one rhyme *sen:bon* 2585, consequently it is not possible to establish precisely its phonetic value. Diphthongization before nasal consonant took place early in Anglo-Norman since we already find in the *Brendan* the rhyme *mien:soen* 751.[7] This rhyme indicates an

---

[1] See below, paragraph 16.

[2] Cf. Pope *op. cit.* secs. 315 and 1086.

[3] See Pope *op. cit.* sec. 1160; Stimming *op. cit.* pp. 209 f.; Matzke *Les Oeuvres de Simund de Freine*, p. xxvii; Koch *op. cit.* p. xxix, and Ewert *op. cit.* I, p. xxii.

[4] Also continental, cf. Pope *op. cit.* sec. 1160.

[5] See Stimming *op. cit.* pp. 209 f. These forms are also Continental, cf. Pope *op. cit.* secs. 515 and 517.

[6] For *essoin* see Gamillscheg, p. 804. Cf. also the rhyme *joinz:poinz* 1987.

[7] See Waters' discussion in his introduction, pp. cxlvii f.

ascending diphthong, which would explain the scribal reduction of *soen* to *sen* in our text, but whether or not the diphthong
was reduced to a simple vowel in our author's language cannot
be ascertained.

In the rhyme *pelote:mote* 253 *mote* is a learned form based
directly on *motu* of the Latin text. The usual form from **movita*
is *moete* or *muete*[1] but its meaning is not 'motion' as is the case
for *mote* in our text.

13. **locum> liu,** *lius:eschius* 1259, the prevailing orthography
in the MSS being *iu*, but *ui* and *u* also occur, neither proven by
rhyme.[2] Freine has *liu* once in rhyme[3] and the *Chateau d'Amour*
has *liu* and *lu* in rhyme.[4] Since *liu* is a reduction of *lieu*, we may
note here that *griu(s)* (var. *gru* and *greu*) occurs in our poem
within the line (cf. ll. 1996, 2270, and 2334).

focum >feu (*:vertu*) 1871. The same rhyme occurs in the
Vie de Saint Georges 219, Adgar offers *fu:ennu*,[5] and the *Vie de
St. Auban sarcu:lu* (< *lupu*).[6]

14. Open **o** checked rhymes only with itself. Here there is
only one rhyme of interest, *fous:avels* 2525, in which *avels*
represents *ad-velle +s*, from which we get *avęls*, which form
passes to *avǫls* as *essęl* became *essǫl*.[7] Since *l* before consonant
vocalizes to *u*[8] our rhyme is *fǫus:avǫus*. This latter word occurs
within the line in our text in lines 240, 2131 and 2717 and the
following orthographies are found, *avols, avous, avels, aveus,
avers, aveals*. As a furṫher example we may cite *chevols* 1146 for
which R offers *cheveuz*.

15. Close **o** free rhymes with close **o** checked, the orthography being uniformly *u*, *lungur:estur* 571, *jur:freidur* 1251,

---

[1] See Schwan-Behrens *Grammaire*, sec. 58[2]R.
[2] Note also the rhyme *Giu:liu* 991.
[3] Matzke *op. cit. Rom. de Phil.* 929.
[4] Murray *op. cit.* p. 47.
[5] See Carl Neuhaus *Adgar's Marien-Legenden* (Heilbronn, 1886), p. 26.
[6] Cf. Pope *op. cit.* sec. 1169: Suchier *Voyelles toniques* sec. 31; and Menger *op. cit.*
pp. 77 f.
[7] Cf. paragraph 1 above.
[8] See below, paragraph 16.

A3

menur:entur 933, *tur:freidur* 2079, *plusurs:curs* 2413, *estrus:nus* 1809, etc. This rhyme is regular in Anglo-Norman, occurring in the earliest texts.[1] It is a characteristic of Western French dialects.[2]

Both vowels in turn rhyme with **u** < Lat. *ū*, *dur:tristur* 671, *jur:oscur* 1879, *plus:gelus* (<*zēlōsus*) 2455, *creature:honure* 2201,[3] *anguissuse:encuse* 2519, *tenebrus:sus* (< *sūrsum*) 1405; *froidure: nature* 1635, *fu* (< *fuit*):*nevou* 815, *sure* (< *sŭpra*):*cure* 137.[4]

u in Latin loan words is treated similarly: *Romulus:estrus* 1099, *Herebus:penus* 1425, *Tartarus:confus* 1419, *Saturne:returne* 1895, *Venus:plus* 1957, etc.

Suchier originates the theory that the coupling in rhyme of ǫ with *u* < Lat. *ū* is peculiar to texts written in the North of England.[5] Most scholars have accepted Suchier's theory, but its reliability has been questioned by Vising, who points out that such rhymes are found also in Southern texts.[6] More recently Prior has noted this phenomenon in a text which he believes Southwestern.[7] It is open to doubt whether Suchier's distinction is valid for thirteenth century texts, even if it can be relied on for earlier works. Stimming, in discussing the possible home of the author of *Boeve de Haumtone*, admits that he most likely lived in the South, near his hero's home. But since the poem combines *u* and ǫ in rhyme he is forced to postulate a Northern reworking of a Southern original.[8] Granted that this rhyme originated in the North, it is quite possible that it soon spread to other parts of England.[9] I hesitate therefore to attribute the *Petite Philosophie* to a Northern author on the evidence of this one trait.

[1] Cf. Waters *op. cit.* p. cxlix; and Walberg *Bestiaire* p. xlvi.
[2] Cf. Pope *op. cit.* p. 502.
[3] See above under final atonic *e*, paragraph 6.
[4] Cf. Waters *ibid.*
[5] *Literaturblatt für germanische und romanische Philologie* IX (1888) 176. See also Suchier *Voyelles toniques* sec. 11c, and his *Vie de Seint Auban* p. 5.
[6] Cf. Vising *Archivum Romanicum* VIII (1924) 330 ff.
[7] See Prior *Anglo-Norman Texts* p. 7.
[8] Cf. *op. cit.* p. lviii.
[9] For further discussion and bibliography see Waters *op. cit.* p. cl; Menger *op. cit.* p. 67.

Close **o** free rhymes also with close **o** checked before nasal consonant, *envirun:sun* (< *sŭmmu*) 761, *sum:numum* 689. The orthography is consistently *u* in all cases.[1]

Close **o** does not rhyme with open **o**, except before a nasal consonant, where they rhyme together whether checked or free, *ʒone:bone* 2439, *mund:sumund* 1997 *funt:respunt* 2445, and perhaps *home:summe* 2103,[2] but the reading is doubtful.

There is no example in our poem of a rhyme between close *o* and *u* < *ū* before nasal consonant, unless the doubtful reading *home:une* 2103 *C* be accepted.[3]

16. Consonants. Here there are no unusual developments to consider. The following points may be noted.

c before **a** retains the velar pronunciation common to Northern French territory in the following rhymes, *musike: fiche* (<*figĭcare*, REW 3290) 1991, *riche:musike* 2001, *Aufrike: riche* 1367, *Carmarike:riche* 1209, etc.[4] The scribes seem to have used *ch* and *k* indiscriminately for this sound.

m and **n** final are not distinguished, *envirun:sun* (< *summu*) 761, *septentriun:sun* 977, *leun:nun* 1097, *septemtriun:numun* 1685, *voisin:venim* 1639, etc.[5] Likewise *m* may be coupled in rhyme with *mm*, *summe:pume* (<*poma*) 635.

m and **n** final after *r* have been lost, *lungur:estur* 571, *jur: freidur* 1251, and *menur:entur* 933.[6]

n-mouillé rhymes with *n* in two cases, *disne:reschine* (*rechignier*) 1341, and *Capricorne:borne* 2391.[7]

l-mouillé has been reduced to *l* before consonant and vocalized, *solalʒ:chalʒ* 449.[8] The rhyme *Pontil:exil* 967 is probably a case of final *l*-mouillé losing its palatalization, but the value of the *l* of *Pontil* is uncertain, the author having taken liberties

[1] See Menger *op. cit.* p. 69; and Stimming, *op. cit.* p. lii.
[2] On these rhymes cf. Menger *op. cit.* p. 69.
[3] For such rhymes see Menger *ibid.*
[4] Cf. Menger *op. cit.* p. 98.
[5] This trait was characteristic of Anglo-Norman from the beginning, cf. Walberg *Bestiaire* p. lvi.
[6] Also early, cf. Walberg *ibid.*
[7] See Vising *Etude* pp. 77 and 87.
[8] Cf. Waters' discussion in his edition of the *Brendan* p. cliv. For a discussion of the form *solalʒ* see above, paragraph 2.

with proper names, as he later writes this name *Pontin:fin* 1001. For the rhyme *solail:fail* see above, paragraph 4.

Vocalization of *l* to *u* before consonant is established by the rhyme *cels:Deus* 2473. Vocalization in Anglo-Norman occurs as early as Gaimar.[1]

s and *z* final are confused only three times in rhyme, *pertuz* (< *pertusiu*):*veluz* 631, *tens* (< *tempus*):*turmens* 2389, and *assens*: *cenz* 2019, although rhymes in *-enz* and *-ent* are very numerous. This confusion of *s* and *z* is also early.[2]

f and *p* before a flectional *s*, though written by the scribes, have no phonetic value, *mis:cheitifs* 2207, *grips:pais* (< *pagēnse*) 585. *p* also has no phonetic value before *t*, *desrumpt:funt* 1759, *amunt:rumpt* 1933.

r has been assimilated before *s*, *lors:os* (< *ossu*) 699, perhaps also *Mercurius:curs* 2007, where, however, the correct reading may be *Mercurs:curs*, compare *Mercur:aseur* 1955.

s disappears once before *n*, *disne:reschine* 1341;[3] and once before *t*,[4] *natres:Choatres* (< *Coatres*) 565.

For the treatment of *t* in verb endings, see below under 'Morphology,' pages xlii and xliii.

B. *Morphology.*—(1) Declension. Complete disorder in the declension of nouns, pronouns and adjectives prevails in the MSS of the *Petite Philosophie*. The original text was probably less faulty inasmuch as the correct flexional forms are often preserved by one or more MSS, and most frequently by *P* and *C*, the earliest and best. Nevertheless the rhymes prove that the author was responsible himself for some of the irregularities in declension found in the MSS. The oblique form for the nominative is attested by rhymes such as *sanc* (nom. sg.):*fanc* 1577, *mund* (nom. sg.):*sumund* 1997, *pecheur* (nom. sg.):*folur* (obl. sg.) 2625, *ciel* (obl. sg.):*camel* (nom. sg.) 2035, etc. Less frequently the *s* appears in the nominative plural masculine,

---

[1] See Menger *op. cit.* p. 85.
[2] Menger *op. cit.* p. 108.
[3] Schwan-Behrens gives this reduction as early, *Grammaire* sec. 280R.
[4] See Menger *op. cit.* p. 105.

tens:turmens (nom. pl.) 2389. In the long tirade in -*ez* which ends the poem, irregular forms are frequently admitted (cf. lines 2732 ff.). Occasionally even an oblique singular appears in this laisse, compare *de grez* 2735, 2859, etc., which elsewhere has the form *de gré*. The etymological nominative singular form of imparisyllabic words is preserved in a few cases: *crieres*: *manieres* 238, and within the line, *faitres* 215 and *faiters* 2583, *grip* 587, and *prestres* 778. *Compaings CG* 1707 is apparently the form used by the author instead of *cumpainun* of the other manuscripts, which gives a nine syllable line. In *grips:pais* 585 the nominative form functions as an oblique. Conversely the oblique functions as nominative singular: *empereur:valur* 825, *greinur:entur* 1819, *greinur:luur* 1873. The most frequently recurring word of this type is (*h*)*um* < *homo* for which the manuscripts strongly favour the monosyllabic form in the nominative singular, but never with analogical *s*, and the disyllabic form *humme* in other cases. But whenever the meaning is 'no one,' the oblique form stands as nominative singular, compare ll. 444, 486, 491, etc.

Non-agreement of the past participle is frequent, for instance, *feint* (m. sg. nom.):*remeint* 475, *numé* (m. sg. nom.):*plungé* (m. pl. nom.) 1409, *ausi:departi* (fem. sg.) 1985, and *cité:honouré* (f. sg.) 961.[1] Similarly the present participle does not agree consistently, *manant* (m. pl. nom.):*lusant* (f. pl. nom.) 911, *manant* (f. pl. nom.): *grant* (f. sg. obl.) 1355, *boillant* (m. sg. nom.): *grant* (m. sg. obl.) 1265, etc. Agreement of participial forms appears to have been optional for the author.

Agreement of adjectives is established by rhyme in a great majority of cases, but we may cite the following contrary examples, *lez*(< *laeti*, m. pl. nom. in a -*ez* laisse) 2736, *dit:parfit* (f. pl.) 2589, *clers* (m. pl. nom.):*encumbrers* 2239. All the cases in question are predicative.

Analogical feminine *e* for adjectives of the type *grandis* is

---

[1] The last two cases may represent loss of final atonic *e* after the tonic vowel, cf. above under 'Phonology,' paragraph 6.

infrequent in the MSS, and is not attested by rhyme except in the following cases, *pesante:hante* 353 and *fole:parole* 2183 and 2539. This latter rhyme is inconclusive as *fols* was assimilated early to the *bonus* type.[1] The forms *quele*, *tele*, and *duce*, which appear regularly in the MSS, were usual in Anglo-Norman from an early date.[2]

The pronominal forms *li* and *lui* are hopelessly confused by the scribes, and the rhymes prove nothing since *ui* may rhyme with *i* by virtue of the former's reduction to *i*.[3] The MSS also offer the contracted forms *els* for *eles*, and *el* for *elle* or *ele*,[4] which may belong to the author, since these words occasionally appear to have monosyllabic value in the line. The tonic form *sei* (*soi*) replaces the atonic twice in the text, *soi garir* 128 PR and in *sei getter* 2637 (all MSS), and occasionally appears elsewhere as a variant, compare *sei* 328 (*V*). Interesting also is the form *si* 2349 and 2580 which may represent *sei* (cf. note to l. 2349). I know of no other occurrence of such a form, but *mi* for *mei* is claimed by Vising for Fantosme and Adgar.[5] This form is Continental as well as Anglo-Norman, and is derived by Meyer-Lübke from *mihi*.[6]

The forms of the relative pronoun are regularly *ki* and *ke* in *P* but *qui* and *que* or *qe* occur, especially in MSS *G* and *R*. *Ki* is frequently written *ke* and *ke* occasionally stands for *ki*.[7] *Ke* = *ki* does not usually elide, and similarly *ke* = *kar*. *Ki* is also used as a genitive equivalent to *cui* (cf. ll. 802, 947, etc.).

Cel as demonstrative adjective is occasionally replaced by the late Anglo-Norman form *ço* in *P* (*ceo* appears also in the other MSS), ll. 465 and 1725.[8] *Iço* likewise replaces *icel* in line 2457. These forms are certainly scribal in our text. *Ço* in its

[1] Cf. Jenkins *Roland* p. cxv.
[2] Cf. Matzke *op. cit.* p. xxxix.
[3] Cf. above under 'Phonology,' paragraph 11.
[4] These forms are current in Anglo-Norman documents, cf. Menger *op. cit.* p. 117.
[5] See *Literaturblatt für germanische und romanische Philologie* III (1884) 68.
[6] Cf. *Grammaire* II, 102, sec. 75.
[7] See note to l. 2094.
[8] See Menger *op. cit.* p. 117; and Stimming *op. cit.* p. xxv.

turn is frequently replaced by *ce* in *P*, cf. ll. 561, 916, 1081, etc.

The inflection of the definite article is regular except that the oblique forms often replace *li* singular or plural, compare ll. 231, 317, 325, 420, 422, etc. MS R also uses the fourteenth century form *lui* for *li*. Occasionally *le* for *la* appears,[1] but rarely in *P*. Exceptional is the form *del* = *de* + *la*, *P* 224, and *C* 804. The combination *de* + *le* (= *la*) could become monosyllabic in value by enclisis, which would account for the orthography *del*. I know of no other example of this form.

We may note for the indefinite article the frequent use of *uns* and *unes* as plurals, compare *uns hummes* 570, *uns autres* 593, *unes ewes* 2459, etc.

The tonic form of the possessive adjective occurs four times with the definite article, ll. 172, 424, 1950, and 1985, three times with the demonstrative adjective, ll. 488, 1301, and 1302, and once with an indefinite adjective, l. 189. Worthy of note is the unusual phrase *les voz e lur pechez* 2801. *Si* and *sis* are confused by the scribes as nominative singular or plural, compare ll. 240, 1045, 1699, 1707. Note also *mi* as nominative singular in l. 303 *CDVG*.

(2) Conjugation. In contrast to the wavering declension the inflection of verbs remains relatively regular. There are few cases of shifting conjugation, but we find as past participle for *espenir espenez* 2893 alongside *espenie* 2703, etc., and *aneinti* 2561 for *aneanter*. *Furnie* (ind. pr. 3) 1178 seems to be an irregular form of *furnir*, perhaps coined to give a rhyme.[2] *Veste* 1782 and *perte* 2053 are merely scribal for *vest* and *pert*.[3] The scribe of *P* likewise confused the forms of *finer* and *finir*,[4] but both verbs were freely used by the author. Two verbs in *-ir* have mixed forms, compare *englute* 502 and *englutist* 511, *resplent* 1764 and *resplendi(s)t* (in the line) 1792.[5] *Marchir* has the non-inchoative

---

[1] Cf. Menger *op. cit.* p. 110.
[2] See note to this line.
[3] See above under 'Phonology,' paragraph 6.
[4] Cf. ll. 868, 890, 1162, 1206, etc.
[5] *Suffrist* 1574 (PG) alongside *sufre* 2628 is probably scribal, as the context requires *suffist*. For the above mixed forms see Pope *op. cit.* sec. 882.

ind. pr. 6 *marchent* 892.[1] Finally *veintre* uses two radicals in conjugation *vein-* and *venqu-* which explains *venquent* 625, *venquirent*
858 and *venquist* 1083, alongside *veintra* 242, *veint* 1855 and
vaint 2603.[2]

In the present indicative analogical *e* and *s* are not attested
in the first person, but only one example in rhyme occurs, *fail*:
solail 1868. Within the line we have *vois* < *vado* + *is* 1343, *faz* <
facio 217, and *voil* < *voleo* 2341. The third singular of *aveir* is
written *ad*, *at* or *a*, but the rhymes prove that the consonant was
silent, *la:a* 1119 and 2471, *Amana:a* 959, etc., which in turn
proves *va*, *ad:vad* 763, etc. The form *vait* is found in the line
2512, and *veit* occurs as a variant for *va* 1838 *C* within the
line. *Stat* > *estat:ad* 1235, but also *estet:tret* < *trahit* 803, *estait*:
trait 1609 and *esteit:feit* 1707. This form is frequent especially
in twelfth century Anglo-Norman.[3] The first person plural of
both indicative and subjunctive ends in *-um* in *P*, sometimes
-om in the other MSS, and rhymes freely with both *-um* or *-un*,
sum:numum 689, *nun:apelum* 831, *Laciun:disum* 1085, and *Bara-*
trum:numum 1427, etc.[4] Occasionally also *-uns* appears, *nuns*:
numuns 2337, *regiuns:diuns* 891, etc.[5] For *sumus* we regularly get
sumes, 1663, 2227, etc. In the present subjunctive third person
singular, alongside the etymological forms, *trespast:guast* 484,[6]
aturt 251, *ost* 1450, and *doint* 2915, appear the analogical forms
afole 17, *espire:dire* 156, *desplie:pie*(< *pica*) 161, *quide* 2189, *deigne*
164 and 2438,[7] and *ottraie* (BG) 2919. The forms in *-ge* likewise
occur in the line but not in rhyme: *tenge* 1944, *perge* (*pareat*)
1821 and *prenge* 2430.

In the imperfect indicative it is interesting to note that no
rhymes are found for the first conjugation, which suggests that
they had not been assimilated to the *-eit* type and were conse-

---

[1] Palsgrave still gives this verb as mixed, cf. Pope *ibid*.
[2] On the radicals of this verb see Pope *op. cit*. secs. 1038 and 943.
[3] Cf. Tanquerey *Evolution* pp. 144 and 145.
[4] *-um* is the regular Anglo-Norman desinence of the latter twelfth century,
cf. *ibid*. p. 179.
[5] For *diuns* see Pope *op. cit*. secs. 960 and 961. Cf. also *avum:dium* 2243.
[6] See note to this line.
[7] See notes to these lines.

quently difficult to use. Most early thirteenth century texts still offer examples of -*out* imperfects, compare Chardri *Josaphaz* 73, 955, etc., *Gui de Warewic* 8151 and 10221, *Chateau d'Amour* 1008, 1310, etc. The third plural desinence -*eient* has not been contracted to -*eint* or -*ent* in our text, save scribally in MSS *D* and *G*, and is disyllabic within the line. The imperfect of *estre* is dimorphic, compare *estoient* 167, etc., and *erent* (:*donerent*) 2326, etc.

In the preterite final *t* in the third singular of first conjugation verbs, though usually written, is graphic only; *la:funda* 1063, *ja:comença* 1321, etc. No rhymes occur for weak II and III, but the forms appear without *t* within the lines, *cunverti* 970, *suffri* 2206, *perdi* 95, *respundi* 97, etc. Strong perfects are in general regular. We may cite *refirent* 1226, *mist* and *mistrent* from *metre* 348, 198, etc., alongside *mist* and *mistrent* from *maneir* 814, 1321, etc., *purent* (*paistre*) 2727 and *turent* (*taisir*) 2723. *Fuit* > *fu*: *nevou* 815 and *habuit* > *out* in the line 1045, 1314, etc. It is also important to note that sigmatic forms do not appear in rhyme in our text.[1]

In the imperfect subjunctive no rhymes of interest occur. Within the line *dust* 1767 appears to have lost its atonic vowel. We may also cite *vosist* 107 and *volsist* 2094.[2]

The past participles *mu* 2175 and *cunu* 2176, as they stand in octosyllabic lines, appear to have lost their atonic vowels, while *conuz* 216 and *commu* 1677 may stand for *conëuz* and *commëu*, since they occur in lines of seven syllables. On the other hand, *coneu* 2464 (*DG conu*) is disyllabic despite the orthography, unless we admit a nine syllable line. It appears that the Anglo-Norman scribes used *eu* as equivalent to *u*, possibly because it was a traditional spelling.[3] To be noted also is the form *espuns* (*espundre*):*nuns* 2275.

---

[1] On perfect forms in Anglo-Norman see Tanquerey *Evolution* pp. 610 ff.

[2] The forms *pussum* 2236, *pusse* 2327 and *pussez* 2805 are probably all presents, but the reduction of *ui* to *u* has rendered their identification difficult.

[3] Koch arrived at a similar conclusion for the MSS of Chardri, cf. Koch's edition, p. xxx. Cf. also Paul Meyer's remarks in the introduction to his edition of *Saint Thomas de Cantorbéry* p. xxix.

The future of *estre* is dimorphic, *ert* 126, 130, *donerent:erent* 2325, etc., occurring alongside *serrad:ad* 1850, *serrunt* 51, etc. *Aveir* has the intrusive *e* regularly, *avera* 111, 701, etc.,[1] which however does not seem to have syllabic value in the verse, while *faire* is contracted without exception in the MSS, 416, 2514, etc. An intrusive *e* is frequently found in other verbs also, compare *meinderunt* 2653, *defenderunt* (*desfendre*) 1662, etc., *Larrai* 159 is probably from *laier* not *laissier*, compare also the present indicative *lest* 1560. Of interest is the form *arsereit* (P only) 1817, for which *RCDG* read *ardereit*. This form must be on the analogy of the perfect. For *terrai* (*taisir*) 2416 *C* reads *teserai*, compare also *C*'s reading *lusera* 2908 (*B reluira*), for the future third singular of *luire*.

C. *Versification.*—The number of syllables in the lines of the *Petite Philosophie* is not constant, which is equivalent to saying that, from the point of view of Continental French prosody, the versification is irregular. The basic line is the octosyllable except for 205 lines at the end which are decasyllabic. The text of this edition has not been emended for metrical reasons, consequently, although a very large majority of the lines of the text read as octosyllables, there are many which are irregular in syllable count. For most of these lines one or more of the MSS offer an octosyllabic variant, which creates a strong presumption that many of these lines were regular in the original text. Nevertheless it is impossible to absolve the author from partial responsibility for the varying length of the line. Occasionally one comes to a line which, by agreement of all the MSS, is too long or too short, and for which an emendation does not readily suggest itself. These lines fall into three distinct types, (*a*) lines in which the eighth syllable is feminine; (*b*) lines of seven syllables; (*c*) lines of more than eight syllables. Examples of each of these types are:

Type (*a*)

France l'um dit, e Cumee.   1145
L'ydle par est tant plentive.   1387

---

[1] *avrez* occurs twice, cf. ll. 1970 and 2864.

Galaras est une zone.	2439
Tut fet, tut tient, tut aurne.	2511

Type (b)

Deu duna a Salamun.	105
U li froit fet sun estal.	454
Saturne nun lui duna.	1082
E si al matin ruvist.	2315

Type (c)

Ke de la cité Palestin nun tret.	804
La est Pelopenens la cité.	1061
Vers occident ad citez de pris.	1268
K'en enfer averont li suduiant.	2105

There are no octosyllabic variants for any of these lines: they are grammatically correct and the ideas are expressed with clarity and precision; it seems necessary, therefore, to attribute them to the author himself.

Those who have dealt with Anglo-Norman rhymed texts are familiar with the vexing problem of their versification. Various attempts, none entirely satisfactory, have been made to account for the varying number of syllables in the lines, nevertheless no uniformity of opinion has yet been reached.[1] The introduction to an edition is not a suitable place to debate this highly controversial question, consequently only a brief statement will be given here and the versification of the *Petite Philosophie* will be reserved for detailed discussion elsewhere at a later date. It is in order however to say that, after having read and re-read the text, my conviction has grown that its author was no semi-illiterate trying to write correct French verse according to imperfectly known Continental standards, but rather that he was a man of considerable culture entirely content to write in the form of French familiar to him, that current in England in the thirteenth century, of which he possessed an adequate knowledge and in which he could express himself with pre-

[1] For a bibliography and commentary on this problem down to 1909 see Matzke *op. cit.* p. xliv; and for a convenient summary with additional references see Vising *Anglo-Norman Language and Literature* pp. 79 ff.

cision and assurance. I am convinced also that he was perfectly well aware of what an octosyllabic line was and that when he wrote lines having fewer or more syllables he did so deliberately and could have done otherwise had he so wished.

Scansion of many lines in our poem is clearly impossible unless atonic *e* can be suppressed in certain cases. Everyone is familiar with Suchier's analysis of this problem in his study on the *Vie de Seint Auban*. The system there evolved has been applied[1] in studying the lines of our text which are apparently hypermetrical and it has been found that only a few do not fit into the categories he suggested. As printed in the text the lines of the *Petite Philosophie* vary in syllable count from six to eleven (cf. ll. 1771 and 1903). There is no reason to attribute any of the six syllable lines to the author as in every case an emendation is evident or at least one more syllable is supplied by the other MSS. The seven syllable masculine line has been accepted for the author in forty six cases by virtue of the agreement of all or of the better MSS. Similarly the seven syllable feminine line is assured in twenty-five cases. This latter type had been admitted into Anglo-Norman octosyllabic verse from the beginning, cf. the *Brendan*. Here it should be recalled that, if certain atonic *e*'s may be suppressed in reading lines apparently hypermetrical, the syllabic value of these same vowels becomes problematic in the octosyllabic lines, hence many lines may be considered as either heptasyllabic or octosyllabic according to the value given these vowels. Of course the syllable count cannot be employed to determine the author's scansion, therefore we cannot be sure how to classify such lines.

In considering lines of more than eight syllables well supported octosyllabic variants have been accepted as representing in all probability the original line. The reader should also note that a long series of double forms of different length were

---

[1] In the notes I have indicated how Suchier's system may be applied to explain lines apparently irregular; cf. notes to ll. 153, 164, 224, 295, 308, 388, 762 and 763.

available in our author's language, which provides an easy way of rectifying the syllable count in many lines. Finally, after application of Suchier's principles, there remain in all eleven lines still hypermetrical as follows: 224, 575, 618, 804, 817, 1061, 1268, 2026, 2035, 2105, 2710, for which possible emendations have been suggested in the notes.

The above discussion has not taken into consideration the last 205 lines (2716-2920) of our poem which are in decasyllabic monorhymes. The shift to this meter occurs abruptly in the midst of a laisse (monorhymes begin at line 2597), and without change of style or subject matter. The *Petite Philosophie* is not unique in having a change of meter, since other cases occur in Anglo-Norman, notably in *Gui de Warewic*, lines 10069-10112.[1] This phenomenon is rare in Continental texts.[2] To be noted also is the extreme length of the final laisse of our poem, which runs for 189 lines of text. Apparently the author's chief concern was not to avoid monotony.[3]

The decasyllabic portion of the poem is relatively regular in versification. The author admits into this group a few nine syllable feminine lines, and occasionally also a line of nine syllables. After taking variants into consideration only two lines, 2799 and 2815, have eleven syllables, and both can be easily emended. The decasyllabic lines regularly have a clearly marked caesura after the fourth syllable, though occasionally it falls after the sixth syllable. Both the epic and lyric caesura are used, that is, if the fourth syllable be tonic, an atonic syllable following may not count, but if the fourth syllable be atonic the following syllable invariably counts.

The author of the *Petite Philosophie* rhymed correctly, there being no rhymes in the poems which can be shown to be inexact or approximate. Almost nine and one-half per cent.

---

[1] Other examples are given by Vising *op. cit.* p. 83.
[2] Cf. Adolf Tobler *Vom französischen Versbau* (6th ed.; Leipzig, 1921) pp. 10 f.
[3] The rhymed laisse is frequently employed in Anglo-Norman, cf. the *Vie de Saint Auban, Boeve de Haumtone,* and the *Sermon de Guischart de Beaulieu,* ed. A. Gabrielson (Upsala, 1909).

of the rhymes are rich, and two per cent. are leonine. Of the
2920 lines 849 are feminine and 2071 masculine.[1] The author
occasionally rhymes a word with itself, compare ll. 547–8 and
2167–8, and also frequently continues the same rhyme for
several couplets, compare ll. 173–180, 1137–1142, 2057–2062,
etc.[2] In the portion of the poem devoted to the presentation
of factual information the rhyme serves little purpose beyond
marking the end of the line, and is consequently almost devoid
of artistic value. The frequent recurrence in rhyme of the
verbal desinences -*unt*, -*um*, -*eit*, etc., produces a decidedly
monotonous effect. Elsewhere, however, notably in the first
part of the poem, the rhymes are quite good, and show that
the poet had acquired a reasonable degree of skill in the art of
writing verse.

5. Date

From the evidence obtained in the foregoing study on the
language of the text, it is possible to determine the date of the
Petite Philosophie within narrow limits. Comparison with
Anglo-Norman literary productions of the late twelfth and
early thirteenth centuries, definitely locates our poem in the
latter period. We shall now present some of the evidence on
which this conclusion is based.

Outstanding in the language of the *Petite Philosophie* is the
combination in rhyme of the OF diphthongs *ai* and *ei*. Three
types may be distinguished as follows:

(1) Before *st*, *r*, *t*, and final in a syllable, with the phonetic
value of *ę*.

(2) Final in the word with diphthongal value.

(3) The rhyme -*ail* with -*eil*, value problematic.[3]

The diphthongs referred to above remained distinct during the
greater part of the twelfth century, except before nasal con-

[1] The uneven number results from the monorhymes at the end where the poet
disregards couplets. In arriving at this estimate the rhyme *e:ee* has been considered as masculine.
[2] This occurs frequently in Anglo-Norman, cf. Vising *op. cit.* p. 89.
[3] On these traits see under 'Phonology,' paragraph 4.

sonant, in which case they were coupled in rhyme as early as the *Brendan*.[1] In tracing the coalescence of these diphthongs we may select as point of departure the *Vie de Saint Gilles* of Guillaume de Berneville, *ca.* 1170. Gaston Paris establishes for this poem absolute distinction of *ai* and *ei*, both in final position and before a consonant.[2] In Fantosme's *Chronique* (before 1183) *ai:ei* only in the endings *-aire* and *-eire*.[3] In the *Protheselaus* of Hue de Rotelande (between 1174 and 1190), only a few examples of *ai* and *ei* occur in rhyme, this time before final *s* and *t*.[4] But when we turn to Simund de Freine (last decade of the twelfth century) a marked change is found to have occurred: *ai* rhymes freely with *ei* before *s*, *st*, *str*, *r*, *re*, and also when final (trait 2 above).[5] Matzke claims the value of *ę* for all these cases except the last, which he considers as diphthongal. But Freine still does not rhyme *-ail(le)* with *-eil(le)*. Passing on to Chardri (early thirteenth, before 1216), we find that his treatment of the diphthongs in question is more conservative than that of Freine, inasmuch as he combines them only in final position and before *str*.[6] But in Frère Angier (1212) we find complete identity of the two sounds in all positions, including the rhymes *-ail(le)* with *-eil(le)*.[7] Our poem offers but one example of trait 2, and only two of trait 3, whereas in Angier such rhymes are numerous. They continue to appear regularly in later works, compare the *Chateau d'Amour* (*ca.* 1230?),[8] *Gui de Warewic* (1232–42, no examples of trait 3),[9] and *Boeve de Haumtone* (1235–50),[10] etc. Thus on the basis of the traits under discussion the *Petite Philosophie* falls between Freine and

[1] Cf. Waters *Brendan* p. cxl; and Vising *Etude* p. 75.
[2] Cf. Gaston Paris and Alphonse Bos *La Vie de Saint Gilles* (Paris, 1881) p. xxvii.
[3] Vising *op. cit.* p. 75.
[4] Franz Kluckow *Protheselaus* (Göttingen, 1924) pp. 2 and 54 f.
[5] Matzke *op. cit.* pp. xxiii ff.
[6] Koch *op. cit.* p. xxvi.
[7] M. K. Pope *Etude sur la langue de Frère Angier* (Paris, 1904) p. 62.
[8] Murray *op. cit.* p. 46.
[9] Ewert *op. cit.* p. xx.
[10] Stimming *op. cit.* p. viii.

Chardri on one hand, and Frère Angier on the other. We consequently accept *ca.* 1210 as a *terminus a quo.*

Consideration of other traits lends support to this *terminus.* The *Petite Philosophie* rhymes freely *e* < tonic free *a* and *e* < *ié.* Neither of these *e*'s rhymes with *ę* except before *l*.[1] Freine and Chardri separate completely open *e* from the others in question, but in Frere Angier, on the other hand, confusion prevails.[2] Again Freine and Chardri each offer a few cases of rhymes between infinitives in *-er* and *-eir*.[3] The *Petite Philosophie* has no examples at all,[4] whereas in Angier they are relatively frequent.[5] Finally in the matter of versification the practice of our author is very similar to that of Chardri, while somewhat freer than that of Freine.[6] Angier's versification is much more regular than any of the other three, which fact is probably explained by his Continental origin.[7] Thus all these traits mark our poem as later than Chardri, and earlier than Angier, exception being made for versification.

In establishing a *terminus ad quem* for the *Petite Philosophie,* we shall first compare it to *Gui de Warewic.* The date fixed by Ewert for this poem (1232–42) is based on internal evidence.[8] Ewert admits that the language of the poem could, taken by itself, be accepted as somewhat earlier, consequently he is inclined to believe that it is slightly archaic for the date established.[9] The

---

[1] See above under 'Phonology,' paragraphs 1 and 3, cf. the rhyme *vol:asol.* For the rhymes *deboneire:matire* 289 and *matire:afeire* 313 see paragraph 7. The value of the rhymes *perent:querent, signifer:cler,* etc. (i.e. *e* <tonic free *a* before *r*), accepted as close above, paragraph 1, may also be questioned, since examples of confusion of *e* sounds before *r* occur in twelfth century texts; cf. Menger *op. cit.* p. 48, and Pope *Etude* p. 53. Suchier, admitting this confusion, thinks the value is close before *r*, though open before *l*, see *Voyelles toniques,* secs. 15 and 17. But Miss Pope in the above mentioned discussion, claims that *e* before *r* is open in Angier.

[2] Pope *op. cit.* p. 9.

[3] Cf. Matzke *op. cit.* p. xxi; and Koch *op. cit.* p. xxviii.

[4] See 'Phonology,' paragraph 5.

[5] See Pope *op. cit.* p. 9.

[6] Matzke *op. cit.* pp. xliii ff.; Koch *op. cit.* pp. xli ff.

[7] See Pope *op. cit.* p. 73.

[8] *Gui de Warewic* I, vii.

[9] *Ibid.* p. xxiv.

phonology and morphology of the *Warewic* is quite similar to that of our poem.[1] It seems slightly earlier in that it presents no confusion of *e* sounds and has no examples of *-ail(le):-eil(le)*. On the contrary it rhymes *ai:ei* more freely in final position, uses *-uns* in preference to *-um* as first plural verbal desinence,[2] and is decidedly more irregular in versification. These latter traits may result in part from the fact that the author of the *Warewic* was probably a protégé of a noble family, and perhaps less influenced by literary traditions than was our author, who was familiar with Latin writings and theological learning. Thus it is possible that our poem may be as late as the *Warewic*, but it is difficult to admit a later date, consequently I choose as our *terminus ad quem ca.* 1235.

On comparison with the *Vie de Saint Auban* (1230–50) and *Boeve de Haumtone* (same period),[3] the *Petite Philosophie* is definitely earlier. These poems show very free versification;[4] admit regularly rhymes of *-er* and *-eir* infinitives; rhyme in *ę* words which in Latin have an open *o* free; join regularly *-el<-alem* with *-ęl*; and rhyme freely *ai* and *ei* final (there is no laisse in *ai* in the *Vie de Saint Auban*).[5] Finally, the *Petite Philosophie* is distinctly earlier than the *Sermon en Vers*, which, according to Tanquerey, antedates slightly the two works under consideration.[6]

Thus the *Petite Philosophie* is certainly later than the works of Chardri, and seems somewhat less advanced phonologically than the works of Angier. On the other hand, our poem can hardly be later than *Gui de Warewic*. The author of the *Petite Philosophie* was apparently a churchman and very probably of mature years in view of the intellectual interest of his subject

---

[1] For the following comparison, cf. Ewert's discussion of 'Language,' *ibid.* pp. xiv ff.

[2] Tanquerey claims that *-um* is earlier than *-uns*, *Evolution* p. 179.

[3] Cf. Tanquerey *Evolution*, p. xiv.

[4] See Suchier *Vie de Seint Auban* pp. 14 ff.; and Stimming *op. cit.* pp. xxxii ff.

[5] See Stimming *op. cit.* pp. viii ff.; and the *-el* and *-er* laisses of the *Vie de Saint Auban*, ed. Robert Atkinson (London, 1876).

[6] See Tanquerey *Deux Poèmes* p. 41.

matter. His poem should therefore be dated as late as the linguistic evidence will permit, in other words, close to the *terminus ad quem.* I conclude consequently that the *Petite Philosophie* was composed *ca.* 1230.[1]

6. AUTHOR

The *Petite Philosophie* is anonymous, neither the poem itself nor any of the MSS affording us any hint as to the author's name or place of origin. In view of his familiarity with theological learning, and his eulogy of the state of celibacy, it is evident that he was connected with the church, and quite possibly in orders. In true clerical fashion he berates the lawyers, those ministers of Antichrist who mislead the laity, and especially the rich laymen who leave the poor and their shepherds without money and lands. But our author was certainly not a member of a monastic order, inasmuch as he makes no suggestion of retirement from the society of men, rather does he crave learning and strongly urges diligent enquiry in order to become wise. For him philosophical and theological learning are both essential to attainment of wisdom. Neither was he a man of low estate inasmuch as he praises *curtesie*, as well as *sen*. Apparently he was acquainted with the more refined social life of his period.

That the author was Anglo-Norman is proved beyond doubt by constant reduction of *ie* to *e*, and the free rhyming of close *o* with *u*.[2] The latter trait, according to Suchier would localize our poem in the North,[3] but as far as we have any record, no MS has ever been in that part of England, and there is no reason to believe that any of them was written by a Northern scribe. On the contrary *P* was written in Canterbury, and shows Kentish spellings. Likewise *C* is known to have been in London

---

[1] The *Petite Philosophie* is somewhat more conservative than the *Chateau d'Amour* of Grosseteste, which Miss Murray, on linguistic grounds, dates *ca.* 1230, cf. her edition, pp. 62 ff.

[2] To this might be added one case of *e* <tonic free *a* giving *ę*, cf. *asol* < **axale*, 'Phonology,' paragraph 1.

[3] Cf. 'Phonology,' paragraph 15.

before it became part of the library of Syon Monastery. When
the regional traits of Anglo-Norman MSS are more definitely
fixed, it may be possible to determine precisely the place of
origin of our MSS, and consequently to arrive at some conclusion regarding the locality in which the poem was written.[1]
But in the present state of our knowledge no definite results can
be achieved in this direction.

7. SOURCE

The *Petite Philosophie* is for the most part a relatively faithful
translation of book one of the *De imagine mundi libri tres*.[2] In
general our author was content to render his original literally,[3]
presenting the same facts in almost unchanged order. Some
material has been omitted: of the 140 captions of the *Imago*

[1] Cf. Prior's discussion of this problem in *Cambridge Anglo-Norman Texts* pp.
xxvi ff.

[2] This work was formerly attributed to Honorius Augustodunensis, and was
printed by Migne with the works of that author in *Pat. Lat.* CLXXII, 121 ff.
Migne merely reprinted the text of the *Bibliotheca maxima Patrum* published at
Lyons in 1677, XX, 1120–30. The *Imago mundi* was at one time included in the
writings of Saint Anselm, cf. the edition of the latter's works by J. Hochfeder
at Nuremberg in 1491. The first editor to include the work in the writings of
Honorius Augustodunensis was Jean Herold (Bâle, 1544). It is now well established that the author was not this Honorius but another called Solitarius or
Inclusus. German scholars identify this latter with a certain Honorius who was
a member of the order of Saint Peter at Ratisbon in the early twelfth century,
mainly because this city is added to the list of places in Germany mentioned by
Isidore of Seville, whose work is the main source of the *Imago mundi*; cf. J. A.
Endres, *Beitrag zur Geschichte des geistigen Lebens im* 12. *Jahrhundert* (Kempten,
1906), pp. 1 ff. and 45 ff. Another theory is that the author was an English monk,
in view of the unusually precise knowledge he possessed of the islands to the
North and West of Europe. This conjecture was first put forth by Tritenheim in
Fabricius' *Bibliotheca latina mediae et infimae aetatis* (3rd ed., Florence 1858) III,
261, and has received support in the most recent scholarly study on the *Imago
mundi* by Pierre Duhem, see *Le Système du monde, histoire des doctrines cosmologiques
de Platon à Copernic* (Paris, 1913–17) III, 24 ff. Duhem has likewise established
Honorius' sources with precision, namely, Isidore of Seville, Bede, and Pliny
the Elder. For information on the MSS and editions of Honorius Augustodunensis and of the *Imago mundi* see, in addition to Migne, Endres, and Duhem,
the *Histoire littéraire de la France* XII, 165 ff.; Potthast, *Wegweiser* I, 620; and
Manitius, *Geschichte der lateinischen Literatur des Mittelalters* III, 364 ff.

[3] Translation from the Latin begins at l. 253 and ends at l. 2474. Within these
limits there is one long passage, ll. 2031–2242, and three shorter ones, ll. 425–460,
1609–24 and 2413–2438, for which there is no equivalent in the Migne text. In
addition about 300 lines of the poem are mere amplifications of the Latin.

mundi thirty-seven have been passed over completely, including almost the entire passage on the constellations, thirty captions in all, numbers CVI–CXXXV. Apparently the author thought that such information was unlikely to interest the lay reader.[1] Within the captions a choice of details is often made, for instance the list of names in the passage on islands is considerably reduced.[2] Of interest also is the rejection of the mythological explanations for the signs of the zodiac, on the ground that fables are false and consequently harmful.[3] Almost no factual information has been added by the author.[4] Jason and the Golden Fleece are not mentioned in any version of the *Imago mundi* I have examined, but this item was very probably in the MS used by the author. A short passage on water, lines 1609–24 has been added, but contains only one idea not found elsewhere in the poem.[5] The most important addition is the passage, lines 425–60, which constitute an amplification of the summary account of the terrestrial zones given in lines 417–24. Here again little information is added which the poem does not give elsewhere and it is unnecessary to postulate a second source. Since the amplification in question could have been made quite as well in the Latin as in the Old French it is not certain to whom it should be credited.[6] Numerous chevilles are likewise found in the text, their presence being easily explained by the difficulty of finding rhymes for many of the proper names. In a number of cases statements are made in those chevilles which seem to have no foundation in fact and appear to represent nothing more than figments of the author's imagination.[7]

Mention of the sky at the end of the passage on celestial

[1] Cf. ll. 2416 ff.
[2] Cf. ll. 1285 ff.
[3] Cf. note to ll. 2339–44.
[4] The Migne text lacks certain passages found in the older editions. These I have indicated in the notes.
[5] See note to ll. 1609–24.
[6] See note to ll. 425–60.
[7] Cf. ll. 798, 830, 836, 904, 964, 1160, etc.

measurements provides the author with a pretext for inserting a long tirade, lines 2031–2242, on the impossibility of the sin-laden soul rising to heaven, and the necessity of repentance, confession and absolution before death. Likewise a reference to God at the end of the translation from the Latin text (line 2474) leads to the appending of a long sermon of 446 lines, the phraseology and ideas of which are similar to those of the homilies of the twelfth and thirteenth centuries, both in Latin and in the vernacular.[1] That the author was here handling material perfectly familiar to him is evident from the spon-taneous profusion of the language, and it is not necessary to assume that he was using a written source. However it is worth noting that numerous points of resemblance exist between our text and the *Elucidarium* of Honorius Augustodunensis,[2] for instance, the list of torments in Hell is similar, including the idea of alternation of extreme heat and cold, the idea that the saved and damned can see each other, that the earth will side with God against the sinner at Judgment, that the joys of heaven will be increased when soul and body are re-united, that man cannot conceive of the joys of the blest and the tor-ments of the damned, that angels have bodies of fire and devils of air, etc. Such ideas were too widespread to prove that the *Elucidarium* was an immediate source of our poem, nevertheless it appears to be the most probable written source if such were employed.[3]

Special mention must be accorded the promise of heavenly mistresses to those who live chaste lives on earth, lines 2676–2704. As far as I am aware nowhere else in Christian literature

---

[1] Cf. the *Sermon de Guichart de Beaulieu*; the *Chateau d'Amour* of Grosseteste; the *Reimpredigt* published by Suchier; the *Sermon en Vers* published by Tanquerey; the *Evangiles des domnées* of Robert of Gretham, ed. M. Y. H. Aitken (Paris, 1922); and the Latin homilies in the *Vitae Patrum*, Migne *Pat. Lat.* LXXIII. Close similarity is a well known characteristic of mediaeval sermons, owing to the widespread use of the same models; cf. Lecoy de La Marche, *La Chaire française au moyen âge* (Paris, 1886), p. 270.

[2] Cf. especially coll. 1157–83 in Migne *Pat. Lat.* CLXXII.

[3] References are given in the notes to the passages in question.

is such a reward promised for celibacy. Following this passage
is a second, lines 2705–2719 which asserts that self-denying
Christian marriages will be re-constituted in heaven. This idea
is also extraordinary since the orthodox Christian heaven was
not a place for 'marrying and giving in marriage.' Whether
or not our author is responsible for such assertions we have no
way of knowing, but it is obvious that they are heretical in
character and one wonders how they were received by the
religious authorities. In any case they serve to break the
monotony of the tiresome sermon in which they are found, and
consequently are amply justified from the literary point of view.

Of interest also is the prologue of 166 lines which constitutes a sort of preamble in which our author seeks to justify
himself for displaying his mediocre literary talents. Two main
ideas are developed, namely, the superiority of learning over
wealth and the jealous criticisms directed by the enviously
ignorant at those who had sufficient knowledge and ability to
write. Prologues of this sort had always been especially popular
in Anglo-Norman. Philipe de Thaün apologizes similarly for
deigning to write, and answers in advance the anticipated
envious detractors of his work.[1] He seems to have been chosen
as model by Denis Piramus in the 'Prologue' to his *Vie de
Seint Edmund*.[2] Robert of Gretham also writes a lengthy defence
of his intention to translate into French a book of sermons for
a certain Dame Aline, and he likewise warns against the *enviüs*
who will criticize his work.[3]

Since this prologue is found in only two MSS, *P* and *R*,
the question arises as to its authenticity. In the first place, it is
unlikely that a thirteenth century Anglo-Norman author
would begin his poem as in line 167 of the edition, without

[1] See E. Mall *Li Cumpoz Philipe de Thaün* (Strassburg, 1873) pp. 5 and 22.
[2] Ed. F. L. Ravenel (Philadelphia, 1906) pp. 57 ff.
[3] *Op. cit.* p. 108. Cf. also a passage in the *Image du monde*, ed. O. H. Prior (Paris, 1913), p. 74, in which the author Gautier de Metz expresses sentiments com-
parable to those of our author; P. J. Jones *Prologue and Epilogue in Old French Lives
of Saints* (University of Pennsylvania Dissertation, Philadelphia 1923) pp. 53 ff.

addressing to his readers the usual apologetic justification for his poem. The absence of such an opening in the archtype of *y* led the scribe of *D*, or an earlier scribe, to compose another prologue, that found in the 'Appendix.' Secondly, there is no linguistic reason for rejecting this passage. Finally, it is found in the best MS of the poem. Since there are thus no good reasons for considering it an addition, it has been incorporated in the edition as part of the poem.

Following the prologue just discussed is a second passage, lines 167–252, the purpose of which is to introduce the material translated from the *Imago mundi*, and which is a brief summary of the current notions respecting the search for knowledge by the ancient philosophers. No direct source for this material can be established since only a general outline of this story is given. Such information, it may be noted, is found in the works of Alexander Neckam,[1] a compatriot of our author. A presumption in favour of Neckam as source is created by the fact that he also relates how the fox befouls the badger's den in order to force him to leave it.[2] Neckam likewise compares the slanderer to the serpent as does our author.[3] But such points of contact are not sufficient to constitute proof of direct borrowing. Since the *Petite Philosophie* contains no passages for which an immediate source can be established, except in the case of the *Imago mundi*, we are probably justified in crediting to the author the remaining portions of the poem.

8. ESTABLISHMENT OF TEXT

This edition is based on MS *P*, the orthography and readings of which have been given unaltered except in those cases where, in order to produce a readable text, it has been necessary to correct obvious errors. The deficiencies of the text of *P* such as lacunae, omissions, displacements, repetitions, etc., have

---

[1] See Alexander Neckam *De naturis rerum*, ed. T. Wright ('Rolls Series'; London, 1863) II, 207.
[2] Cf. ll. 31–32, and Neckam, *loc. cit.*
[3] *Op. cit.* II, 320, and the text, ll. 10 ff.

been made good. The text itself has been emended in the following cases: (*a*) When *P* is isolated against R plus *y* in a reading which involves a real difference in meaning. (*b*) When *y* plus the Latin are opposed to *x*. (*c*) When *x* and *y* differ and *y* can be proved correct. These latter cases are generally discussed in the notes. When the text of *P* appears corrupt, but the other MSS fail to indicate what emendation should be made, *P* has been printed unaltered with full variants and possible emendations suggested in a note. When the text of *P* has been emended, the source of the emendation is given, followed by the rejected reading of *P* and the variants from the other MSS, immediately below the last line of text on the page. In this case it is understood that non-mention of a MS means that it lacks the line in question. If the emendation is supported by the Latin, this is cited within round brackets immediately following the sigla of the MSS giving the emendation. An emendation reproduces the orthography of the first MS cited as source. Occasionally the orthography of an emendation has been made to conform to the practice of *P* in order to avoid placing unusual forms in the text. In these cases the orthography of the MS cited as source appears in the emendation and the sigla of the supporting MSS are followed by a comma rather than a square bracket (cf. *vult* restored to the text in l. 247 from C's reading *voet*).

Abbreviations have been expanded according to the practice of the scribe of *P*. In doing so only one case arose where there was reason to hesitate, namely the expansion of the sign '9.' The scribe wrote this syllable out as either *cun*(*m*) or *con*(*m*). Consequently the form most frequently used in a given word was adopted in expanding abbreviations of that word. The use of *u* and *v* and *i* and *j* has been regularized on the basis of vocalic or consonantal value. The modern forms *de l'* and *a l'* have been written before vowels although the MSS regularly use *del* and *al*. All proper names and initial words have been capitalized and modern punctuation has been added to the text. Illumination in the MS has been indicated by indentation

in the text when it corresponds to a logical division in the
subject matter, otherwise it has been disregarded.[1] On the
other hand indentation has been made in a number of cases
where there is no illumination in P.[2] The acute accent has been
written on final tonic -é and -és of polysyllabic words to distinguish them from atonic -e and -es, and likewise in a few cases
on monosyllabic words to distinguish like forms, cf. pié(pied)
and pie (< pica). The cedilla has been placed under c before a,
o, or u whenever it has the sound of c before e or i.

Diaeresis has not been used in the edition, since the usual
criterion, the syllable count, is unreliable in our text. In a few
cases use of diaeresis can be justified by the evidence afforded
by rhyme. Thus the rhyme meime:abime 2069 proves meïme in
this case. But one example can hardly be accepted as proving
meïme in all cases, as the author might have used both the long
and contracted forms. The learned endings such as -ial, and
-iun seem generally to be disyllabic, but lines occur in which
they appear to have undergone syneresis. As for atonic e in
hiatus before or after the tonic vowel it is not possible to
determine with certainty those cases in which the author gave
the vowel syllabic value. The rhyme escripture:vesture 381 proves
nothing as to whether we should read vesture or vesteüre, since
the seven syllable feminine line is attested for the author. Thus
it is precisely in those cases where diaeresis would be most
helpful that it is least possible to prove its validity. Since an
attempt to use diaeresis must of necessity result in many
arbitrary decisions it has been deemed wisest to omit it
altogether.[3]

In addition to the emendations discussed above certain minor
corrections in the text have been made systematically without

---

[1] Such cases are ll. 57, 65, 70, 71, 227, 234, 247, 249, 255, 283, 290, 295, 405
409, 469, 479, 539, 547, 769, 939, 1003, 1007, 1009, 1011, 1019, 1067, 1077,
1113, 1119, 1121, 1125, 1158, 1313, 1402, 1515, 1711, 2465, 2769, and 2057 and
2137 where C serves as base MS.
[2] In ll. 597, 767, 2295, 2307, 2329, 2403, 2597, 2605, 2639: 2661 and 2705.
[3] Ewert, in his recent edition of Gui de Warewic, refrains for similar reasons
from using diaeresis. See his introduction, p. xxvii.

emendation. These are (*a*) restoration within square brackets of the following final consonants which were occasionally omitted by the scribe: (1) *l* in 110, 775, 827, 2297, 2489, 2501, 2533, 2561, 2586. (2) *r* in 1404, 2393, 2394, 2438. (3) *s* in 2308. (4) *st* in 1814, 2501, 2569. (5) *t* in 230, 1746, 1958, 1986, 2176, 2449, 2489. (*b*) letters restored within a word: (1) *e* in 2821, 2830. (2) *n* (no overstroke) in 31, 121, 275, 442, 833, 1010, 1315, 1787, 2329, 2394, 2512, 2532, 2632, 2707, 2729. (3) *s* before consonant in 1156, 1997, 2634. (4) *t* in 2848. (5) *u* in 326, 2502. (6) *v* in 1487, 1952. (*c*) correction of evident errors (MS reading within round brackets): *del(des)* 27, *dist(dst)* 33, *Le*(illuminated *K* for *L*) 405, *en* (last stroke of *n* missing) 414, *Rin(Bin)* 1131,*Leunais(Leumais)*1147, *Galice(Calice)*1167, *Arsinoe(Arsimoe)* 1213, *Aufrike(austrike)* 1277, *retrover(re retrover)* 1386, *arusent* (*aruseent*) 1590, *amertume*(last *m* has 4 strokes) 1591, *sulfre* (*sulfle*?) 1632, *Eir* (illuminated *A* before *Eir*) 1665, *ferir(ferit)* 1720, *element(elelement)* 1789, *la(la la)* 1831, *cercles(ce cercles)* 1914, *espeudre* (*espeuare*) 2285, *alcun(n* has one stroke only) 2594, *Plus* (illuminated *E* for *P*) 2655, *Deu* (illuminated *L* for *D*) 2661. (*d*) *s* corrected to *f*, *chief* 80, *fent* 515, *fet* 1002, *finant* 1010. (*e*) *f* corrected to *s*, *resunt* 2403, 2409. (*f*) *t* corrected to *c*, *purceint* 268, 492, 540 (*purtient* corrected to *purceint*), 1624, *Chambises* 883, *curt* 1780, *trescurt* 1839, *presence* 1879.

The following corrections made in the MS by the corrector have been incorporated in the text (corrections are indicated within round brackets): *fuiez* (*z* added after final *t* altered to *z*?) 387, *late* (*t* written above *c*) 746, *Mes* (*s* inserted) 2508, *Bel* (MS *Del*, *b* in margin) 2314, *Dez* (written above *.ii.*) 2431, *Deus* (*v = u* written over *n*) 2474, *pussant* (first *s* inserted) 2475, *dehors* (*h* and *s* inserted) 2498, *cuntent* (first *t* written above *c*) 2499, *environ* (overstroke for first *n* added) 2500, *esquis* (first *s* inserted) 2504, *aurne* (MS *auure*, *rn* written above *ur*) 2511, *quanque* (abbreviation for *ua* added) 2515, *encusera* (MS *enseuera*, *seu* underlined and *cus* in margin) 2527, *lé rechesses* (MS *lenchesses*, *n* stroked out and *re* written above) 2529, *mal* (*l* inserted)

2538, *sert* (*t* inserted) 2559, *fort* (written in margin) 2584, *trahit* (MS *trahir*, *t* in margin) 2621, *met* (*t* inserted) 2649, *est* (added in space left by scribe) 2673, *dirrait* (MS -*at*, *ai* written above *a*) 2692.

Corrections made by the scribe have been followed. For the most part these are quite clear and there is no need to record them. The following cases justify citation: *mauls* or *maulz*? written over another word 28; *tutdis* written above *trestuit* not expunctuated 332; *munt*, *mult*? corrected to *munt* 364; *ni vient*, MS *n vient*, perhaps for *ni vent* 876. The scribe hesitated between *t* and *z* final and wrote one over the other several times, with the result that sometimes it is difficult to determine which letter was written last. Such cases are *element* 311, *numez* 1103, *floz* 1499, *cuntenanz* 1841, *finez* 1894, *joinz* 1987.

Economy of space has made it necessary to disregard a mass of variants which do not affect in any way the sense of the text. Such are, variations in orthography and alternate forms of words, presence or absence of inflection in substantives, adjectives and pronouns, agreement, elision, enclisis, etc. In such matters no uniformity exists even within the MSS and it is clearly impossible to determine the author's practice. Consequently only those variants are recorded which serve to establish a critical control of the text. These have been selected according to the following system:

(1) Isolated readings which occur in $RCDVGB$ are usually not recorded. For the most part they are corrupt and without value for the establishment of the text.

(2) When $x(PR)$ and $y(CDVGB)$ differ, the variant of y is recorded. Within y, DV have been considered as one MS and V has been cited instead of D only in a few cases where the latter's reading is corrupt. D breaks off at line 2546 after which its place is taken by the fragment B which begins at line 2468, and which like D is closely related to G. The group y has been considered therefore as consisting of three MSS, C, G, and DV or B. Of these C, the most reliable and probably the oldest,

stands by itself within y and must be accorded at least equal authority with DG. A reading is accepted as representing the group y whenever C is supported by DG, or by one of them when the other is isolated or does not contain the line in question. In these cases the variant is cited for y according to the orthography of C. Elsewhere the appropriate sigla accompany the variants. When x is supported by C the reading is assured and it is evident that no group variant for y exists, consequently a variant for DG represents a common error and can be disregarded. But G, though clearly a y MS, appears to represent a contaminated text and sometimes agrees with x against CD. When this occurs the reading of CD probably represents a y variant and has been recorded, it being understood that G agrees with x in this case. Similarly CG variants are recorded in the few cases where D supports x, although such agreements appear to be fortuitous. When x stands alone and y divides with C opposed to DG, either reading may represent the y variant and both have been recorded, unless for good reason one of them is inadmissible. A list of lines which are added or wanting in MSS C, D and G has been given in the notes.[1] Similarly for lines wanting in the other MSS and for all displaced or transposed lines see the section on 'Manuscripts' in the 'Introduction.' These have not been mentioned in the variants.

(3) When R agrees with y against P, the variant is recorded as Ry.

(4) When R agrees with any MS of y against P, the variant has been recorded unless it is of minor significance.

(5) When the reading of P is probably corrupt but left in the text all helpful variants have been given.

In the lacuna in x which extends from line 2031 to line 2144 the text is based on MS C supported by D and G, from which relatively full variants are given. A similar situation exists for the last 101 lines of the poem except that MS B replaces D.

---

[1] See below, pp. 99, 100.

The variants are arranged at the foot of the page, below the rejected readings of *P*, in the following general order of preference, *RCDVGB*. When necessary they are located in the line by giving the words immediately preceding and following, these reduced to initial letters if possible. Sometimes the word or words, for which the variant is to be cited, are given first, followed by a square bracket. Variants for the same part of a line are separated by commas, those for different parts by semicolons. The orthography of a variant cited for more than one MS is that of the first mentioned. When one of the MSS cited for a common variant differs by a word from the variant as given, such variation is noted within round brackets immediately after the word in question. Variants reproduce the MS readings exactly, except that abbreviations are expanded, and initial words are capitalized. MS sigla, and other words which do not form part of the variants proper, are italicized.

Since the Migne text of the *Imago mundi* is readily accessible, it has not been reproduced in the edition. It has been found necessary, however, to establish a control of this text, and the emendations which are essential have been indicated in the 'Notes' to the edition. For this purpose I have examined MS Cleopatra B iv of the British Museum, the edition of 1477? (before 1479) by Koberger at Nuremberg, the edition by Hochfeder at Nuremberg in 1491, the edition of 1497 at Basle by Amerbach, the edition by Herold at Basle in 1544, the edition at Spire in 1583 by Albin and the versions in the *Bibliotheca Patrum* published at Cologne in 1618 and Lyons in 1677.[1]

A complete analysis of the orthography of *P* is not provided, but attention is here drawn to some orthographical characteristics of the text which might cause difficulty to the reader. *Vowels.* (1) *i* is written *y* frequently in proper names, *Ylyun* 943, *Moyses* 776, etc., and occasionally elsewhere, *croyz* 164, *yle* 312, yver 410, etc.

---

[1] For bibliography see the references given on p. liii, n. 2.

(2) *ie*, being reduced to *e*, is frequently so spelled, *manere* 47, *vent* 918, etc.; also *ei*, *reveint* 2627, and *i*, *retint* (pr.) 1223 (see note).

(3) Close *e* is occasionally written *ie*, *fieble* 147, *clier* 1543, etc. (see note to l. 2316).

(4) Close *e* is twice written *ee*, *poeez* 1974 and *outreez* 2827.

(5) Tonic *ei* is sometimes written as *i*, cf. note to l. 648; and once as *ie*, *purtient* (corrected to *purceint*) 540.

(6) Open *e* is written *e*, *ei*, *ai* and *oi*, cf. 'Phonology,' paragraph 4.

(7) Open *e* is once written *ei* before *n*, *teint* (< *tendit*) 1076.

(8) Atonic *e* in the verbal ending *-ent* is written *u* twice in P (see note to l. 586), and once *ee*, *aruseent* (corrected to *arusent*) 1590.

(9) Atonic *e* in intertonic position is raised to *i* once, *briefiment* 1787.

(10) Intrusive *e* after the tonic vowel occurs once, *leiez* (= *laids*) 2152.

(11) Flexional *e* feminine is occasionally not written in hiatus, *chescun ewe* 1602, etc.

(12) *an^c* is occasionally written *on^c*, see note to l. 2316.

(13) *an* is occasionally written *aun*, cf. *haunter* 2392 and *manauntie* 2665.

(14) The product of open *o* free is written as *o*, *son* 1416, *nof* 1842, etc.; as *u*, *tun* 1952, *sun* 2583, *estut* 116, etc.; as *e*, *sen* 2585, *tens* 1984, *nef* 1329; as *oe*, *poet* 258, *boef* 1054, etc.; as *eu*, *seun* 83; as *eo*, *neof* 1472, *ileoc* 1537; as *ou*, *pout* 2418, 2623; as *ui*, *muit* 360.[1]

(15) For *oi* spelled *e* see note to l. 2731.

(16) Tonic close *o* (**u**) is regularly spelled *u* in P, but *ou* occurs, *nevou* 816. For an explanation of *gloiz* 2815 see note to this line.

(17) *ui* is frequently written *u*, cf. *nut* 1186, *lust* 1183, etc., and also *i*, *cesti* 1423. Since *ou* and *u* are equivalent orthographies *ou* may appear for *ui*, *nout* 2538.

---

[1] *muit* is an inverse spelling for *mut* arising from the reduction of *ui* to *u*.

(18) It appears that *u* may be written *eu* after the atonic *e* in hiatus before the tonic vowel drops out, cf. 'Morphology,' p. 50. Note also that the form *feu* alternates with *fu* in the text, cf. ll. 212, 228, etc., and the rhyme *feu:vertu* 1872.

Consonants. (1) *c* and *s* are sometimes confused, *alci* 2460, *cecle* 2468, *si(ci)* 2641, *sertes* 2563, etc.

(2) *f* and *v* interchange occasionally, see note to l. 115.

(3) *j(i)* is written occasionally for *g* before *e* or *i*. Cf. note to line 487.

(4) Flexional *s* of adjectives and articles is sometimes omitted, *tute rens* 288, *un munz* (pl.) 551, *une meres* 609, *uns fauve tors* (pl.) 665, *ces noble dras* 2836 C, etc.

(5) Intrusive *s* before consonant occurs in *fest(<facit)* 299, and possibly in *cest = set* 2322.

(6) *s* before consonant is dropped occasionally, *relut:nut* 1869, etc.

(7) *t* is sometimes written as *ct*, cf. note to l. 1346.

(8) Confusion of final *t* and *z* has resulted in the ending *-tz* in *wibetz* 365, *fustz* 927 and *frutz* 1393.

(9) Final *t* is replaced several times by *th*, *north:forth* 425, 455, etc.; and also by *dh* once, *nordh* 1687.

LA PETITE PHILOSOPHIE

185 a

Mult volenters escrivereie,
E multes choses enditereie,
Dunt mulz purreient bien aprendre,
4   Ki me suffrist al bien atendre;
Mes dous vices el mund habundent
Ke tuz biens heent e confundent;
L'une est envie venimuse,
8   L'autre est averice cuveituse.
La cheitive gent enviuse
Plus het ke serpent venimuse;
Serpent ad lange en treis furchee,
12   Chescune furche est barbelee;
L'envius, ke a tuz maus tire,
Plus ad ke trente pur mesdire;
Ses langes resunt barbelees
16   E del duz venim si medlees
Ke nul n'est ke tantost n'afole
Pur la ducur de sa frivole;
El mesdire est mult delivre,
20   Cum tigre ignel, mordant cum guivre;
Sul vers les bons ses mesdiz guie,
Ke des cheitifs nul n'ad envie;
Dunt l'envius put bien aprendre,
24   Se il a verité vult entendre,
Ke il est pres de cheitifvesce
Quant les bons mort, ledit e blesce,
Ke li bons n'ad del mal envie,   *185 b*
28   E li mauls tuz benfez detrie.

Neither P nor R has title or rubric. All variants for ll. 1–166 are from R 2 moultz des c.
4 Que a moi soeffreit al b. entendre   16 E de   17 nul est   18 la f.
21 Sil; ces diz   24 Si a; e.] atendre   25 Qest pris de c.   27 E li; de nul mal
28 t. biens d.

Si acuns cunte bone parole,
U ren escrit de bone escole,
L'envius hu[n]ist e deprave
32   Cum gupil [a] tessun sa cave;
U il dist: 'Ce ne fist il mie,
Tel sens ne ist pas de tele vie,
U il n'est pas de tel clergie
36   Ne issi fundez ke il issi die.'
Tant parole seurement
Cum il cunust tute la gent,
E si ne fra ja mesmes nient
40   Ke a bien n'a buntez apent;
Les altres set de buntez retraire,
Si ne vult mesmes nul bien faire;
U il ne vult u il ne set,
44   Dunt il altri bien plus het.
Deus destruie lange furbie
Ke mult destruit bien par envie!
    Li aver unt une manere
48   Ke mult est malveise e motere.
Asquanz dient: 'Ke valt despendre
Pur ren en cest siecle aprendre?
Tuz serrunt sages en l'altre vie,
52   Icest aprise ert tost finie.'
Sache cil ke si n'est sage,   *185 c*
La perira par sun folage.
Poi sunt ke sul Deu face entendre,
56   Dunt chescum deit lire e aprendre.
Li sages dist : 'Ne finez mie
De aprendre tant cum dure ta vie.'
E nul ne purra bien aprendre
60   Sanz oir, veer e entendre;

32 a R   58 ta R] sa P
34 nest il pas de bone v.   40 Que b.   41 des b.   49 Ke] quai   51 serroms
52 est   53 qe issi est   58 De prendre   60 et bien e.

E ki quidum ke ço nus face,
S'il n'espeire reprendre od grace?
Mes ore est veire la sentence
64 Dunt li poetes par vers tence:
'Mult vulent oir e aprendre,
Mes nul ne vult le travail rendre.'
Suz cel n'ad tele marchandie
68 Cum de sen e de curtaisie;
Mult est estreite la entree,
L'aprise large e honuré,
La fin est pardurable vie
72 U ja mes n'ateindra folie.
Ove sen ai mis curteisie,
Ke fol curteis fet deverie;
E ne pot estre ke ne pleise
76 Sapience ke n'est curteise.
    Asquanz dient: 'Ke valt saver?
Mult est sages ke ad aveir.
Par aveir put hom trestut fere,   *185 d*
80 Quant sens ne pot a nul chief trere;
Li riches sunt trestuz honurez,
Li sage povre, desuz pez;
Fols est ke vult le seun despendre
84 Pur meseise u poverte aprendre.'
Ço dient il tut par feintise
Pur cunceler lur cuveitise.
Mult est en peis li povre sages,
88 Quant richesce ad plusurs damages;
Ke richesce est chose treslable,
E saver est tutdis estable.
La gent sunt granment esperdues
92 Quant lur richesces sunt tolucs;

69 la e. R] ladentree P
77 Ke] quai   80 c.] fyn   86 consailer   89 c. passable   91 Les riches s.

Mes cil ki unt riche science certe
Ne se esmaient de nule perte.
   Scilbon perdi trestut par guere,
96   Femme, enfanz, homes e terre;
Si respu[n]di il a un rei:
'Tutes mes choses sunt od mei.'
Cist k'aveit trestut perdu,
100   Quant sun sen tint, out tut tenu.
Sul le sen propre li esteit,
Dunt perte ne out, quant ço teneit.
Li sages recuvre a l'aveir,
104   E li fols ja mes al saveir.
   Deu duna a Salamun   *186 a*
De treis choses electiun,
Le quel il vosist: estre sage,
108   Ou riche, ou de grant vasselage.
Salomon al saveir se prist;
I[l] l'out, e par tant tut cunquist.
Li sages avera en baillie
112   Quanque li aver esparnie.
Sul li fols het e reprent
Sen, saver e apernement.
Ke, jofne, ne vodra aprendre,
116   Veil, a trebble le estut despendre;
E dunc luera altri sens,
Quant de aprendre n'ad liu ne tens.
Certes mult li esterra bien
120   Ke en soi set alcune rien;
Mes cil ke en tuz sens me[n]dive,
Dreiz est ke il a hunte vive.
Nul ne set les set arz trestutes,
124   Si revalent al cors les tutes.
   Pur ço doit chescun bien aprendre

93 vnt s.   95 Si hom p.   96 h.] chatel   97 r. a   99 Cil ne a. rien p.
oo tient   102 tenout   106 Des   116 lui e.   121 qe t. s. mendie   122 qe a

Pur soi, quant mesters ert, defendre;
E ne pur itant sulement,
128 Mes pur soi garir e sa gent.
La gent dient en lur voir diz:
'Ki est garni ne est pas huniz.'
Ja n'ert meillur garnissement   *186 b*
132 Ke cil ke sage quor enprent;
E suz ciel n'ad si riche dun
Cum savoir quant est a bandun,
Ne suz ciel n'ad tele richesce
136 Cum savoir ke tuz mals adresce;
Tutdis lui crest e acurt sure
Ke sen despent en bone cure.
Trestut ausi ke se abaundune,
140 E a l'aprendre sun quor dune,
Cum plus aprent, plus i truvera,
E greinur sens lui abundera.
Pur ço deit hum par bon delit
144 Lire e oir chescun escrit;
Mult par est male la sentence
U l'om n'i pot truver science;
E mult est fieble l'escripture
148 U il n'i ad point de apresture;
Neis cil ke dient vileinie
Garnissent nus de tel folie.
Ke pot e vult, sei meimes triche,
152 Ke de tuz prent e plus est riche;
Ke de tuz lit, tuz out e escute,
Plus ke tuz savera senz dute:
Cum ert sages ke sen ot dire!
156 Poi sunt ke par soi Deus espire;
Mes ke en sen met sa voillance   *186 c*

154 qe touz R, ke de tuz P

126 est   129 Les gentz   131 ni ert   133 ni ad   140 al prendre   146 ne p.
148 Ou ni; apristure   149 Mes cil   150 cele f.   153 out] oit   155 est

Le Deu de sen par tut l'avance.
Pur ço ne larrai pur envie,
160   Ne pur avers ke Deu defie,
Ke mun petit sen ne desplie:
Aver de sen pire est ke pie
Ki autre luer ne vult rendre.
164   Prie Deu ke m'alme deigne defendre
E ove ces seinz en glorie prendre,
Ke me deigna en croyz rendre.

Li sages ke jadis estoient
168   De grant savoir se entremetoient,
E mult estreitement enquistrent
Des choses dunt il puis escristrent.
Chescun mustra sa sentence
172   Solunc la sue sapience,
E en plusurs lius deviserent,
Deskes li sages ke pus erent
Lur escriz tuz assemblerent,
176   E lur sentences acorderent,
Les dutances tutes osterent,
E la verité confermerent;
Ke il en tuz [poinz] l'apruverent,
180   E cum pruvé l'acerterent.
Ces escriz mult longes corurent
Dunt plusurs avant garni furent
De bon e de mal aventure,   *186 d*
184   Ke tuit disoit lur escripture.
Par tut le mund apris avoient
Les aventures que il savoient.

179 p. *CDVG] not in* PR   180 l'a. *CDV*] la crecerent *P*, la certifierent R, la cercherent *G*
181 c. *CG*] curerent *P*, current R, conurent *D*, conustrent *V*

158 Le *not in* R; l'] len   163 ne me v.   167 *CDVG begin, see note*   170 p.]
plus *RG*   173 En *y*; diuiserent *RC*, diuerserent *G*   176 ordeinerent *y*   179 Kar
en *y*   181 m.] plus R, puis *y*

Deu meimes en alcune guise
188 Mustre al mund ço k'il devise
Par alcune sue feiture
Ke faut u crest en sa mesure.
Il en urent grant garde prise,
192 Pur ço en surent la devise;
Le mund trestuit parmesurerent,
Terres, ewes, [fuz], eir, tuit numbrerent,
Les qualitez de tuz cercherent,
196 Dunt la force de tuz truverent;
E l'espruvé truveure
Mistrent en sage lettrure,
Pur garnir ceus ke pus vendreient,
200 E lur sens aprendre vodreient.
Mes nul ke seit a cest cuntempre
A lur sens gueres ne se atempre;
Nul ne purvoit nule aventure
204 Par ren ke Deu avant figure;
Dunt terre est mult afeblie,
E la gent tantost devie
Par les pledurs, par les legistres,
208 Ke tuz sunt Antecrist ministres.
Cil purvertent tute droiture   187 a
Pur terriene pureture;
Nul ne purvoit la Deu manace,
212 Dunt la gent est cum fu sur glace;
Nul n'esgarde la creature,
Par tant del creatur n'unt cure,
Ke li faitres par sa feiture
216 Est conuz sanz defalture.

194 fuz eir CG] eir PR, eir fu V, e fu D   201 ke CDVGR] nc P
190 u] e y   193 p.] ames. C, mes. DG   194 Tere ewe RDG, Terre e ewe CV;
t. n.] an. y   199 g.c.] cels g. y   201 a] en y   203 p. malav. y   207 e les (par
D) l. CD   209 peruertent RG   211 p.] doute y   212 est not in R, sunt y
213 ne garde y   215–6 not in y   216 Nest c. s. defaiture R

Pur ço faz en cest escripture
De tuit le mund la purtreture;
Coment la tere set entere,
220   Des ewes tute la maniere,
De l'eir e de l'ethere ensement,
E la force del firmament,
D'enfer, del ciel e des planetes,
224   Del lune, del soleil e des cometes,
Des .xii. signes e lur curs,
Pur quei sunt curz e lungs les jurs,
Dunt li vent vient, dunt la toneire,
228   Dunt fudre, dunt feu, dunt escleire,
Dunt pluie, dunt noif, dunt gelee,
Dunt gresil, niule, dun[t] rusee,
Dunt le feu vent ke l'um chair veit,
232   Ke l'em quide ke estoile seit,
Dunt vent cele blanche veie
Ke parmi le ciel se desploie:
Ke a ces choses vult entendre,   *187 b*
236   Mult i purra granz biens aprendre,
E saver en tutes manieres
Ke mult est sages li crieres,
E ke il est pussant par nature,
240   E ke si avols par tut dure,
E ke li sert a volenté
Tut veintra par sa pousté,
E ki defalt de sun servise
244   Mult doit duter sa grant justise.
Nun don' al livre ke l'endite
LA PHILOSOPHIE PETITE.
Ki plus [vult] oir par requeste

---

219 e.*CDG*] entrere *P*, en terre *RV*   247 voet *CDVG*, *not in* PR
217 face *RC*   223 de c. *RDG*   224 De la *RDV*; Del s. de la l. *CG*   225 e
de lor *CD*   226 c. e. l.] l. e c. *y*   230 n.] dont n. *Ry*   231 ke l'um] cum *y*
233 Et d. v. *Ry*   236 M. p. *RD*   245 doune *Ry*

248 Li frut li dirrai e la reste;
Ki vult del mund oir l'image,
E sa feture e sun estage,
Aturt oie od bon curage,
252 Jo l'en frai certain e sage.
Li mund est rund cume pelote,   [*Imago mundi*, Lib.
Nent estable mes en mote;   I, Cap. I, *Pat. Lat.*,
Unc ne fu ne ja n'ert estable,   CLXXII, 121]
256 Mes tutdis moble e remuable.
Par elemens est destinctez,
Cum par un of ver purrez:
L'aubun defors enclost l'escale,   *187 c*
260 En l'aubun li muels s'enmale;
Li muels enclost une gute,
Ke de gresse est furmee tute.
Tut ausi est li ciel cum escale,
264 L'ethre pur cum aubun enmale;
L'ethre, cum albun fet muel,
Le espés eir envirune bel;
Li muels enclost la grasse gute,
268 E l'eir purceint la terre tute:
Saver put ke sen ad parfund
Ke li cels enclost tut le mund.
De cest mund la creaciun   [Cap. II]
272 Feite en cinc manieres truvum:
L'une fu einz ke ren nule fut,
Ke Deu en sun penser conçut
Devant tuz siecles a purtreire
276 Come[n]t il volt tuit le mund feire.
Cist est *architepes* dist

248 d. *CDVG*] dirrat *P*, durrai *R*   265-6 *see note*   251 A. *V*] E a. *PR*, Escote
CDG   266 es. *DVG* (turbidus)] purs *PR*

248 d. sanz areste *CG*   250 E la *CD*   251 oie] ore *C*, a mai *DVG*   252 E
ieo *CD*   253 *Latin text begins*   264 pur *not in DG*   265 fet] sor *y*   272 m.
le t. *y*   273 nule rien *Ry*   275 tuit le secle *y*

De Deu prince ke tut purvit;
Prince est dit *archos* en gregeis,
280   *Typos* est dit figure en françois;
Dunt cest mund cel non ad,
Kar Deu par soi le figurad.
L'altre est quant Deu par cest essample
284   Cest mund criad noble e ample,
E trestut furmat en matire   *187d*
Quanque purvit sun sage empire;
Dunt l'escrit dit: 'Cil ke fin n'ad
288   Ensemble tute rens criad:'
Ensemble par voil deboneire
E par apparisante matire.
Le tierce fu quant trestut furma,
292   E par .vi. jurs tuit ordena;
Dunt l'escrit dit ke a .vi. jornees
Fist Deu tutes bones criees.
La quarte manere Deu mustra
296   Quant une rien de altre cria,
Ausi cum il uncore fet
Quant il un home d'altre estret,
Beste de beste fest venir,
300   Arb[r]es e herbes reverdir;
N'est chose ke sulunc sa semence
Dunt le Deu a mund ne recomence;
Dunt l'escrit dit : 'Mun pere uvre
304   Uncore, e ces buntez ne cuvre.'
La quinte maniere adunc ert veire
Quant Deu vuldra le mund refere,
E tuit oster la pulentie,
308   E vestir tuit de nuvelerie,
Dunt le prophete dit verai:
'Tutes rens renuvelerai.'

278 deu le pr. *y*   280 dit *not in* R*y*   281 itel non *y*   284 n.] ueable *y*
285 E *not in* C*V*   298 un *not in* RD   301 ke *not in* D*V*   302 Dunt] Ke D*V*;
le *not in* R*y*; a m.] le monde R*y*   304 b. pas ne *y*   305 est R*y*   306 voet C*D*

Ore escutez des element, *188 a*

312 Ço est de *yle* les liemenz; [Cap. III]

Tant dit *yle* cum fet matire,

Dunt tutes rens pernent afeire;

Yle est matire divine,

316 Dunt tutes riens pernent orine.

Les elemenz sul quatre sunt,

Par ki trestutes riens estunt;

Ço sunt feu, ewe e eir e terre,

320 Dunt chescun a altre se serre

Par si amee concordance

Ke nul n'est a altre grevance;

Ke si cum sercle returnee

324 En soi se turnent sanz medlee:

Le fu en l'eir tutdis s'enturne,

L'eir en l'ewe bien suj[u]rne,

L'ewe en la terre cule e plie,

328 La terre en l'ewe se demie;

Par meime ceste manere

Terre se turne en ewe clere;

E l'ewe en l'eir tres bien se mue,

332 E l'eir en feu tutdis tressue.

Ces quatre par grant cumpaignie

Chescun a altre bien se alie

Par lur quatre propretez

336 Cum par un braz entrelacez,

Si ke lur naturel descorde *188 b*

Remaint tutdis en bon acorde.

La terre, ke est secke e froide,

340 A l'ewe froide pas ne plede;

L'ewe, [ke est] froide e muistie,

A l'eir muiste tient cumpaignie,

341 ke est f. *DVR*] ke f. est *C*, f. en sei *G*

318 Par quai *y*; tutes R*y*   319 eir ewe *y*   320 se s.] saserre *C*, la serre *V*, afere *D*
322 a autre nest *CG*   324 se *not in y*   325 se turne R*y*   334 se lie *CD*   338 en
bon] e bien *CD*   341 E lewe *CD*

E l'eir, ke est muiste e chaude,
344   Al chaut fu est par itant baude;
Le feu par chaude seckeresce
La secke terre pas ne blesce.
De ces, cum tut plus pesant,
348   La terre mist en bas seant;
Le feu, si cum le plus legier,
Sur les altres volt Deus ester;
Les altres deus cum milluiens,
352   Quant tuz atemprent, ne sunt veins.
Des quels deus l'ewe plus pesante
La terre de plus pres hante.
La terre ad les bestes alanz,
356   E l'ewe ad les bestes noant,
En l'eir sunt les bestes volanz,
El feu les resplendisanz.

La terre est runde cum pelote,   [Cap. V]
360   Ne muit ne croulle ne ne flote.
Ele est runde en verité:
Se alcuns fust halt en l'eir posé
E la terre tute surverreit,   *188 c*
364   Ne munt ne val plus n'i parroit
Ke wibetz funt en un grant munt;
Par tant sachez ke ele est runt.
Ele estat sanz sustenement
368   For de sul Deu omnipotent;
N'ad pié ne basse n'apuail,
Dunt dist le prophete fedail
Ke deit ke ne dute la gent;
372   Deu, ki la terre en nient pent,
Il l'ad par sun sen establie

346 La t. s. *y*   347 ces quatre cum plus *y*   350 e.] poser *y*   352 s. pas v. *y*
354 t. plus *CG*   356 b.] peisons *y*   357 b.] oiseals *y*   358 feu sunt les *R*
362 en leir f. h. *y*   364 ne p. *y*   371 doutent *y*   372 Deu ki] Dieux *R*, Kar *C*,
De ceo ke *D*.   Deu kar *G*; en ewes p. *CG*   373 sen si e. *y*

Si ke ja mes n'ert esturmie.
Cil ke la terre mesurerent,
376 [Envirun il i aconterent]
Duze mile liues e cinquante
E dous; geometrie le grante.
Occean, ço est la mer grand,
380 La terre clot en purceignant,
Si cum cunte l'escripture:
'Abime fet sa vesture.'
Abime est la parfunde mer,
384 Ke Deu tut sul put amirer.
La terre ad en soi plusurs veines,
Ke sunt de l'ewe tutes pleines;
Dunt avient, quel liu que fuiez,
388 Tut soit parfund, ewe truverez.
Par ces veines l'ewe s'enserre,
E aruse la secke terre.   *188 d*
Si cel arusement n'estoit,
392 Ja mes nul frut n'aporteroit.
La terre par la Deu asise   [Cap. VI]
En cinc zones bel se devise;
Zones cercles u compas sunt,
396 E Deu compassa tut le mund.
Les deus foreins nul n'enhabite
Pur le grant froit kis desherite;
Nun fet hom pas le miluein,
400 Ke tutdis est de chalur plein,
Ke le soleil en celui meint,
E as foreins unkes n'ateint.
Les deus ke sunt parentre cels

376 *CDVGR*   384 put a.] *see note*   401 m. *CDVGR*] uient *P*

374 Ke ia *CD*   377 Cent mil *RDV*; l.] milers *D*, millers l. *V*   380 enclot *y*
386 de ewe *Ry*   387 fouerez *R*, fuez *DG*   389 cestes v. *RC*   392 nul *not in*
CD; ne p. *RG*   397 nabite *y*   399 pas *not in CD*   401 c.] cel lu *RC*, lui *DVG*
403 p. eals *y*

404 A habiter sunt bons e beals;
 Le chaud se ameine a la froidure,
 Si est bone l'atemprure.
 Entendez, e de bone fei
408 Par ensample le mustrai:
 Fetes un fu fors al serain,
 Quant yver est del gel tut plain,
 Cinc lignes i verrez tut dreit,
412 Une de chaud e dous de froit;
 Li dous ke entre cels serrunt
 Bone attemprure en soi frunt;
 S'il turnast cum li sols fet,   *189 a*
416 Cinc cercles altresi freit.
  Li premer cercle en sun estal
 Est numé septemtrional,
 Le secund est solsticial,
420 Le tierz est equinoccial,
 Le quart est apelé brumal,
 Le quint ad nun austral.
 Le solsticial sulement
424 Reçoit le nostre habitement.
 Septemtriun ço est le north,
 U tutdis est le froit si forth
 Ke, mer e terre, est engelee,
428 Ke ne put estre enhabité.
  D'iloc vers equinocciun
 Dure nostre solsticiun,
 Ke pur itant est si numé
432 Ke li solail en nostre esté

---

417 en *RCDVG*] est *P*

405 se meille *C*, meigne *corrected to* medle *G* 407 Ore en. o b. *DG* 408 le]
vus *CD* 410 de g. *Ry* 411 i *not in CGD* 413 c.] cestes *C*, ces dous *VG*; sunt *y*
414 Bien atempre en eus (sei *G*) sunt *VG*; B. atempraunce en sei funt *C* 415 solail *Ry*
418 Est apele *y* 420 E le terce *RC* 422 Et le *RCDG* 427 sunt *y* 428 Ne
pot pas e. *y* 429 equinoccial *RCD* 430 solsticial *RCD*

Vers le north plus ne passe mie,
Mes ver le su sun curs reguie.
Icest espace est si tem_pree
436   Ke de nus genz est habitee.
Le equinoccial est si ardant
Ke nul alme n'i est manant.
Pur tant est dit equinoccial
440   Ke jur e nuit sunt paringal.
Iloc est la zone bruant   *189 b*
Ke mer e terre fet builla[n]t;
La est li sols si chaud pur veir
444   Ke nul home n'i put maneir.
D'iloc s'estent pus le brumal,
Si se acumpaine a l'austral,
Ke pur ço est brumal numee
448   Ke tendrement est engelee.
Alcune feiz quant li solalz
Vers nus ici fet ses chalz,
Icele zone est atempree,
452   Mes des hommes n'est pas habitee.
D'iloc avant s'estent austral
U li froit fet sun estal,
Altresi cum fet utre cel north
456   U tutdis est gelee forth;
E si est austral apelé
Kar le su est auster numé
Par un vent ki d'iloc vient
460   Ke memes itel nun retent.
Ceste zone ke nus manums   [Cap. VII]
En trois parties divisums
Par une mer ke l'ad severee,
464   Mediterraine est apelee;

435 atempre *y*   439 Pur ceo *RC*   441 z. si *y*; ardant *CD*   442 bruant *C*,
bruillant *DG*   443 solail R*y*   450 refet *CG*   452 des] de *CG*   453 laustral *y*
456 si f. *CG*   457 Si *y*   460 i.] cel *CD*; tient *RD*   461 ke] ou *y*

E ço nun de ço li surt
Ke en miliu de la terre curt,
Si ad [le non] par destinctiun   *189 c*
468   De occean ke curt envirun.
De ces treis parz ke ai destinctee,
L'une est Asie apelee,
L'autre Europe, la terce Aufrike,
472   Dunt chescune est endroit soi rike.
    Asie ad nun d'une reine   [Cap. VIII]
Ke franche ert e de bone orine.
Gariz est k'en bien n'est feint,
476   Ke bon nun a tutdis remeint.
De ceste le cumencement
Est leis loin en orient
Le realme de paradis
480   U Adam fu de primes mis ;
Mes tant i ad de cel occean,
E de terre si tresgrant pan,
Ke de rubes, ke de guast,
484   Ke nul nen est ke la trespassast.
Del trespasser la terre est quite,
Kar n'est home ke la habite;
Nis le deluje nel tuchat,
488   Ke tut cest nostre mund neat.
Paradis ad en soi tuz biens,
De tuz deliz n'i falt ja riens;
Humme n'i vient, humme n'i meint,
492   Ke tut est de feu purceint;
Un mur de feu fort e ardant,   *189 d*
Halt desque al ciel, li est garant.
En cel liu est le fust de vie;   [Cap. IX]

467 le non CDVG

465 E cel *y*; de cel lu s. *G*, de ceo liu sort *C*   468 loc. *y*   473 A. est dite *y*
474 Ke mult ert (esteit *D*) de f. o. *y*   478 leis leis *C*   480 de *not in y*   481 loc. *y*
484 trespast *CDV*   487 ni atocha *y*   488 ceste terre n. *y*   490 ia *not in y*
492 trestut *CV*   493 feu trestuit a. *y*   494 Halt *not in CD*   495 f.] frut R*y*

496   Ke en mangue ne murt mie;
        Ki de sun frut point gustera
        Ja pus cel hure ne murra.
        Une funtaigne de cel liu surt,
500   Ke en quatre fluies decurt;
        Mes tuz quatre, chescune gute,
        Dedens les murs la terre englute,
        Ke pus surdent en lur pais,
504   Mes mult loinz de cest paradis.
        Phison, ke nun de Ganges tent,   [Cap. X]
        D'Orcoban, munt en Inde, vent,
        E tret sun curs vers orient,
508   U il en occean descent.
        Geon, ke Nil est apelé,
        Juste munt Athlant surt de gré;
        Mes terre tantost l'englutist,
512   Dunt a la Ruge Mer s'en ist;
        Ethiope bel envirune,
        E en Egipte se abandune;
        E pus en se[t] buches se fent,
516   E si en la Grant Mer descent
        Juste Alisandre la cité,
        Ke d'un fort rei fu si numé.
        Eufrates e Tygre le ignel   190 a
520   De munt Caucas issent mult bel,
        E lur curs funt par Armenie,
        E chescun vers midi se guie,
        E en la mer Mediterin
524   Iloc entrent, ço est la fin.
            Deça le liu de paradis

506 mount en G] ke m. est P, qe m. en R, mult en C, amunt en V, see note   515
set DVC (septem)] se PG, ces R; f. RCDVG (divisus)] sent P   520 C. V] tankas
PR, cantas C, cancas DG see note

497 de cel f. y; p. not in CG   498 cel iour y   499 de] en y   505 nun] soen
n. G; ke (V only) de g. son non CV   508 loc. CG   509 Seon CD   513 aui-
roune RCG   522 uers inde y

C

Sunt deserz de tuz biens esquis,
Pleins de serpens e de draguns,
528 De guivres, tygres e de leuns,
Tant guastés, tant venimez
Ke ja n'i ert chemin truvez.
Pus est Inde la renumee,   [Cap. XI]
532 Ke de Inde un fluvie est numee,
Ke del munt Caucas del north surt
E vers midi sur terre curt;
E quant ad curu sun esploit,
536 En la Mer Ruge sa fin fet.
Cest Inde enclost vers occident
Le grant occean verrement:
Ço est occean l'Indien,
540 Ke un idle purceint tres bien;
Taprobane l'idle est numee,
De .x. citez nobles est casee.
Chescun an i ad dous estez,
544 E dous yvers e dous fez blez;
Saver poez, grant bien en ist,   *190 b*
Kar ele a trestut l'an verdist.
Crise e Argire iloke sunt,
548 Ke dous idles en la mer sunt;
De or e d'argent sunt replenies,
E a tutdis tres bien fluries.
La sunt un munz de fin or granz,
552 U draguns e grips sunt mananz,
Kis defendent si faitement
Ke nul alme de l'or ne prent.
Iloc est le munt Caspy,
556 Dunt cele mer ad nun ausi.
Entre cel munt e cele mer

533 C.] *see l.* 520   552 g. *DVG* (gryphes)] serpens *PR*, griffons *C*
528 g.] gryffons *RG*, grips *D*, griuers *V*   529 enuenimez *y*   532 est si n. *y*
534 m.] inde *y*   539 le o. i. *y*   547 A.] augur *CG*, augor *D*   551 est R *C*
554 a.] homme *RDG*   557 munt] terre *y*

Fist li rois Alisandre le fier
Gog e Magog si enfermer
560 Ke il ne poent issir ne passer:
Ce sunt une gent malostrue,
Ke humme e crue beste mangue.
Inde content en sun bandun
564 Quarante e quatre regiun.
Inde ad en soi multes genz natres,
Garmanz, Orestes e Choatres;
Lur bois en haut cressent tant
568 Ke le pur ethre sunt tuchant.
En Inde est Pigneos un munt,
E en cel munt uns hummes sunt
Ke dous cutes unt de lungur,   *190 c*
572 E as grues tenent estur;
Od les grues bataile funt,
E al tierz an lur enfant unt;
A l'utime an velz e defrait sunt,
576 Se il plus vivent, petit durrunt.
Entre ces genz li poivre crest,
Si est trestuit blanc quan[t] il nest;
Mes pur les serpens dechacer
580 Funt il les champs tut alumer,
Dunt le poivre tut enercist,
E par l'arsun trestut flestrist.
Les Macrobins ilokes sunt,
584 Quatorze cutes de lungur unt;
Cist guerroient cuntre les grips,
E defendunt lur pais.
Le grip de leun ad cursage,

571 de RCDVG] le P   578 Si RCDVG] Sil P

559 si *not in* RC   560 Ne p. CVG   562 Ke *not in* CVG   563 ses bandons *y*
565 m. g.] mult grant CDG   568 e.] ayr RC   570 En RDG; h.] genz CDG
575 d.] defait RD   576 il *not in* RDG   577 cele RDG, cels C   578 tut b. R*y*
579 d.] ench. CD, esch. D   580 tut *not in* CVG   581 trestut CD; nercist *y*   582 par
raisun *y*   584 de lung CG   585 E il g. *y*

588   Ele e ungle de egle salvage.
          La resunt Agrot e Bragman,
          Ke meimes se ardent a grant han
          Pur amur de cel autre vie:
592   Fole esperance fet folie.
          Uns autres lur pere oscient,
          Quant a vielesce lur tens guient,
          E lur chars manger se aparaillent;
596   Fel sunt tenu ke de ço faillent.
          Altres i sunt ke le cru pessun   *191 a, l. 2*
          Mangunt tutdis a bandun,
          E beivent la mer tressalee:
600   A tel manger tele bevee.
          Uns mustres en cel munt resunt,   *190 d*
          Tels hummes, tels bestes lé funt.   [Cap. XII]
          Asquanz unt les piez besturnez,
604   E .viii. ortilz e sezze piez;
          Asquanz tele teste cum chens unt,
          Lur ungles curbs e aguz sunt,
          De pels de bestes vestuz sunt,
608   E pur voiz abai de chens unt.
          Ilokes une meres sunt,
          Ke une feiz lur enfanz unt;
          Chanuz sunt quant des meres issent,
612   E en viellesce ennercissent;
          E plus vivent mult lungement
          Ke ne fet nule de nostre gent.
          Altres i sunt ke en cinc anz
616   Enfantent trestuz lur enfanz,
          Mes neis un de cest enfanter
          Utre le utime an ne put endurer.

597–600 *displaced in* PR, *see note*   604 .viii. RCG (octonos)] vint P

591 lamur RCD   597 Vns a. *y* ; le *not in* R*y*   601 sunt en cel mont CD; sunt G
605 tele *not in* CD; cum chiens testes C   606 c.] corz C, curs D   611 de mere R*y*
612 en lur v. R*y*   613 p.] moltz R, puis *y* ; m.] plus R*y*   617 Mes vn soul de *y*
618 durer *y*

La sunt gent ke un oil unt,
620 E cil lur set enmi le frunt;
Arismaspi sunt apelé,
E Ciclopes resunt numé.
Lé Cynope la resunt,
624 Ke sulement un pe unt;
L'orree venquent en curant,
E quant del repos unt talant,
La terre cum un sarcu uvrent,
628 U il de lur plantes se cuvrent.   *191 a*
Uns altres tut sanz chef i sunt,
Ke les oilz es espaules unt;
Pur nes e buche dous pertuz,
632 E cum bestes sunt veluz.
Lez la funtaigne de Gangis,
Ke est un fluvie de grant pris,
Une gent mainent, ço est la summe,
636 Ke vivent de l'odur d'une pume;
E si nul de els doit loinz errer,
Ne ublie la pume aporter;
Se il bien vult e il eit mester,
640 L'occean grant put tresnoer.
Une beste ilok habite,   [Cap. XIII]
Centocroce par nun est dite;
Cors ad asnin, costez cervins,
644 E piz e quisses leonins,
Piez de cheval e un cors grant,
De dous parz aguz e trenchant,
La buche ad grant e mult baanz,
648 D'orrille a l'altre atteignant,

633 G. CD (Gangis)] egantis PR, sangis G

619 unes g. *y*   623 C.] Syclope R*y*; la r.] ilokes sunt *y*   626 de *CG*; reposer *CD*
628 E si de *C*, E la de *DG*   631 unt d. *C*; d. p. unt *DG*   637 Si *CD*; l. aler *y*
638 la] pas la *CG*, mie la *D*   639 e eit *y*   642 non d. *y*   645 Pys *R*, Dens *y*
646 p.] piez *y*

Plein os pur denz, maissele pleine,   *191 b*
E voiz purpostement humeine.
      Un altre beste est en cel val,
652   Ke tel cors ad cum cheval;
      Eale le solt hum nomer,
      Si ad meissele de sengler,
      Ausi cum olifant cuee,
656   Si est de dous cornes armee;
      Les cornes ne sunt for d'une cute,
      L'une retret, l'autre bute,
      L'une tent red quant se cumbat,
660   E l'altre lung sun dos tient flat;
      E kant cele est rebukee,
      Arere est mise e l'altre avancee:
      Horrible est, de neire culur,
664   En ewe e en terre ad sa valur.
      Uns fauve tors sunt el munt sus,
      De pail envers forz e hydus;
      Le chief unt gros, la buche grant,
668   D'orille en autre baant;
      E ces lur cornes quant cumbatent,
      L'une estendent, l'altre abatent;
      Tant unt le quir serré e dur
672   Ke nul dart ne lur fet tristur;
      Si l'um par engin les susprent,
      Del danter n'i ad ja nient.
      Manticora est une beste,   *191 c*
676   Ke en itel pais s'areste;
      Vis ad de humme par face bele,
      E trebble denz en la meissele;
      Trestuit le cors ad de leon,
680   E la cue de escorpiun;

---

665 t. *CDG* (tauri)] cors *P*, corps *R*

658 de lautre *CG*   659 t. astret *D*, est esteit *C*, estreit *G*   660 Laltre *y*; l.] tres
C ; le dos *CG*   661 celui est trebuche *y*   668 b.] atteynante *RC*   669–70 *not in y*
669 ceuz *R*   673 Si hom *RDG*   674 ad n. *y*   676 cel p. *Ry*   677 par *not in CD*

Oilz ad jaunes, culur sanguin,
La voiz cum siffle serpentin;
Ducement siffle en sa facunde,
684 E plus curt tost ke vole arunde.
Ke l'atent trop ne fet ke sage,
Ke char humeine ad en usage.
La sunt bofs ke trois cornes unt,
688 E pié de cheval tut rund.
Monoceros i meint en sum,
Ke nus unicorne numum:
Cors de cheval, chief ad cervin,
692 Piez d'olifant, cue porcin;
D'une corne de quatre piez
Enmi le frunt est bien armez;
Mult est lung e resplendisant,
696 E mult aguz e mult trenchant:
La beste est fiere durement,
E si muist mult ferement;
Quanque encuntre tresperce lors,
700 Ne ad obstacle, ne quir ne os.
Tuer le put ke l'avera pris,   *191 d*
Mes en danture n'ert ja mis.
Anguilles en Ganges resunt,
704 Ke trente piez de lungur unt.
En memes l'ewe uns verms sunt,
Ke autels braz cum crabbes unt,
Mes lur braz de mult greignur sunt,
708 Ke sis cutes de lungur unt,
Dunt il pernent les olifanz,
E es undes noient asquanz.
Mer Indien ad limaçuns,

685 l'atent *CG*] la tient *PR*, lentent *D* 707 b. *CG* (brachia)] testes *PR*

684 Plus *RCG*; tost c. ke ne u. *y* 685 t. latent *y* 689 i *not in CD*; en] el *C*, al *DG*
690 appelom *RD* 691 C. ad de (cum *C*) c. chef c. *RCD* 700 Ni ad *CD* 702 en
dante *C*, pur danter *D* 704 de lung *CG* 705 m. cel ewe *C* 707 de *not in Ry*
708 vnt de l. *y*

712   Dunt les paisanz ce funt maisuns;
     Les escales tant lees sunt
     Ke il hostel larges en funt.
     Inde magnete en soi nurist,
716   Ke chescun fer en soi ravist;
     E adamant tuit ensement,
     Ke sul sanc de buc freint e fent.
     Ki les merveilles pardirroit
720   De Inde, trop enuius serreit.
     Del flum de Inde desque a Tygrin   [Cap. XIV]
     Est Parchie procain veisin,
     Ke content en ses enviruns
724   Trente e trois nobles regiuns.
     Aracusye [la] regiun,
     Ke de Aracuse tret le nun;
     Le regne ad nun de la cité,   *192 a*
728   Ke est en Parchie fundé.
     La est Medie la regiun,
     Ke del roi Mede tret le nun;
     Une cité en sun nun ferma,
732   Dunt le regne le nun enprunta.
     Sage est ki bienfet agree;
     Mult dure bone renumee.
     La est Perse d'un roi dite,
736   Perse out a nun, si la tint quite,
     E Persipolin i funda,
     Dunt al regne le nun lessa;
     Si comença premerement
740   L'art ke l'um dit enchantement.
     Une piere pyride en vent,
     Ke art la main de li quil prent;

725 la C] *not in* PR, la premere D   733 ki CDG] ke PR

712 p. f. *y*   713 e. si l. *y*   714 il *not in y*; h. l.] mult l. h. C, osteles mult l. G
720 i. ennuie s. C; enui fereit G   726 tient son non *y*   728 en p. est *y*   730 tient
sun non y   731 furma R   732 son non ad CG; nun portad D   735 si d. RC
739 Cil R, E il CD   740 que hom C   742 de ki la tient *y*

E senilite, ki blanchur
744 Od lune crest e pert luur.
Del flun Tygre desq'en Eufrate [Cap. XV]
Est Mesopotamie la late;
En griu est issi apelee,
748 Cum entre les dous flums posee.
Ceste ad cité Ninivé,
Ke trois jurnees tient d'esté;
Le roi Ninois la funda,
752 E de sun nun si l'apela.
Babiloine la regiun, *192 b*
Ke de la cité tint le nun,
Ilokes set, ilok esta;
756 Nembroc le geant la ferma,
Mes Semiramis la reine
La cité estora de ruine;
Cinquante cutes de laur
760 Ad le mur de la cité entur;
Quatre cent liues d'envirun,
Ad la cité, e quatre vint en sun;
Cent portes de araym fortes i ad,
764 E flum Eufrates parmi vad;
Babel, ço est la mestre tur,
Quatre mil pas ad de hautur.
En Parthie reset Chaldee;
768 Astronomie i fu truvee.
Arabie est en lui fundee,
Ke Saba fu jadis numee.
Saba, fiz Cus, la herberga,
772 E al regne sun nun leissa.
L'encens cult hum en icesti,

767 P. R] perchie P, parthe CG, parche D

744 p. color *y*   746 la cite RCD   748 e. dous *y*   749 la c. *y*   754 son n. *y*
756 furma RD   758 restora RC   759 ad de C, est de G   760 Ad *not in y*
761 d' *not in CG*   764 Le f. de e. *y*   766 Ke mil *y*   771 le fiz CD

E en li est munt Synai;
I[l] esteit Horeb enceis dit;
776   Moyses la ley [i] escrit.
Juste cel liu fu Madian,
Dunt Jetro fu prestres meint an;
En ceste mainent Moabite,   *192 c*
780   E Ydumei e Amonite,
Sarazin e Madianite,
E multes genz de Deu despite.
De Eufrate jesque a la mer—   [Cap. XVI]
784   Mediteraine l'oi numer—
Est Syrie d'un roi si numé,
Ke primes l'avoit cunquesté.
En li est Damas la cité,
788   D'un sers Abraham feit e numee;
E Antioche i esta,
Ke rois Antiochus funda;
Ele fu ja Reblate dite,
792   Mes le nun real ore herite.
Comagent i est, un pais,
E Fenice lez li asis,
Ke est d'un oisel si numee,
796   K'en nul liu n'est for la truvee,
U de Feniz, fiz Agenor,
Ke la cunquist par sun tresor.
Tyre e Sydoine en li resunt,
800   Dous citez ke a priser funt.
En li estat le munt Liban,   *192 d*
A ki pe surt le flum Jordan.
Et Palestine i estet,   [Cap. XVII]
804   Ke de la cité Palestin nun tret,

775 en. *RDG*] en cest *P*   776 i *R*] iloec *CD* ; La ou M. la lei aprist *G*   778 J.
CG] Ierico *PR*, *not in D*   788 D'un *CDG*] Dunt *PR*

774 En *CG*   782 moltz des g. *RC*, mult de g. *DG*; de] ke *D*   788 a. si nome *y*
789 iloec e. *y*   790 Ke le r. *y*   791 fu iadis *y*   792 ore i h. *y*   803 iloec e. *y*   804
del c. *C*

Ke ore est Escalon numee,
Kar eschaloine i fu truvee.
En ceste terre reest Judee,
808   De Juda, fiz Jacob, numee;
Ceste reest dite Chananee,
De Chanaan, fiz Cham, numee.
En ceste esteit Jerusalem,
812   Ke Sem fist e numa Salem;
David Jerusalem la dist,
Pur Jebusen ke pus i mist:
Sem fiz al gentil Noé fu,
816   Chanaan, fiz Cham, sun nevou;
Dunt des dous est dit Jerusalem
Ausi cum Jebuz-Salem.
Rois Salemon enprés i mist,
820   E d'or e de gemmes la refist;
L'ost de Babilun la roba,
Zorobabel pus la força;
L'ost de Rome pus la cunquist,
824   Ke nis les fundemenz enquist;
Hely Adriane, empereur,
Pus la refist en sa valur;
E quant i[l] l'out bien estoré,   *193 a*
828   De soi l'a Helyam numé.
En Palestine reest Samarie,
Une realme de noble afeire;
De Samarie la cité tret nun,
832   Ke nus Sebaste ore apelum.
E[n] Palestine est Galilee,
Ke tient Nazareth, la numee,
Ke juste Thabor est fundee,

819 S. *CDG* (Salomon)] salem *PR*   829 En *RCDG*] E en *P*

807 r.] est *CD*   809 r.] est *y*   811 e.] esta *RDG*   815 al] a *Ry*   817 des] de *RG*
819 e.] apres *y*   825 li e. *DG*   827 Q. il lout *D*   829 r.] est *y*   830 n.] grant *y*
831 De vne c. s. *y*; n.] son n. *C*, le n. *DG*   834 n.] renomee *Ry*; la *not in C*

836   Un munt de mult grant renumee.
  Ilokes est Pentapolis,
  Cinz citez furent ja de pris:
  Sodome e Gomorre i furent ja,
840   E trois altres ke Deu nea
  Par feu e sulphre tut ardant
  Pur lur pechié ke fu puant;
  En liu des citez est morte mer
844   E palu noir cum adverser,
  Ki flum Jordan en li reçoit,
  Mes del pur ewe point ne boit.
  En cest pais sunt Sarazin,
848   De Sare unt nun, ço est la fin;
  E Agaren iloc resunt,
  Ke de Agar nun enprunté unt;
  E la resunt Ysmaelite,
852   Ke de Ysmael sunt issi dite.
  Iloc resunt li Nabathé,   *193 b*
  De Nabaioth issi apelé,
  Ke fu le fiz danz Ysmael,
856   Ki linnage fu grant e bel;
  Kar duze genz de ces issirent,
  Ke mult grant tens le mund venquirent.
  Les regiuns ke numé sunt,   [Cap. XVIII]
860   El orient orine funt,
  E si descendent droit chemin
  Desque en la mer Mediterin.
  Del su de ces Egypte gist,
864   Ke .xx. e quatre genz nurrist;
  Ceste cumence en orient,

839–40 *CDG*] *transposed in* PR 859 Les *CDG*] Des *PR*

838 ja de p.] iadis R*y* 841 e] de *y* 845 li] sei *y* 846 de pur R; Mes (*not in*
C) de cel ewe *y*; point] nul hom C, hom p. *G* 847 cel p. R*y* 854 si a. *y* 855
danz *not in y* 857 de els i. *y* 858 mult grant tens *C*] par geant teus *PR*, luns
tans *G*; Ke le grant m. *D, see note* 860 En o. R*y* 861 d. le droit *y* 863 El
C, Al *D*

E fet sa fin en occident;
Ele cumence a la Ruge Mer,
868 Mes Libe la fet finir;
Eurize fu primes numé,
Mes roys Egipteis Acelé,
Frere roy Dane, la cunquist,
872 E pur remembrer sun nun i mist;
Del flum de Nil tut est purceinte,
E en furme de .D. enpeinte;
Cent mile viles en soi tent,
876 Ne ja nue ne eir n'[i] vient;
Plue n'i chet, mes Nil surunde,
Dous fez en l'an, si la fecunde.
La est Thebaide la cuntree,   *193 c*
880 De Thebes la cité numee;
Lez ceste gist guastine grant,
U moines furent jadis manant.
Chambises rois Egypte prist,
884 E une cité noble i fist,
E Babilun nun lui duna,
E de Egipte chief la leva.
Rois Alixandre la cunquist,
888 E une noble cité i fist,
E de sun nun la fist numer:
Bienfet ne purra ja finer!
Del north as dites regiuns   [Cap. XIX]
892 Quels lius marchent ore diuns.
Munt Caucas de la mer Caspin
De l'orient tient sun chemin,
Par aquilon sa voie tient,
896 E a mes[mes] de Europe vent.
La sunt Amozenes manant,

---

876 n'i *CG*] ne *D*, y *R*   893 Caucas] *see l.* 520   896 mesmes *GCDR*
873 tut *not in CD*   876 Niwele ne pluie ia ni *C*   883 *C.* le (un *DG*) r. de e. le p. *y*
891 Des le n. de ces r. *C*; as] des *G*   894 Vers o. *C*   896 a *not in CD*

Femmes plus ke hummes cumbatant,
Lez els habitent Messageth,
900   Colchi e li Sarmareth,
Trois genz ke sunt si apelee
Des lius ou il sunt habité.
  Seres apelent un chastel
904   En orient mult fort e bel,
Dunt Serice ad nun quanque i apent,   *193 d*
E regne e vesture e la gent.
  Baarie a li est acosté,
908   D'un flum de cel nun apelee.
Yrcanie est joint a cestui,
Ke d'un bois Yrcan ad nun si;
En cel bois sunt oisel manant,
912   Ke pennes unt de nuit lusant.
Ciht e Hunnie lez ceste sunt,
Ke .xliiii. genz unt.
  La sunt munt Yperborei,
916   Ke pur ce sunt numé ici
Ke l'eir surmuntent par hautur,
Vent n'i vent ne n'ad valur.
  Pus est Albane la cuntree,
920   Ke de blanchur est si numee;
Tuz ke en la terre sunt net,
De blanche crine sunt feffez.
  De Armenie les munz pus sunt,
924   Ke munt Ararath en soi unt,
U l'arche ke dan Noé fist,
Enprés le deluje se assist,
Dunt les fustz uncore perent

916 n. ici *RCD*] ici n. *P*, n. sunt issi *G*   924 m. *GRC*] mult *P*, grant *D* ; unt *RCDG*]
sunt *P*

899 h.] maignent *y*   900 E c. *y*; e s. *CD*   902 s.] vnt *C*   903 S. i est (set *G*) vn *y*
905 D. ad a (*not in G*) non *y*   906 e g. *y*   907 Bactrie est a lui costee *G*; sest acostoie
C   921 cele t. *y*

928   A cels ke la veer les querent.
   A lui se cuple Hyberie,
   Pus Capadoce la vermie,
   U venz funt ywes concevanz,   *194 a*
932   Les puleins vivent sul trois anz.
   Pus est Asye la menur,   [Cap. XX]
   Ke de mer est pres clos entur,
   Ceste ad Ephesie la cité,
936   U seint Johan est reposé.
   Le premer pan de cest Asye
   Li paisant nume[n]t Bithinie.
   La est Nicee la cité,
940   U ja fu grant sene assemblee;
   La reest Troie la renumee,   [Cap. XXI]
   Del roi Troi fez e numee;
   Ele est numé Ylyun,
944   Cum sun fiz ke out nun Ylun.
   A ceste se ajuste Liconie,
   E la riche terre Chalie,
   U flum Hermes curt, ki graver
948   De fin or est mellé e cler.
   Pus est Libie l'asenee,
   Del roi Lide si apelee;
   Ceste ad une cité prisee,
952   Ke Thyatyr est apelee.
   Pus est Ysaure, si numee
   Ke de or est par tut aventee.
   Aprés els Cilice vient,
956   Ke de sa cité sun nun tient,
   La quele rois Silis funda,   *194 b*

931 y. *G* (equae)] ewes *PC*, et ewes *R*; c. *CG* (concipiunt) cuntenanz *P*, continuantz *R*
932 v. sul *GR*] u. sur *P*, ne u. fors *C*

928 la *not in CG*   930 v.] guarnie *C*, vrnie *G*   931 En v. *G*; f.] sunt *RCG*
941 r.] est *CD*   944 Cum] D'un *RG*, De *CD*   945 se a.] sacostoie *C*, sacoste *DG*
946 t.] cite *y*   [954 de fin or *y*; par tut *not in y*   955 A. celi *y*   956 sa] la *CD*

Ke rois Agenor engendra.
En ceste est munt Amana,
960 Ki e de Taurus le nun a;
En ceste est Tharse la cité,
Ke de seint Pol fu honuré.
Pus est Licie e Perside,
964 E [P]amphilie ki n'es[t] Lide.
Pus est Pontus la regiun,
Ke multes genz ad en bandun,
Dunt la mer ad nun Pontil ;
968 La fu Ovides en exil,
E pus i murrut seint Clement,
Ke cunverti tute la gent.
Ore avum [Asie] trescuru,
972 Desque a Europe sumes venu.
   Europe sun nun ad cunquis   [Cap. XXII]
De Europe, un roi de cel pais,
U de Europe, fille Agenor,
976 Pur ki Jupiter se feint tor.
En ceste vers septentriun
Sunt munz Rifei al premer sun,
E un flum ke ad nun Thanais,
980 Dit de Thanai, roi del pais,
E un paluz grant a plenté,
Ke Meodides sunt numé,
Ke a la Grant Mer sunt cuplé   *194 c*
984 Lez Thiodisie la cité.
   De Thanay, des flums la flur,   [Cap. XXIII]
S'en vent Sithie la menur,
E vers midi tent sun chemin,
988 E en Danubie fet sa fin.

964 DCG (Pamphylia)] amphilie PR   971 Asie GCD (Asiam)] *not in* PR

960 e *not in* R*y*   963 L.] latide R, litide G   964 qe neis lyde R, e melide C
972 a *not in* CG   973 ad quis CG   974 de cel p.] iadis *y*   976 f.] feist *y*
978 al] el CG   981 Ou sunt vns (*not in* D) p. a grant p. *y*   982 n.] apele *y*   983
mer set acostoie C   987 m.] mede *y*

Lé pais de ceste Sichie,
Germanie, Alane, Dacie.
   De Danubie desque a munt Giu   [Cap. XXIV]
992 Grant Germanie tent sun liu;
Iceste en dous flums se termine,
Vers occean en Ren se fine,
En Albine vers north se fine,
996 E Suave tient en saisine;
Ele reest Alemaine numee,
D'un lai ke est en la cuntree.
Danubie en cest realme nest,
1000 E de seisante flums se acrest,
Einz ke il veigne a mer Pontin,
U en .vii. buches fet sa fin.
Ci est Norich, une cuntree
1004 Ke est Beivere apelee;
La mestre cité del regné
Est Ratisbon apelé.
Pus est France oriental,
1008 Ke vers Turigne fet estal;
Pus [est] Sessoine la vaillant,   *194 d*
Ke en Albie vet fina[n]t.
D'iloc la basse Germanie,   [Cap. XXV]
1012 El north el occean se guie;
Danemarche i est e Norweie,
Nul hum [ne] set avant la veie.
   De Danubie jesque a la mer,
1016 Ke soil Mediterin numer,
Vers orient s'estent Messie,
Dit cum de messun replenie.
Pus est Pennine, pus Bugrie,

1009 est *RCDG*   1014 ne *RCDG*

991 a] al *RCD*   994 loc. *CG*   995 A.] albie *D*; n.] le n. *C*   996 en sa s. *y*
998 un roi qui fu en *y.*   999 cel r. *CD*   1001 a la mer *y*   1003 La *CD*
1005 del pais *C*   1010 v. fuant *RD*; Vers albie estendant *C*   1016 *s.*] len sout R,
soleit hom *G*; m. soil *C*, m. oi *D*   1019-20 *not in y*

D

1020 Pus Trace de gent replenie;   [Cap. XXVI]
      Tyras, fiz Japheth, la cunquist,
      E de sun nun Trace la dist.
      Ceste ad Heberon, un flum noble,
1024 E la cité Constentinoble,
      Ke li roys Constentin funda,
      E de sun nun la numa.
      De ceste mer Mediterin   [Cap. XXVII]
1028 En la Grant Mer, Grece fet fin.
      De Grec, un roi, est apelee,
      Terre Sechin fu ja numee;
      Vers le su turne sun chemin,
1032 En mer Illico fet sa fin.
      Ceste ad en soi une cuntree,
      Ke Dalmathie est numee;
      E un autre Epir ad nun,   *195 a*
1036 De Pirro, le fiz Achillun.
      En Epir ad une funtaine
      De ewe duce garnie e pleine,
      Ke les tisuns ardanz afume,
1040 E les tisuns esteinz realume.
          La est Chaonie la cuntree,
      De sa cité memes numee;
      Elen, fiz Hector, la fundat,
1044 E de sun frere la numat.
      Sis freres out Chao a nun,
      Dunt nus Chaonie apelum.
          La est Boette de bof dite,
1048 Ke Cadmus rois tint sul e quite.
      Cadmus, ke fu fiz Agenor,
      En icel liu truva un tor,
      Ke il a ses deus sacrefia,

1028 G. R] de grece *PCDG, see note*

1021 Treis fez I. *y*   1023 ad un flum ebron la n. *y*   1030 *S.*] cethim *C*
1031 t.] tient *y*   1034 Ke Alemaine *y*   1035 E.] empire *y*   1036 fiz ascalon *y*
1039 a. alume *CD*   1040 t. *not in RCD*   1041 est caoyne *y*   1042 la c. *RD*
1043 Eleine la (*not in C*) fille h. *CD*   1045 out C.] caonon out *y*   1046 nous
caoyne lap. *y*   1047 b. si dite *y*   1049 C. fu *y*   1050 cel *RD*

1052   E Thebe la cité aferma;
          Le regne Boette apela,
          Del boef ke il iloc truva.
          E memes icele cuntree
1056   Est Aonie reappellee
          D'une funtaigne renumee,
          Ke as muses fu ja sacree:
          Ke jadis de cele bevoit,
1060   Tuz sens e tuz engins savoit.
          La est Pelopenens la cité,   *195 b*
          Del roi Pelope si numee;
          Et Thessalie reset la,
1064   Ke Thessal, fiz roi Grec, funda.
          Achaia reest en cel pais,
          U rois Cheo sun nun ad mis.
          Corinthe, ke fu fiz Horest,
1068   La cité Corinthe fist el est.
          La est Archadie la cuntree,
          Ke fu Sironie ja numee.
          Archadie ad une pere arbest,
1072   Ke n'esteyndra pur nul tempest;
          Si une feiz est de fu esprise,
          Pus n'esteindra en nule guise.
          Pus est Pannonie sun veysin,
1076   Ke teint jesque al munt Appenin.
          Hystrie del north se est assis,
          Ke de Hystre, un flum, sun nun ad pris;
          Ceste fu dite ja grant Grece,   [Cap. XXVIII]
1080   Mes Saturne l'out une pece,
          E pur ce ke il aukes regna,

1065 A. *CDG* (Achaia)] Et chaia PR   1067-8 *CG*] *displaced in* PR, *see note*

1052 a.] i fermat *C*, ferma *DG*   1056 apelee *y*   1057 De aonie f. *C*   1059 cel
ewe b. *y*   1061 la] une *y*   1064 t. un roi *C*   1067-8 C. la cite i est Que fist c.
li fiz oreste *G*   1070 fu S.] liconie fu *y*   1072 pur] par *CD*   1073 est] soit R*y*
1076 t.] tent R, sestent *y*; A.] pennin *C*, perin *D*   1077 se] i *DG, not in C*   1078
de Ister f. *C*, de vn f. Yster *G*; ad son (*not in G*) n. p. *y*   1079 fu ia la g. *y*   1081
il *not in CD*; a. i r. *y*

Saturne nun lui duna;
Jupiter Saturne venquist,
1084   E il en cel pais tapist,
Dunt pus out nun Laciun,
Kar *laterre* tapir disum.

A la parfin del roi Ytal   *195 c*
1088   Out Ytali nun comunal;
De munt Giu ceste prent orine,
E en la Grant Mer se termine;
En ceste Rume ben herite,
1092   Del roi Romul fundé e dite.

Les citez de vels purtreture
Des meillurs bestes unt figure;
Li antif par signifiance
1096   Les furmerent par lur creance;
Dunt Rume ad furme de leun,
Ke roi des bestes est par nun;
Le bruc ke ferma Romulus,
1100   En est le chef tut a estrus;
Les edefices par defors,
Ces sunt les costez e le cors;
Dunt Lateranes sunt si numez,
1104   Kar *latera* ço sunt costez.
Brandiz est cum un cerf furmé,
Cartage cum boef purtreté,
Troie de cheval ad figure,
1108   Chescune ad sufferte sa aventure.

Champaine reest en Ytalie,
Terre de tuz biens replenie.
De Capua est la cité dite,
1112   Ke rois Capi prist e tint quite.
La est Puille, la est Y[m]brie,   *195 d*

1113 Y. *CD* (Imbria)] ybrie *PR,* Vmbrie *G*

1085 pus] pais *R, not in y*   1086 lateri *D*   1089 Del *RD*; prent cest *y*   1091
c. est *R. CG*   1093 de vels] des vals *R,* les uiles ont *C,* de veille *G,* e uiles par *D*
1100 Ele est *y*   1103 s. si n.] n. sunt *C,* si n. s. *G,* sunt n. *D*   1104 coe c. s. *C,* c. s.
G. ces s. c. *D*   1105 come c. *y*   1107 ad de c. *C*

De tant dite k'i[l] n'i plut mie
Quant le deluje surunda,
1116   E pluie e ewe tut nea.
Etthurie est la posee,
Del roi Etthurche si numee;
E Lumbardie reset la,
1120   Ke de lungs barbes nun a.
Padus, ke Eridan est dit,
Par Ytalie curt a delit;
De munt Apenun nest e surt,
1124   E desque en la mer a fort curt.
Venete del roi Bene dite,
Primes esteit Benete escrite.
Gallia de blanchur est dite,
1128   Kar bele genz en li habite.
    Le Rin a munt Giu surt a fort,
E entre l'occean vers le north;
Rin le flum de munt Goie surt,
1132   E ver le nort en la mer curt;
Ele ad a nun la mer de Bretaigne,
Ke de pessuns n'est pas baraigne.
    La est Gallia le pais,   [Cap. XXIX]
1136   Ke ad le surnun de Belgis;
Ele reest France numee,
Del roi Franc ke l'out cunquesté,
Ke de Troie vint od Enee,   *196a*
1140   E Troie ad sur le Rin fundee;
La terre ad de sun nun numee,
E de Franc France apelee.
Ceste France vers occident
1144   Vers munt Leun se tret e tent.

1114 quil *RC*, kele *D*, ke *G*

1114 Por *CD*   1117 est] rest *C*   1120 b. son n. *y*   1123 Del *y*   1124 f.]
force *RD*, forte *G*   1125 Venice *R*, Penice *C*, Benice *G*; Vene *RC*; est d. *y*   1126
Puis e. *y*; Venge *R*, Benice *C*, Venice *G*   1128 en li] i *CG*, iloke *D*   1129 Leon
a *y*   1130 l'] en *R*, en l' *y*   1133 a *not in Ry*   1137 n.] apelee *y*   1143 o.]
orient *y*

France, l'um dit, e Cumee,
Pur lung chevols k'iloc agree.
De Leunais vers le su
1148   Est France Nerboneys tendu,
Ke de Nerbone la cité
Est France Nerboneys numé.
Et iceste vers aquilun
1152   Ad Equitaigne a cumpaignun
Dous flums nun de Equitaine funt,
Kar Ronne e Lengres par li wnt.
Espaine pus aprés li vent,   [Cap. XXX]
1156   Ke del roi Y[s]pan le nun tent.
Enprés Espaigne vent Yberie,
Ke d'un flum Yber sun nun trie,
Ke del rey Yber est si numé;
1160   La terre prist, la fu neé.
Ceste terre vers le avesprer
Finist en occean la mer.
Cinc cuntrees en ceste sunt,
1164   Ke nun de cinc citez unt:
Teracune e Cartage,   *196 b*
E Lusitane salvage,
Galice i est, si est Boece,
1168   E Tinquitane, bone pece.
Cuntre Espaigne en la grant mer,   [Cap. XXXI]
Ke l'em sout occean numer,
Ces ydles sunt: primes Bretaigne,
1172   Ke de nul bien n'est baraigne;
Pus Engleterre la plentive,

1148–50 Nerboneis—Nerbone *CDG* (Narbonensem Galliam—Narbona)] Verboneys
—Verbone *PR*   1160 neé *RC*] ne *P*, neiee *G*, nez *D*

    1145–6 *not in CD*   1146 qe lur a. *R*, qui lout a. *G*   1147 leoenis de uers *y*;
luinays *R*   1151 Et *not in y*; Iceste terre u. *C*   1153 f. en Aq. sunt *CD*   1156
Yspan son n. *y*   1157 v.] est *CG*   1158 del f. *C*; De f. *D*; non crie *y*   1159 E del
C, Ou del *D*, Del *G*   1162 lcc. *CG*   1164 des .v. c. *R*, de lor c. *y*   1166 s.] la
s. *y*   1167 *G*. rest e b. *C*   1169 Entre e. e la *y*   1170 s.] soleit *DG*, *not in C*
1172 n' *not in RD*, ni *G*

E dunc Yrlande rive a rive,
E Thanet, ki terre defeit
1176   Les serpenz, ou ke portee soit.
Pus sunt Escoce e Orkenie,
Ke trente e trois ydles furnie.
Utre Escoce uns arbres sunt,
1180   Ke de lur foiles a tutdis unt.
Tel liu i at k'en esté
Sis mois entiers fet grant clarté,
Kar li soleil tutdis i lust,
1184   E le umbre de la nuit n'i nust;
E en yver sis mois enters
La nut i fet ses encumbrers.
Utre Orkenie ver le north
1188   Est li gel e li froit si fort
Ke mer e terre est engelee,
Si endurcie, si lee
Ke n'ert ja deliveré   *196 c*
1192   Se par Deu nun ke l'ad fundé.
Europe avum passé suef,
Vers Aufrike turnum le tref.
Aufrike de Afe est numé,   [Cap. XXXII]
1196   Ke fu un sergant Abrahé.
Ceste cumence en orient,
De Inde le flum ke tant est gent;
Par midi fet sun chemin
1200   Si fet en occident sa fin.
Ceste ad Libie, une cuntree
D'une reine si numee;
Ceste cumence en verité
1204   De Parithone la cité,
E par munt Cathabathinon ist,

1178 f.] furmeye R   1180 de *not in* y   1184 la lune ni y   1188 si freit e f. y
1189 sunt e. *CD*   1190 e. e si liee y   1191 Kele y   1194 le chef *CD*
1195 de affre *C*   1199 fet] torne y   1204 A p. y   1205 par le m. y

E en mer Philene finist;
E pur ço k'ele est la finee,
1208   Mer Libien est apelee.
     Puis est un regne Carmarike,
Dit de la cité noble e riche;
Iceste reest Pentapolis,
1212   De cinc citez dite jadis:
Beronice, Arsinoé,
E Ptolomaide la cité,
E Cyrene e Apolonie,
1216   Des cinc citez n'i falt mie;
Chescune cité sun nun ad   *196 d*
De li ke primes la fundad.
     Lez ceste est Censis la vaillant,
1220   Ke cuntent Cartage la grant,
Ke de Didon fu ja fundee,
La quele Edisse reest numee;
E Cartage retint a nun
1224   D'un chastel fort e felun;
Mes li Rumein tut l'abatirent,
E de rechief tut le refirent;
Nun lui dunerunt de Cartage,
1228   Uncore le tent en nostre age;
Dis e .vii. cutes de laur
Ad le mur de la cité entur.
     Puis est Genilie e Indie,
1232   U Jugnice regna sa vie;
La est Ypone la cité,
Ke fu seint Austin eveské.
     Lez ceste Moretaigne estat,
1236   Ke de neiresce le nun ad;

1229 c. *DGCR*] citez *P*

1206 en la mer *y*   1207 finie *y*   1208 Est apele la mer libie *y*   1211 En cest est p. *y*   1216 ne falt il mie *y*   1222 r. Elise n. *C*, est ore e. apele *D*   1223 Et de c. *R*; retinent *R*, retient *CD*; le n. *Ry*   1225 a.] habiterent *DG*   1226 tut *not in CD*   1231 e medie *y*   1232 Ou gogrite *y*; r. en sa *RD*

Iceste tent une cuntree,
De Stif chastel Stipens numee;
Cesariene iloc herite,
1240 De Cesarie sa cité dite.
La terce Tinguine est apelee
De Tinguin, sa cité prisee.
Ethiope reest vers midi,   *197 a*
1244 Del roi Ethan numé issi.   [Cap. XXXIII]
Un Ethiope en orient,
Un autre se est en occident;
Entre ces dous sunt Garemanz,
1248 E Gamare, cité vaillant.
Ilokes est une funtaigne,
De ewe duce tute pleine;
Nul ne la put taster de jur,
1252 Tant par ad en soi grant freidur;
Ne de nuz nul hume nc la beit
Pur la grant chalur ke la defeit.
Pardelez ces en orient
1256 Sunt Trogodite, une gent,
Tant delivres, parigneler
Ke beste nes put eschaper.
Utre Ethiope sunt uns lius
1260 De tutes genz voidez e eschius;
Mult par est grant la gastine
E tute pleine de vermine;
E le soleil tant chaut i art,
1264 Ke nul ne passe cele part;
Puis est l'occean tant boillant
Cum est chaudere sur feu grant.
Aufriche en ses forens pais
1268 Vers occident ad citez de pris:

1240 c. la c. *y*   1241 t.] terre R*y*   1242 sa] vne *C*, la *D*   1245 en] ad en *C*, est
en *D*   1248 De g. *y*; la c. *D*   1252 par *not in* R*y*   1253 hom *y*; n'en b. *C*, ne
b. *D*   1254 Por grant *CG*; la desoit *RG*   1265 t.] si *y*   1266 feu ardant *C*

Gabes i ad, une cité   *197 b*
Ke les Fenices unt fundé,
Dunt la mer ad nun Gaditan,
1272   E altres ki nuns ne sunt plan.
En occean est munt Athlas,
Tant haut ke hum nel survoit pas;
Dunt la mer ad nun Athlantike,
1276   Des bons pessuns plentif e riche.
Rois Athlas Aufrike tenoit,
Ke frere Protomeu estoit;
Cil Prothomeu en cel munt mist,
1280   E astrologie iloc escrist;
Dunt dit est ke il le ciel sustint,
Pur sen celestre ke en vint.
De Aufrike asez oi avum,
1284   As ydles ore tresnoum.
Chipre est en mer Mediterin,   [Cap. XXXIV]
Riche des bles e de bon vin;
E Taphe de sa cité dite,
1288   E Crete de sun roi escrite.
Cele meimes est Centipolis,
Kar ele ad cent citez de pris;
Ceste set en mer Libien,
1292   Ke de Adre cité est Adrien.
Anidos est un ydle ausi,
En Ellespont se set de fi;
Ellespont est la mer nomé   *197 c*
1296   D'Elle la bone cité.
Un ydle read, Colcos ad nun,
Dunt Jason prist l'orin toysun.
Les Cyclades ydles resunt,

1281 s. *CDG* (sustinere)] sunt *P*, fu *R*   1282 v. *CDG*] vnt *P*, est veu *R*

1270 f. i ount *C*   1273 o.] orient *R*, occident *y*   1274 lum *CD*   1276 De *y*
1278 promotheu *CD*   1281 il *not in CD*; le] en le *R*   1286 des b. *y*   1294 se
not in C, i *D*   1297 r.] y ad *RDG*, est *C*

1300 Dites de ço k'il sunt rund,
Kar *cyclon* en cel lur gregeis
Dit rund en cest nostre franceis;
Ke petit, ke maen, ke grant,
1304 Cent en i ad e quatre estant;
Les nuns a quel os cunteroie?
Kar plus ennui ke bien feroie.
E cil ke vuldra bien cunter,
1308 Ennui e surfet doit lesser.
    Sezille de roi Sicul ad   [Cap. XXXV]
Sun nun, kar il la cunquestad.
Li roys Ytal sun frere estoit,
1312 Dunt Ytalie le nun tret.
Puis fu nomé Sycanie,
Del roi Sican kin out bailie;
Ele reest dite Mo[n]trine,
1316 De trois munz k'ad en sa seisine.
Munt Ethne set en ses banduns,
Ke gette sulfrins arsuns;
En ceste mer dous perilz sunt,
1320 Stille e Karibde les nuns unt;
Li Cyclope i mistrent ja,   *197 d*
E *comedia* i cumença.
Ceste ydle set cuntre Ytalie,
1324 Ke ore est dite Lumbardie.
    Lez Sezille resunt posees
Del roi Coile ydles numees,
Ke resunt dites Vulcanies,

1316 m. *C* (montibus)] nunz *PR*, *not in D*   1318 g. *RCG*] grece *P*, iuste *D*
1321 Li *CG*] La *PR*, Le *D*

  1300 ke elles s. *C*   1301 cel *not in Ry*   1302 Est dist mond en n. *R*; Dit tant
come rond en f. *C*   1305 A quai les n. c. *R*; a quei reconterei *C*   1306 ke
delit frei *C*   1307 bien conter uodra *C*   1308 s. tot lerra *C*   1309 Roy Syrus
; ad] son non ad *C*, non ad *D*   1310 Sun nun *not in CD*   1312 son n. *y*   1315
est d. monterine *y*   1316 qele ad en seisigne *RD*, dunt ad s. *C*   1317 set] est *R*, se
est *G*, i ad *D*   1320 les *not in R*, lur *y*   1325 r.] sunt *y*   1326 C.] Olle *C*, elle *D*
1327 Que sont *RD*

1328　　Kar d'enbraser sunt replenies.
　　　　Ydles Stecades nef i sunt,
　　　　Ke vers Marsille lur lius unt.
　　　　Sardine i est, la region,　　　　　　　　[Cap. XXXVI]
1332　　Ke ad del rei Sardin le nun;
　　　　Cist Sardin fu fiz Herculis.
　　　　L'ydle vers Numide s'est mis;
　　　　Lou ne serpent iloc ne nest,
1336　　Mais un altre malvé i crest,
　　　　Solivag est par sun [nun] dit,
　　　　Si reest cum araigne petit,
　　　　Si reest venimus ensement,
1340　　E par mordre tue la gent.
　　　　Un herbe i crest, cil ke s'en disne,
　　　　Cum riant mort si bel reschine;
　　　　L'erbe dunt jo vus vois disant,
1344　　Ache resemble en sun cressant.
　　　　Funtaignes chaudes la resunt,
　　　　Ke as malades sancté funt;
　　　　Mais si larrun i boit ou baigne,　　　　198 a
1348　　Del ver ert tutdis baraigne.
　　　　Ebosus est cuntre Espaigne,
　　　　Ke reest de tuz serpens baraingne.
　　　　Aparmemes est Colubrie,
1352　　De plusurs serpens bien emplie.
　　　　Gorgoines, ydles de bel grant,
　　　　En occean sunt lez Athlan.
　　　　En ces furent jadis manant
1356　　Trois femmes de bealté grant;
　　　　Si ensembles fussent aunees,

1337 nun DGCR

1337 sun *not in* RD　　　1339 Et si RD; r.] est RCD　　　1343 vus *not in* y
1348 De RG; De la (*not in* C) veue CD　　　1349 est] seet Ry; encuntre y　　　1350 Quest
de R; Que de t. s. est b. G, De t. s. void e b. C　　　1352 s. replenie C　　　1354 En
occident lez mund a. C　　　1356 b. mult g. C　　　1357 a.] veues R, aunets C

Ja mes [ne] fusent devisees,
Tant par s'entresemblerent,
1360 E Gorgoines lé appelerent.
 Lez cestes Ysperides sunt,
Ke de lur citez lur nun unt;
Blanches berbiz asez i sunt,
1364 Dunt il le gentil purpre funt.
 Utre ces fu un ydle grant,
Dunt Platun dit en sun lisant
K'ele fu greignur ke n'est Aufrike,
1368 Ne Europe ke tant fu riche;
Mes ele ove sa gent enfundra,
E morte mer en sun liu ad.
 Un ydle el Nil ad nun Menee,
1372 El chief de Ethiope posee;
Umbre n'i pert en nul esté;   198 b
L'iban i crest, un fust prisé.
 Delez ceste est Syrine la cité,
1376 Ke ad un puz de antiquité;
Les philosophos la fuirent,
Seisante cutes parfunt firent;
Le soleil i luist el mois de juin
1380 Tut droit as funz sanz nul essoin.
 Un ydle est el occean,
Mais l'um ne set en quel pan;
Ydle Perdue est apelee,
1384 Une fez put estre truvee.
 Sage est kel truve se il l'enprent,
Kar del retrover n'i ad nient.
L'ydle par est tant plentive,

1358 ne RC   1361 Lez RC (iuxta)] Des P, Iloke G   1362 c. RCG (civitate)]
cutes P   1372 c. CDGR (capite)] chiel P

1359 sentre asemblerent C, face entresemblerent R   1360 Ke G. sap. C   1362
Ki de une cite C; nouns Ry   1364 il *not in y*   1365 ces] cest *y*   1368 fu]est *y*
1369 ele *not in y*; enfundeat CD   1377 la] i *y*   1378 c. de p. CG; le f. DG   1380
as] al RDG, el C   1381 est] rest CG   1385 il *not in Ry*

1388   La fin ne seit humme ke vive;
        N'est metal el mund ke rien vaile,
        Gemme ne piere ke la faile,
        Tutes especes e tuz blez,
1392   Ewes duces e pessuns e prez,
        Arbres chargez de trestuz frutz,
        Tutes delices e tuz deduiz;
        Le mund ke tant par est espars,
1396   Ver li de tuz biens est eschars.
        La terre brefment avum trespassé,
        Oum d'enfer la verité.
        Enfer set enmi terre en veir,   *198 c*
1400   Cum fet la terre en miliu l'eir;   [Cap. XXXVII]
        Dunt il est dit terre foreigne,
        De tuz mals, de tuz turmenz pleine;
        Ka[r] cel liu est de fu espris,
1404   E de sulfre k'art tutdis;
        Mult est horrible e tenebrus,
        Desuz mult large, estreit desus.
        Ceste est numé terre de mort,
1408   Ke la entre n'ad mes resort;
        Estanc de fu reest il numé,
        Kar li malvois i sunt plungé,
        Cum est la piere en parfunde mer,
1412   E la ardent sanz recuvrer.
        Cesti est terre de tenebrur,
        De fume, de niule, de puur;
        Cesti est terre de obliviun,
1416   Kar li son sunt sanz rançun;
        Si cum il ci Deu ublierent,

La de tuz bienz ubliez erent.
Cil liu reest numé Tartarus,
1420   Kar en tuz hidurs est confus;
Jehenne reest ausi numé,
Ço est terre tut enbrasé;
Nostre fu ke nus avum ci,
1424   N'est fors umbre vers cesti.
Sa parfundesce est Herebus,   *198 d*
De draguns ardanz tant penus;
Sa buche est dite Baratrum,
1428   Ke noir devurement numum;
Ses lius sunt numé Acherun,
Ke ord espiriz unt en sun.
E Flageton, un flum, i est,
1432   Ke nule fez n'est sanz tempest;
Kar l'ewe est a tutdis ardant,
E la puur horrible e grant,
E le froit tutdis ensement;
1436   L'un par l'altre ne se desment,
Nul mal par altre ne se pert.
Fols est ke cel regne desert;
Les peines n'erent ja pensees,
1440   Dunt almes sunt la turmentees.
Et altres lius en terre sunt,
Ke grant turmenz en soi refunt,
En ydles, en munz e en vals,
1444   De sulfre, de feu e de altres mals;
E en cel eir tut ensement
U les almes sunt en turment.
Quantke eida ci a pecher,
1448   Trestut aie al turmenter.

1428 noir R (atra)] uoir P   1442 refont RCG, resunt P, unt D
1419 r.] est R*y*   1420 Kar *not in* C, E D; de touz illes est *y*   1424 celui *y*
1426 a. mult perillus C   1428-9 *not in y*   1430 e. ad *y*   1433 a *not in* R*y*
1437 por a. C   1438 r.] liu C   1440 i sunt C   1441 E *not in* CD   1444 e *not*
in RDG   1445 en leir *y*   1448 Tut eide iloec (la G) a t. *y*

Enfer ja trespassé avum—
Deus [nus] en ost par sun saint nun!—
E la terre tut ensement,   *199 a*
1452   Oum del secund element.
     Ewe est le secund element,   [Cap. XXXVIII]
     Ke entur la terre se estent;
     Iceste en mer tute se cult,
1456   Par flums curt, par funtaignes bult,
     Par tutes terres se espanist,
     E par l'eir grantment atenvist;
     Ceste depart les regiuns,
1460   Les cuntrees, les mansiuns;
     Sa parfundesce abisme ad nun,
     Pur ço ke funz ne ateignum.
     L'occean munte, si retret,   [Cap. XL]
1464   E siut la lune en sun espleit;
     Par sun espirement el mund
     Retret les ewes e refunt.
     La mer ove la lune descret,
1468   E si crest quant la lune crest;
     En equinocce est la mer grant,
     Kar la lune est dunc pres curant;
     En solstice ses salz reprent,
1472   Pur la lune ke loinz se tient;
     Par dis e neof anz sun curs tent,
     E sun començail dunc reprent,
     Tut ausi cum la lune fet,
1476   Kar od li crest, od li retret.
     La mer ad un devurement,   *199 b*
     Ke les ewes devure e rent;   [Cap. XLI]
     Si ad un el orient,

1450 nus *CDGR*

1449 E. a. t. *C*; ia passe a *G*   1452 Oum] Ore dirrom *R*, Ore oum *CG*, Ore oyez *D*
1454 Ki en tote la *y*   1462 ni a. *y*   1463 si] e *y*, et se *R*   1465 el m.] amont *CD*
1466 les] ces *Ry*   1470 est p. *CD*   1471 salz] cors *y*   1476 c. e si r. *C*   1479
Sen i a *C*, Si en ad *G*; el] en *RCD*, en le *G*

1480 E un altre vers occident;
En prime lune mult tret, mult rent,
E en la pleine tut ensement.
Si l'achesun saver vulez,
1484 Jo le vus dirai, ore l'escutez:
En terre est un abisme grant,
Ço est parfundesce baant;
Dunt tru[v]um en escrit lisant,
1488 Deus overi le abisme tresgrant.
Lez cesti sunt fosses mult lees,
E caves e boves celees;
En cels, par grant espirement
1492 Des ewes, nessent tut li vent,
Dunt cil sunt numé esperit
De tempest en seint escrit.
Ces venz par lur espiremenz
1496 La mer treent la par dedenz,
E l'abisme tut funt paremplir,
E quant est plain, par force issir.
De ço sunt floz en occean,
1500 E retreanz e jur e an.
De ces venz terremute vent,   [Cap. XLII]
Kar quant les crus les venz retent,
Ke issir ne puent franchement,   *199 c*
1504 La terre enpeignent durement,
E funt fremir horriblement,
E par tant trembler ferement.
De ço se avent ke terre bee,   [Cap. XLIII]
1508 Quant est par ewe afebliee;

1481 r. *RCDG* (removit)] tent *P*   1487 l. *RCDG*] libant *P*   1490 b. *RCD*]
bones *P*, boefs *G*   1492 Des *CDG*] Ses *P*, Ces *R*   1502 les crus *R* (concavis locis)]
les trus *P*, le croiz *C*, le croes *G*, les treos *D*, *see note*

1480 v.] en R*y*   1481 m. creist e r. *y*   1482 En *RG*   1484 ore e. R*y*   1488
le *not in CG*; a. g. *y*   1492 tut *not in y*   1494 Des *y*   1495 v.] ouerent *y*
1498 a f. *y*   1499 loc. *y*   1502 le uent *y*   1503 poet *CD*   1507 se *not in y*
1508 ewe] tut *y*

E

Li venz deden les crus rebutent,
E sa tenvesse tut derutent,
E funt en ces crus jus chair,
1512   E grant baees aoverir.
Multes citez par tels haschees
Sunt perdues e enfundrees.
Dunt la terre, ke est cavee,
1516   E cum espoigne tut crusee,
La u ad sulfre u betumee,
Pleine de feu, devent percee,
Quant li venz s'enpeint durement,
1520   Cum en forge le feu se esprent,
E fet issir flambe e fumee,
Ou altre male destempree;
En asquanz lius gette sabelun,
1524   Si en fet muncels a bandun.
Dunt Ethna, ke est un grant munt,
E ensample d'enfer parfund,
De feu est tutdis enbrasee,
1528   De venz suzterins aventee;
Kar des ewes ke desuz sunt,   *199 d*
En muant tutdis vent funt;
E ces venz entrent en crusesces,
1532   E tant dis sunt en lur destresces
Ke il ne puent mes suffrir,
E dunc se efforcent de issir,
Par grant fruis funt le munt fremir,
1536   Feu esprendre, flambe sailir.
Ileoc ad un devurement,
Ke la mer e devure e rent;
Scille ad nun, dunt li fableant

1509 les crus R (loca cava)] les turs P, le croiz CG   1511 crus R] trus P, crois CG
1512 o. CG] anurrir P, amireer R   1530 En CG] E en PR, Al D
   1509 r.] debotent y   1511 crois tut dechair y   1529 des] les G   1530 m.]
mouant C, mouent G, munt D; v.] grant u. C   1531 Ces y   1532 t.] tut RG
1534 Dunc CD; del i. CG   1535 E par y   1536 e. et f. RC   1538 mer d. y

1540 Dient ke chiens i ad baant,
Pur ço ke mer tant fremist,
Quant ele i entre u en ist,
Ke la noise ount tut clier
1544 Li marinail loinz en la mer;
Ço est de l'ewe e del vent,
Ke se ferent ensemblement.
Par meimes ices achesuns
1548 Art terre en altre regiuns,
Si cum la chalur de feu nest,   [Cap. XLIV]
E la freidure de l'ewe crest;
Dunt les foreins parz de occean,
1552 De gel e froit unt grant ahan;
Gelee pardurable i nuist,   *200 a*
Kar li soleil unkes n'i luist.
De l'occean cele partie,
1556 Ki par miliu le mund se guie,
De boillant chaud est tutdis pleine,
Kar tutdis li solz la se meine.
Occean par les flums ne crest,   [Cap. XLV]
1560 Ke la salse durer ne le lest;
Li soleil une part ravist,
Partie par les venz sechist,
Partie par uns venz privez
1564 Repeire as ses propres guez.
Pur ço remeint la mer salee,
Des flums, de pluies tant chargee,
Kar li solail trest la ducur
1568 De l'ewe e la tenve liquur,
Dunt sa chalur atempre e pest,
Le grant, le pesant aval lest;

1548 Art t. *RCG*] A retrere *P*, Ardent *D*   1556 Ki *CG* (quae)] E *PR*

1541 mer] la mer *y*   1542 ele entre e (ou *DG*) quant ele ist *y*   1544 m. ki uont par la (*not in D*) mer *CD*   1546 sentreferent *CD*   1551 loc. *Ry*   1556 parmy le *Ry*   1558 li soleil la (*G only*) t. *y*; solail *R*   1559 Loc. par f. *y*   1560 ni lest *C*, ne l. *DG*   1561 p.] partie *Ry*   1566 des p. *Ry*   1569 la c. *y*

Dunt mer en sum est duce e clere,
1572   Vers ço ke ele en parfund est amere.
Duce ewe la lune nurrist,
Al solail la amere suffist.
De l'occean la Ruge Mer vient,   [Cap. XLVI]
1576   Mes de la terre culur tient,
Ke tut est ruge cum est sanc,
La mer la demoist cum fanc.   *200 b*
La mer est de amertume dite,
1580   Pur la sause dunt ja n'ert quite;
Par veines en la terre curt,
E es funtaignes duces surt;
En la terre tant est culee,
1584   Ke l'amerté tut ad lessé.
Quant Deu paradis compostat,   [Cap. XLVII]
Une funtaigne en li posat;
En quatre flums la devisat,
1588   E le mund aruser ruvat;
Dunt ces ewes tres duces sunt,
Ke arusent trestut le mund;
Dunt ad la mer tel amertume,
1592   Ke tant undeie, tant escume.
Les flums ke de paradis vunt,
Par tut lur droite ducur unt,
Ne pur terre ne pur marine,
1596   Ne perdent lur duce seisine.
Lur curs parfunt enterinement,
E entrent tut priveement
En le abime de lur funtaigne,
1600   Dunt pus issent a veine pleine;

1574 s. *CDR*] suffrist *PG*   1578 f. *RG*] sanc *P*, estanc *C*   1589 D. *CDG*] Quant
PR   1597 p.] *see note*

1572 ke le p. est *D*; ele est parfunde e (*G only*) a. *RCG*   1573 Dolcor en la *y*   1574
amerte *CG*   1577 cum s. *y*   1582 as f. *RG*   1583 est tant *RG*, ad t. *D*   1584
ad tut (*not in C*) l. *y*   1587 q. parties *y*   1590 tut *y*   1591 cel a. *y*   1592 e tant
(*not in C*) e. *y*   1596 p. ia lor *CD*   1597 curs *not in R y;* enterrement *y*

Dunt Salomon dit en apert,
Chescun ewe en sei revert.
Al liu dunt [ist], iloc repeire   *200 c*
1604   Pur autre fez sun curs refere.
De ces flums e de lur funtaigne
Vent chescun ewe duce e seine,
E les funtaines autresi,
1608   Ke de ewe duce sunt empli.
La mer ke en un liu estait,
De la chalur amerté trait,
Ke la ducur tute ravist,
1612   E sa tenvesce tute sechist.
De la terre tut ensement
L'occean sa amertume prent:
La terre ad en soi plusurs veines
1616   De cel e sal gemme pleines,
Ke en l'ewe tute defit,
E li solail amunt la quit,
E par itant devent amer;
1620   Essample pernez del sauner.
L'occean sa amertume cult
Desuz la zone u tutdis bult,
Dunt tutes mers salces sunt,
1624   Kar il purceint tut le mund.
Unes fosses en terre sunt,   [Cap. XLVIII]
Ke de sulfre grant plenté unt;
Li venz i pulse durement,
1628   E le sulfre de feu se esprent.
Sulfre en sun naturelment   *200 d*
Trop dure, mes de poi se esprent.
L'ewe ke par cest arsun curt,

1603 ist *RCG* (exeunt)] *not in PD*
1610 Lamerte de la c. t. *y*   1612 tuit bruist *C*   1614 sa a.] lamerte *C*   1616
p.] tutes p. *RC*   1617 Ke lewe dolce t. *C*   1619 tant d. tut a. *C*   1621
samerte *C*   1622 u] que *CD*   1623 t. les m. *y*; salees s. *Ry*   1628 E de s. le
feu e. *C*, El fu del s. e. *D*; del *R*   1629-30 *not in y*   1631 c. ardor sort *y*

1632 Tut est boillant si de pres surt,
Si reest de sulfre tut puant,
Pus atenvist quant curt avant,
Puis en avant si cult froidure,
1636 Kar ço est sa droite nature.
Uns autres lius sunt suzterins, [Cap. XLIX]
Pleins de serpenz et de venims;
Les ewes ke la sunt voisin,
1640 Treent la force del venim;
Ki en boit tantost murt a peine;
Itele est Stix, une funtaine.
Nul vent nel mut ne fet trembler [Cap. L]
1644 Les ewes de la Morte Mer;
Les betumeis i sunt si grant
Ke les ewes tenent estant.
Betum par naturel afeire
1648 E[st] a l'ewe tute cuntreire,
Kar l'ewe est tutdis remuant,
Betum est estant e trop tenant;
Ren nule nel put depescer,
1652 For sul sanc menstre de mulier.
Nembroc sa tur de ço fermad,
Ke de Babel le droit nun ad.
Quant la mer de nut estencele, *201 a*
1656 As aviruns tempest apele; [Cap. LII]
Quant li porpeis sailent amunt,
Tempest proceinement sumunt;
E de iloc le venz vendra,
1660 Vers u li porpeis tumbera.
D'iloc ausi les venz vendrunt,

1648 Est R*CD*

1632 p. cort *y*   1633 r.] est R*D*; del R   1635 E si coilt puis la f. *C*   1636
sa] la R*D*   1638 v.] uermines *y*   1640 Tenent D*C*   1641 tost R*y*; en p. R*D*
1642 Icele *C,* Cest *D*   1649 Kar ewe *y*   1650 est *not in* R*y*   1651 Nulle r. R; Ke
nul ren (*not in C*) ne p. *y*   1656 As mariners t.

U les niules se defenderunt.
Les ewes sumes tresnoé,
1664   De l'eir cerchum la qualité.
    Eir est quantke vus vein veez,   [Cap. LIII]
U vus ren funder ne poez;
Aval a la terre se prent,
1668   E desque a la lune se estent;
De li viel espirement
Treent oisels, bestes e gent;
En li sunt diables sujurnant,
1672   Jur de juise atendant;
De li pernent corsage en veir,
Quant a la gent vulent pareir.
    De l'eir resunt li venz criez,   [Cap. LIV]
1676   Kar quant il est bien demenez,
E commu en remuant,
Cum chose ke n'est pas estant,
Par ses multes remuvemenz
1680   De plusurs parz meut plusurs venz,
Dunt les quatre sunt cardinals,   *201 b*
E uit altres collateral.   [Cap. LV]
    Les cardinals apelé sunt,
1684   De quatre parties del mund.
    Li premer est Septemtriun,
Ke nus ici Bise numum;
Cesti s'en vent dever le nordh,
1688   E fet nues e froiz e forz;
Il e li diu collateral
Funt noif e gresil e grant mal.

1680 m. *RC*] mult *P*, muent *D*, mouent *G*

1662 n.] nues *y*; se fenderont *C*, descenderunt *D*   1664 les qualitez *CD*   1666 fonder rien *y*, sustindre r. *R*   1668 a *not in CG*   1669 li ouuel e. *CG*   1672 Le ior *DG*, Et le i. *R*   1673 por ueir *C*   1674 as homes *CG*   1675 r.] sont *RD* 1678 pas *not in C*, en *DG*   1679 les m. *CG*; remuemenz *Ry*   1680 p. v.] plus v. *R*, li u. *C* les v. *DG*   1683 Les quatre c. *y*   1684 Des *Ry*   1688 n. fr. *CD*, n. mult fr. *G*; fr. moltz fort *R*   1689 li] si *C*, ses *DG*; diu] deus *RDG*

Li secund Subsolan ad nun,
1692 Ke nus Solaire renomum;
Cist est attemprez, mes ki sunt
Lez li, nue e sec tens funt.
Li terz venz Auster ad nun,
1696 Ke nus del su Surreis disum;
Cesti humurs e chalurs tret,
E fuldres e tuneires fet.
Sis cumpaignuns ke sunt delez,
1700 L'un est sec, l'altre attemprez.
Li venz del su plus umbles sunt,
E greignur tempest en mer funt.
Le quart ad Zephirus a nun,
1704 Ke nus Molvent a droit numum;
Kar il yver tolt e defet,
De terre herbes [et] flurs tret.
Si cumpainun ke a destre esteit,   *201 c*
1708 Tempez, tuneres, fudres feit;
L'altre en orient nues porte,
E Inde de bel tens conforte.
Kanz ces vus voil dous venz numer,
1712 Eure en terre, Altain en mer.
Les venz par lur espiremenz   [Cap. LVI]
De l'ewe en l'eir tirent grantment;
Les ewes la ensemble vunt,
1716 E nues granz e espés funt.
Quant li vent est en lur clos,
Cum ren muvable n'unt repos;
Les nues pulse a grant air,
1720 Les uns as altres fet ferir;
El entreferir sunt pesant,

1706 et *RCDG*

1692 s. apelom *y*   1694 Lez les nues *DGR*, Espesse nues *C*; led t. *RC*   1695 t.
a. apelum *y*   1703 q. z. ad n. *y*   1706 f. atreit *CD*   1708 t. f.] f. et t. R, t. et f. *y*
1711 Ces dous uenz vus voil n. *y*   1714 t.] treent *Ry*   1716 espes] espesces *RCD*
1717 c.] reclos *Ry*   1718 ren] chose *y*   1719 a] oue R, par *y*   1721 Al e. *RCDG*

Dunt feu gettent e noise grant;
La noise ço est la tunaire,   [Cap. LVII]
1724   Le feu, escleire e fudre en veire;
Ço feu tresperce quantke ateint,
Kar la force des venz l'enpeint.
L'arc del cel quatre culurs fet,   [Cap. LVIII]
1728   Ke il de quatre choses tret;
Del cel ad il culur fuin,
E de l'ewe la purprin;
De l'eir ad il jaune colur,   *201 d*
1732   E de la terre la verdur.
Volez saver dunt l'arc est nez,
Par essample melz l'aprendez:
En un rai del soleil metez
1736   Un bacin ou eit ewe asez;
Tantost verrez un rai issir,
E en la meisun resplendir;
Mais dunc ert mult bien aparisant,
1740   Quant l'ewe ert ben en pes estant.
Ausi quant les nues estunt,
E le solail les rais i funt,
De l'ewe ke la nue tent,
1744   E del solail l'arc del cel vent.
La pluie de l'eir partent vent,   [Cap. LIX]
L'ewe en gutes se coil[t] e tent,
Ke par l'eir ke nes put porter,
1748   Ke par le vent ke les fet ruer,
Ke par le solail ke les deserre,
L'ewe par gutes chet a terre.
Ceste gutes, quant sunt furmé,   [Cap. LX]
1752   Alcune feiz sunt engelé

1724 en v.] en eir *CD*, a ueire *G*   1725 Cest *CD*; quankil a. *CD*   1726 del uent *y*
1728 c. atreit *CD*   1730 la] color *CD*   1731 E de *CG*; il *not in y*   1732 la] ad la
C, ad il *D*   1733 Ki (Si *DG*) sauer uolez *y*   1736 eit] ert *RD*   1739 mult *not*
in y; m. a. *R*   1745 portent v. *R*, partie uient *y*

Par le froid eir ke aval est,
Si funt de grisil le tempest.
    La neif en l'eir de l'ewe vent,   [Cap. LXI]
1756   Ke en sa liquur se retent,
E n'est par gutes departie,   *202 a*
Einz ke le gel le eit pursesie;
Li venz la fert e tut desrumpt,
1760   Si ke a terre par offes funt.
    La rusee de l'eir revent,   [Cap. LXII]
Quant a grevance l'ewe tent;
Par le chaut de la nut descent,
1764   E par la lune ke resplent.
Si la nut grantment froidist,
En gel la rusee enblanchist,
E ço ke dust estre rusee,
1768   Si revert en blanche gelee.
    Niule vent de muistes aleines,   [Cap. LXIII]
Ke od terre e ewe sunt es eines;
Iloc bas en l'eir pent,
1772   U par le solail jus descent.
    Uns feus de nuz vers terre elident,   [Cap. LXV]
Ke esteiles seient plusurs quident;
Einz sunt feus de l'ethre amunt,
1776   E li forz venz ravist e rumpt,
E ver la terre aval enpeint,
Mes el muiste eir sunt tost esteint.
    Pestilence de l'eir resurt,   [Cap. LXVI]
1780   Quant trop grant sekeresce curt,
U trop grant chaud, u grant tempeste,
Ke l'eir de corupture veste.

1770 s. *CDG*] funt *PR*   1773 Uns f. *CGR*] Vne fez, *P*, Vn grans feus *D*
1775 f. *RCDG* (igniculi)] sunt *P*

1753 a.] de aual *C*, de ual *G*   1755 de leir en ewe *y*   1758 que giel *y*   1760
par o. a t. *y*; se funt *CG*   1766 blanchist *y*   1770 od *not in y*   1771 E i. *y*
1772 E *CD*; aual d. *y*   1775 de leir *y*, de ayr *R*   1776 ra.] le reimt *C*, les raient *G*
1777 e.] lemp. *CD*   1778 tost *not in y*

Ke l'eir corumpu en soi tret, *202 b*
1784 E pureture e mort receit.
Desuz la lune est quantke ai dit,
La clarte l'amunt ne defit.
L'eir avum briefime[n]t tresvolé,
1788 Del feu parler nus vient a gré.
    Feu, ke est le quart element, [Cap. LXVII]
Va de la lune al firmament.
Il reest dit ethre e pur eir,
1792 Kar tutdis resplendit pur veir;
Angeles pernent de li corsage,
Quant funt en terre le Deu message.
    Set esteiles en cesti sunt, [Cap. LXVIII]
1796 Ke funt lur curs encuntre le mund;
Planetes apelees sunt,
Kar wai curs e folif funt.
Cestes par grant ignelesce
1800 Del firmament ke n'ad peresce,
De l'orient el occident
Sunt ravi mult ignelement;
E si est lur naturel curs
1804 Cuntre le mund tut a reburs.
    La planete premer est dite [Cap. LXIX]
Lune, ver les autres petite,
Mais pur ço resemble grant
1808 Ke de la terre est pres curant;
Ele fet sun curs a estrus *202 c*
El premer cercle pres de nus.
Ceste ad le cors tut rund en fin,
1812 E par nature tut fuin,
Mes pur ço ke de ewe est medlee,

1786 La c. *CD* (serenum)] Le chaud de *PR*, La charge *G*   1792 pur *RDG*] par *P*,
le *C*   1799 g. *CD* (immensa)] lur *PR*, la g. *G*
    1783 Ke] E *C*, *not in D*; en] a *y*   1791 r.] est *y*   1795 Les s. e. en li s. *y*
1801 en o. *Ry*.   1807 r. ele g. *CD*   1808 Kar *CD*   1810 c. plus p. *y*

Des neirs puinz e[st] tut techelee;
Si ele od ewe ne fust medlee,
1816 De chaud serreit tant enbrasee
Ke la terre tuit arsereit
Cum li solail, si pres esteit,
Kar sa rundesce est mult greinur
1820 Ke la terre trestut entur,
Ja soit ço ke ele perge petite
Pur ço ke loinz de nus habite.
La lune lust cele partie,
1824 U ele ver le soleil se plie;
E cele partie oscurité treit,
U ele le solail pas ne veit;
Quant del soleil loinz est ostee,
1828 Dunc est trestut enluminee.
Ele ne crest ne ne decrest pas;
[Mes] quant ele est en itel cas
Ke la terre entredous s'estent,
1832 La luur pert ke del solail prent;
De la terre la grant haltur
A basse lune tolt luur.
E ja soit ço ke le firmament   202 *d*
1836 De l'est le treie en le occident,
Par si grant force nepurquant
Encuntre le mund va errant
Ke les duze signes trescurt,
1840 Dunt le zodiac tent sa curt,
En vint e set jurs cuntenanz,
E sun cercle en dis e nof anz.
Si la lune quarte ruvist,

1830 Mes *CDG* (sed)] *not in* PR   1841 vint e set *GCR* (viginti septem)] dis e set
PD   1842 dis e nof *DCR* (decem et novem)] dis e vit *P*, dis nef *G*

1814 De *y*; tut *not in y*   1816 s. tut e. *RDG*   1820 tr.] tot *y*   1825 p.] part
DG, not in C   1827 est loinz *y*   1828 est ele tut e. *C*   1829 ne ne] ne *y*   1830
i.] cel R, ouwel *C*, vel *D*, vouel *G*   1831 entre els d. *CG*, entre nus *D*   1832 l.]
lune *RDG*   1835 E *not in y*

1844 De granz venz tute genz garnist;
E si ele en sa corne suveraine
Des neir teches ad estraine,
Del mois le premer cumencement
1848 Serrat pluius tut finement;
Si ele en miliu les noirs poinz ad,
Bele pleine lune serrad.
L'altre planete Mercur ad nun, [Cap. LXX]
1852 E si reest apelé Stilbun.
Cist reest tut rund par figure,
E trestut fuin par nature;
La lune veint de sa grandur,
1856 E del solail reçoit luur;
En trois cent jurz e trente nof
Le zodiac trescurt cum of.
La terce planete ad nun Venus, [Cap. LXXI)
1860 Si reest numé Hesperus,
E Lucifer en la matinee, *203 a*
E Vesper est a la vespree.
Cist est rund e tut fuin,
1864 Cuntre le mund tent sun chemin;
Trois cent e quarante e uit jurs
Al zodiac parfet sun curs.
La quarte planete est li solail, [Cap. LXXII]
1868 Issi numé, si jo ne fail,
Pur ço ke il sul relut,
Quant as esteiles li jurz nut.
Cist est rund e plein de feu,
1872 Cuntre le mund curt a vertu;
Uit feiz ke la terre greinur,
As csteiles dune luur.

1845 c. *CD* (corniculo)] curune *PR*
1844 tote la gent *R*, la g. *DG* 1846 De *y* 1851 Mercurie *RD* 1852 r.]
est *RD* 1853 r.] est R*y*; tut *not in y* 1855 de] par *y* 1861 jurnee] matinee *CDG*
1864 Encontre *CD* 1869 sul r.] tot soul luist *y*

Trois cent e seisante e cinc jurnees
1876   El zodiac tent ses estrees;
En vint e uit anz fet ses curs,
E puis reprent ses premers jurs.
Sa presence nus fet le jur,
1880   E sa absence nut oscur;
Le jur nus lust sus terre amunt,
La nuit suz terre ses raiz funt.
Quant ver le north sun chemin tret,
1884   Lungs jurs e lungs estez nus fet;
E quant el su refet ses curs,
Yver nus fet e mult curz jurs.

La quinte planete Mars est dite,   *203 b*
1888   E Pyroys en altre escrite;   [Cap. LXXIV]
Cist est rund e tut ardanz,.
Zodiac parcurt en dous anz.
La siste planete ad nun Jovis,   [Cap. LXXV]
1892   Si li reest de Phenon nun mis;
Cist est rund e atemprez,
En duze anz ad sun curs finez.
La setime planete est Saturne,   [Cap. LXXVI]
1896   Ke en Pheton sun nun returne;
Il est rund, gelus e froid,
En trente anz sun curs tut feit.
Puis ces .xxx. anz, al cumencer,
1900   Ke de arraim froit ymage cler,
Ke bien attent quant getté l'ad,
Alsi cum humme parlerad.

Tutes les planetes ke numees sunt,
1904   En cinc cenz anz lur curs parfunt,
E trente douz anz tuit ensement,

1875 j.] iors *CD*   1876 ses e.] son cors *CD*   1877 ses c.] son tor *C*, sun curs *G*   1878 son primer ior *C*   1880 a. la nuit *y*   1881 sur t. *Ry*   1882 r. sunt *y*   1884 lung este *Ry*   1885 r.] fait *RD*, nus f. *C*; son cors *y*   1890 Le z. *Ry*; trescort *y*; .xij. a. *RC*   1892 de pheton *y*   1896 turne *Ry*   1898 E en *CG*; tut *not in CD*, par *G*   1901 a.] ateint *y*   1904 c. font *RCD*

E puis chescun sun curs reprent.
    Le zodiac est *signifer*,   [Cap. LXXIX]
1908   Ke de duze signes est cler;
    Ço est ausi cum un cumpas,
    U cercle rund ke chef n'ad pas;
    En duze parz est divisé,
1912   En sa laur est mesuré.
    Ices rundesces dunt dit ai,   *203 c*
    Ke jo cercles enceis numai,   [Cap. LXXX]
    Od les planetes funt lur curs,
1916   E lur errees e lur turs.
    Tutes par lur muvement
    Funt tel ducur e tel content,
    E tant suef armonie,
1920   Ke nul ne set la melodie.
    N'est voiz de oisel ne voiz humeine,
    Ke ne soit ver ceste veine,
    Kar quant li mund encuntre eus tent,
1924   Ke turne tant ignelement,
    E il cuntre li lur curs funt
    Od tant de force cum il unt,
    Par lur ignel encuntrement
1928   Gettent tant duz frestelement
    Ke tut l'envirun rebundist
    De la melodie ke en ist;
    Mais tut soit grant la melodie,
1932   Ne parvent pas a nostre oie;
    E ço est ultre le eir amunt,
    Ki espeise nostre oir rumpt;
    E nus ne oum ren nule en voir
1936   Fors ço ke sunc par cest eir.
    De la terre, ke bas se estent,   *203 d*

1909 un *not in* CD   1911 p.] parties RD   1916 e.] trespas C, cercles DG
1917 lor esmouement *y*   1923 contre DGC   1925 il entor li *y*   1930 m.] dolcor
RC   1932 Napartent pas C   1933 Kar ceo *y*   1934 Que R*y*; oir] oie e *y*
1935 nulle rien RD, rien C; en] por *y*

Jeske la sus al firmament,
Ceste musike est mesuree,
1940   Dunt la nostre [est] cuntruvee;
Kar si en terre *gamma* soit,   [Cap. LXXXI]
Et .a. en la lune resoit,
E en Mercurie soit le .b.,
1944   E Venus tenge en soi le .c.,
E el solail resoit le .d.,
E Mars de l'.e. soit bien paé,
E en Jove resoit .f. mis,
1948   E Saturne eit le .g. en pris,
La mesure ert tut manifeste
De la nostre gamme e la celeste.
De la terre jeske al firmament,
1952   Set tuns tru[v]um veirement;
Un tun cumence de la terre,
Ke deske a la lune se aserre;
De la lune jeske a Mercur,
1956   Est demi tun aseur;
De Mercur treske a Venus,
Est demi tun e nen[t] plus;
D'iloc deske al solail pur voir,
1960   Trois demi tuns sunt de poeir;
Del solail treske a dan Mars,
Est un tun plener nent eschars;
Des iloc desque a Jovis,   *204 a*
1964   Est demi tun de mult grant pris;
De Jovis desque a Saturne,
Un demi tun sun curs aturne;
Des iloc desque a signifer,

1940 est R*CDG*

1939 Celeste m. *y*   1942 en la lune .a. R   1943 mercure *CG*   1944 v. retienge le *y*   1947 soit R*y*   1948 E en S. le .g. seit p. *CD*   1949 Dunc ert la m. m. *y* 1950 De n. *y*   1953 tun *not in CD*   1954 Ke *not in* RD ; a *not in CD*   1956 a.] tot a. *y*   1957 E de *y*   1959 deske *not in y*   1961 E del *y*   1962 pl.] plein R, *not in y*   1963 De R, E de *G*, D' *CG*   1965 E de *y*   1966 returne *CG*, turne *D* 1967 De R, E de *y*

1968   Trois demi tuns resunt cler:
         Joignez ices ensemblement,
         Set tuns i avrez veirement.
         Le tun ad en ces elemenz
1972   Quinze mile liues e sis cenz
         E vint e cinc, n'i faut de ren;
         Saver poeez, haut sune e bien.
         Demi ton set mil ad en li
1976   E uit cenz e duze e demi;
         Dunt philosophes escristrent,
         E nof muses en escrit mistrent,
         Kar nof consonances sunt
1980   De la terre al cel amunt,
         Les quels en humme sunt manant,
         Ke est naturelment vivant.
         Si cum li mund est destincté   [Cap. LXXXII]
1984   Par set tens ke sunt ja numé,
         E la nostre musike ausi
         Par se[t] est mult bel departi,
         Si est cors de humme ensemble joinz
1988   Par set maneres en tuz poinz;
         Le cors cuplent quatre elemenz,   *204 b*
         E treis forces l'alme dedenz.
         Ces set ausi cum par musike,
1992   Chescun a altre se joint e fiche;
         Tant cum il sunt a un acord,
         Mar dutera nul humme la mort.
         Dunt humme est microcosme dit,
1996   Sulunc les Grius e lur escrit;
         Microco[s]mus ço est mendre mund,

1972 sis *CDGR* (sexcenta)] cinc *P*   1973 f. *CDGR*] fail *P*   1976 duze *GDCR*
(duodecim)] quinze *P*

1968 r.] sonent *y*   1969 ces R*y*   1970 Seet i trouerez *y*; t. ia verretz R   1973
de *not in CD*   1975 en sei *CD*   1977 les p. *y*   1982 Ki sunt *y*   1984 les .vij.
y; ia *not in y*   1986 set] ceo R, .vij. uoiz *y*; est m. bel *not in C*, est ben *DG*; parti R*D*
1989 conprent R, emplent *y*   1993 E t. cum s. *y*   1994 Ia mar d. h. *C*   1996 e] en
RC   1997 M. est li m. m. *y*

F

Dunt cist nun tres bien nus sumund
Ke li mund n'ad ren par feture,
2000 Ke humme n'ad en soi par figure;
Dunt sa jointure est alsi riche
Cum est la celeste musike.
Entre la terre e la lune amunt   [Cap. LXXXIII]
2004 Quinze mile liues bones sunt
Ove sis cenz e vint e cinc,
Si ke n'i falt ne point ne pinc.
De la lune desque Mercurius
2008 Set mile liues ad de curs
E uit cenz e duze e demi;
D'iloc a Venus autresi.
D'iloc al solail liwes genz,
2012 Vint e trois mil e quatre cenz
E trente e sis liwes altresi;
Kis mesura ren n'i faili.
D'iloc a Mars sunt par arpenz   *204 c*
2016 Quinz mile liwes e sis cenz
E puis vint e cinc sanz falture;
Kis mesura mult i mist cure.
D'iloc a Jovem de assens
2020 Set mile liwes e uit cenz
E duze liwes en avant.
D'iloc a Saturne altretant,
E de Saturne al firmament
2024 Vint e trois mil e quatre cent
E trente e sis liwes de acrés;
Kis mesura ne fu pas malvés.
Assumez ço tut en un fil,
2028 Si averez cent e trente mil

2027 fil *CD*] vil *P*   2028 e *CD*] en *P*

1998 tres *not in y*   2000 ad] eit *y*   2002 Cum la *y*   2006 ne f. *RD*   2013
xxxvij. l. et demy a. *R*   2014 ne f. *Ry*   2019 de] est de *y*   2021 l.] l. et demy
R   2023 De *RD*   2025 .xxxvij. l. et demy de *R*   2027 *lacuna begins in R*; tut]
tu ce *C*, tuz ceus *D*

E trois cent e seisante e cinc
Des liwes muntant en [eslink.
Mult estot estre pure e cler   *C, 138 d, l. 19*
2032 L'alme que deit tant haut munter.
Garde soi que carké ne soit
De fol tresor ne de mesfeit.
Plus n'i pot li riche entrer le ciel
2036 Ke en l'agoille pot li camel;
E li pecchanz est si pesant
Ke il ne pot estre montant.
Ki cels dous riens porterat,
2040 [Ensemble] od lui tut arderat.
La voie est tant ardant e pure
Que n'i passe nule pureture.
Par repentir e par amender,
2044 Ki la va, se face leger.
Par petit fes perist e falt
Ki porte e volt monter en haut.
Por ceo doit li riche doner,
2048 Kar il ne porra rens porter;
S'il ne done, a sei le tout,
E cel od tut qu'il aver volt.
Bon donor ne mort en poverte,
2052 Kar del ciel ad la porte overte.   *C, 139 a*
Li avers coilt e tuit en perte,
Kar en enfer est sa deserte;
Kar ki ne pot en le ciel monter,
2056 Si [l]'estot en enfer plunger.

2029 cinc *CD* (quinque)] cent *P*   2030 eslink *C*] *lacuna begins in P*   2031–2144
text based on C   2040 Ensemble *D*   2056 l' *G*] lui *D*

2031–2054 *all variants from D*   2031 M. couent e. pruz e leger   2032 Ke si halt
ueot m.   2034 De auarice ne de autre leid   2035 r. munter al c.   2037 li
pecheur   2038 e. ben m.   2039 Ki de ci ren od sei p.   2041 Le chemin est si &
pur en sei ardant   2042 Ke nul ne p. por. portant   2043 Mes pur r. e sei a.
2044 Ne put il fere tut l.   2046 porter ueolt e m. h.   2049 sei meimes le   2051
ne murra ia en   2055 pust al c. *G*   2056 En e. lui estut p. *D*

La ard le feu que fin n'ad mie
Ki ci enprist la lecherie,
E orgoil e sorquiderie,
2060　E hayne e coveitie,
E avarice e dure envie,
E mensoinges e glotonie.
N'est pecché grant ne petit
2064　Ke la, sache, paine ne quit.
La est le verme de conscience,
[Ke tutdis mort e puint e tence;
Tutdis point par remembrance,
2068　E mort par fole repentance],
Ke totdis tence od soi meime,
Kar d'enfer ad deservi l'abime.
De ces dous l'escripture dist:
2072　' Lur feu n'estaint, verm ne desist.'
Nostre feu n'est fors une ymage
Vers l'enfernal que ard a rage;
Nostre fraid est cum chaud esté
2076　Vers cel ou pecchurs sunt pené,
Ki de un en altre sunt plungé,
Solun la formé del pecché.
L'escrit dist: ' Pecheur fet sun tur
2080　Del feu ardant en grant freidur.'
[Le feu al freit est ajusté,
Si n'est nul par autre atempré];
Le feu ard sanz doner luur,
2084　Dunt tutdis i ad tenebrur.
De debles i ad tel hidur,
Tel brai, tel cri e tel haur,

2066–8 *text from* D, *not in* C　　2079 P. D] pecche CG　　2081–2 DG] *not in* C
2059 E *not in* G　　2061 Dure a. e e. G　　2062 E *not in* G　　2063 p. si g. ne si
p. D　　2064 Ke en enfern ne art e q. D　　2066 t. point e m. e blesce G　　2069
Ke *not in* DG　　2070 qe deserui de e. lab. G; ad serui D　　2072 ne defist DG
2080 De G　　2084 t. sunt en t. G　　2085 E de D, Des G　　2086 h.] hydur D,
horrur G

Ke tonaire semble duz chant
2088   Vers lur noise orrible e grant.
Il reprochent as pechours
Lur mesfez e lour fols amors.
Le deble nuli mesfeit ne ublie,
2092   Kar il entice e al fet guie.
Cest reprover est tant fort
Ke iloec melz volsist estre mort,
Kar cil del ciel e enfernals
2096   Touz tresveient les criminals;   C, 139 b
Les mals en acreis de lur mal,
Les bons a ben quant ne sunt tal.
Trestut serrat iloques apert,
2100   Kantque confesse n'averad covert
Par coragus repentement,
E par parfit amendement.
Unke ne fu ne ja n'ert home,
2104   Ke des paines deist la summe,
K'en enfer averont li suduiant,
Li endurci, li mescreant.
Ki si creire ne me voldra,
2108   Certes al suffrir me creira.
Proverbe dist que trop est tart
La main retraire quant ele art;
E a la fin est parhoniz
2112   Ki ainz ne vot estre garniz.
Melz vaut un bon conseil avant,
Ke aprés le colp ne funt dis tant.
Fols est qui en nul se asseure,

2087 Ke DG] Kar C   2091 n.] de nuli C, nulli D, nul G   2094 Ke D] Ki C, *not in* G   2103 ja n'ert DG] la uist C   2104 deit la s. D, nissist une C, peut penser la s. G, *see note*

2090 Lur peche e DG   2091 Le] Ke D, *not in* G; m. ne u.] mesprent oblie G   2092 il lentice al fet e g. D   2093 Cel G, E el D; tant est G, t. par est D   2094 Pecheur m. vost G   2095 de ciel G   2096 Tuz pechez verrunt c. G   2099 s.] est D; ert la en arest G   2100 Ke par confusiun nad descouert D   2111 E *not in* DG   2115 ke a ren se D

2116   Chescun cumparra sa faulture;
Celui perist a mult grant dreit
Ki tut se met en autri fait.
Home dist bien, a la cort le rai
2120   Chescun respundera por sai.
Jhesu li juges est a dreit,
Li rois qui tut set e veit;
Il jugera totes homes nez
2124   Solun lor fes e voluntez.
Seint Jake dist: 'A Deu est mort
Ki sun veisin het a son tort.'
E nul [ne] deit autre hom hair,
2128   Ne mal voler en son desir.
Plusurs por male volenté,
Sanz plus fere, sunt dampné;
Ki ses avols ben ne refraint,
2132   Vers Deu de malfait est ataint.
Home ne juge fors le fet,
Fort est juger que l'em ne veit;
Mes ki veit trestut secrez   *C, 139 c*
2136   Juge solun les volentez.
Dunc al pecheor esta mult fort,
Ki suratent desques a la mort;
Ses mals vendront susprisement,
2140   Si l'estreindront tant durement
K'il ne purrat nul el penser,
Ne de ses pecchés remembrer;
E li malfez pur desturber
2144   Se peinent de l'enfantomer]

2120 r. *D*] respunderai *C*, respoyne *G*   2127 ne *DG*   2144 de *DG*] pur de *C*
2117 a bon d. *G*   2119 b.] ke *G*   2121 I. est iuges *DG*   2122 e tut v. *G*
2125 A] ke a *G*, en *D*   2126 a t. *DG*   2127 Nul ne d. a. hair *DG*   2130 serunt
d. *G*   2131 sa uolente ne destreint *D*, ses volers ne restreint *G*   2134 est a iuger
kom *DG*   2135 ki] cil ke *DG*; v.] set *D*; tuz *G*   2137 al] as *D*, a *G*; e.] ert *D*; e. f. *G*
2139 s.] sudainement *G*, si priuement *D*   2141 p. rien p. *G*   2144 p.] espleitent
DG

Par sunges, par avisiuns, P, 205 d
E par altres illusiuns,
Ke il ne put a el entendre,
2148 Ne cunfessiun parfeit rendre.
E dunc se mustrent enemis,
Ke einz se feintrent bons amis;
Tant li a[c]umblent ses mesfez,
2152 Tant les funt horribles e leiez
Ke il le mettent en desespeir,
Ke il n'ert salvé par nul poeir;
Se il en tel point a sa fin va,
2156 Ja mes d'enfer ne eschapera.
Pur ço fet bien ke en santé
Geist sun mal e sun peché,
E dunc se peine de amender,
2160 Quant il ad poeir de pecher.
Ke a la mort prent cunfessiun,
Pecché li lest e il li nun;
Li fols, si il vivre plus quidast,
2164 De ses pechez point ne lessat;
Pur ço serrat en grant destreit
Quant bien ne volt quant il poeit.
E se il eit passé tut sun tens,
2168 Purrad il dunc en tant de tens
Remembrer bien en sun purpens
Tuz ses mesfez, tuz ses offens,
Ke il ad fet tant lungement 206 a
2172 En dit, en fet, en talent?
Certes meint hume par ubliance
Sa alme met en grant grevance,
Dunt l'escrit dit ke pas n'est mu:

2145 PR *resume, text based on* P   2151 a. CG] acombrent R
2145 s. e par *y*   2150 f.] feignaint C; se mustrerunt a. G   2152 E t. C; Que
t. sunt h. RG   2155 cel p. CD   2158 Regeist CD, Lest G   2164 De *not in* RD
2166 b.] ben fere D; v.] fist C, fait R, v. fere G   2167 ad p. trestut C; a trestuz ses
sens DG   2170 m. e ses CD   2172 fet e en *y*

2176 'Ke ne cunoist n'er[t] pas cunu.'
  Deu ne cunoist nul pur salver,
  Ke ne cunoist sun amender.
  Ore soit ke il bien se cunoisse,
2180 Purra il dunc en tel anguisse
  En un moment tut regeir?
  U se il le dit, tut espenir,
  Quantke ad einz fet [en] sa vie fole
2184 En fet, en penser, en parole?
  Pur Deu amendum nostre vie!
  Certes malfé nul mal ne ublie;
  Nes tut le mendre penser
2188 Remembre il pur l'alme grever.
   Si nul est ki se quide tel
  Ke il seit digne munter al cel,
  Purvoie soi de quor parfund,
2192 Kar malfez sunt el eir amunt,
  Ke rien ne funt fors espier
  Les almes, ke il voient munter.
  Si ren i truvent de mesfet,
2196 Tantost la mettent en destroit,
  E tenent en lur cumpaignie,   *206 b*
  Desque ele eit trestut espenie,
  Quantque cunfesse [e] repentir
2200 Par bienfet ne volt ci cuverir.
  Lasse! dolente creature
  Ke Deu tant eime, tant honure
  Ke nus furme a sa figure,
2204 E met sur tute creature!
  Tant par ad dever nus le quor tendre

2183 en *RCDG* 2194 ke] le *P*, que *CDG* 2199 c. e *G*] e *not in PR*, par confes e par *C*

2176 ne conut *RDG* 2183 einz *not in RDG* 2184 p. e en *y* 2186 c. li m. *CD*; ne *not in RC* 2190 Ke d. soit m. *C* 2202 et t. h. *Ry* 2203 Kil *CG*; furma *G*, fist *D* 2204 met] mette *C*, nus mist *G*, eyme *D* 2205 par *not in Ry;* d.] vers *Ry*

Ke hume devint e se suffri vendre;
Flaelé fu e en croiz mis
2208 Pur parreindre nus cheitifs;
Puis releva de mort a vie
Pur acerter nostre folie,
K'en altre vie parvendrum,
2212 U ja puis murrir ne purrum;
Veant les suns en cel munta,
E par iço bien nus mustra,
Ke si nus sulunc li vivum,
2216 Par sa grace a li munterum.
Cheitifs dolenz! ke la frum,
Ke sa furme tut defurmum,
Ke sa vente ne li rendum,
2220 E sun achat par mal tolum,
Ke despisum sa rançun,
E de sa mort plet ne tenum,
Ke de altre vie ne pensum,   *206 c*
2224 Ne de sun cel cure n'avum!
Cheitif, dolenz, maleurez!
Ou sunt noz senz e noz pensez!
Pur quoi sumes si estuné
2228 Ver li ke tut nus ad duné!
Il ne nus demande ren
For mal lesser·e fere bien,
E ke nus li rendum s'ymage,
2232 Pur ki il out mortel damage;
D'argent n'ad cure, ne de or,
L'alme eime plus ke nul tresor;
Pur ço vult il ke nus vivum,
2236 Ke l'alme rendre a li pussum,
E a sun cel par li venir,

2206 Ke hom se fist e *y*   2209 a] en *RDG*   2211 K'] Kar *CG*   2213 en] el
G, al *D,* le *R*   2220 mal lui t. *RC*   2223 del a. *CD*   2229 nous ne *RC*; ren] nule
r. *DG*   2230 f. le bien *RC*   2236 a *not in RC*

E sa grant feste paremplir,
Ke nus seum si purs, si clers,
2240   Delivres de tuz encumbrers,
Ke pussum bien a l'habitacle
Del cel venir sanz nul obstacle.
    Mais quant del cel tuché avum,   [Cap. LXXXIV]
2244   Droit est ke alkes en dium.
Le ciel est fuin par nature,
Sutil e rund en sa feiture;
Si est a terre ke set bas
2248   Cum a sun point si est cumpas;
Quant al cumpas le point poi valt,   *206 d*
Si fet la terre al cel en halt;
Quant la terre al cel est nient,
2252   Kar cel trestut le mund cumprent;
Le point el cumpas set enmi,
E terre est centre al cel alsi.
Il est tres bien cel apelé,
2256   Kar a tuz pecheurs est celé;
Purquant en latin *celature*,
E en nostre franceis peinture,
Kar des esteiles est depeint,
2260   Ki lumere ja n'ert esteint.
Il est rund veraiment,
Kar en chambre trestut s'estent;
Tant par turne ignelement
2264   Ke nul fors Deu le veit ne entent.
Dous portes ad, si escrit ne ment,
L'une orient, l'altre occident;
A l'orient solail se leve,
2268   A l'occident la nut le greve.
    Quatre parties le cel ad,   [Cap. LXXXV]

2240 E d. *y*   2242 De R*y*   2245 f.] fin *CD*   2248 si est] fet (*not in G*) le *y*
2251 al c. la t. *y*   2252 le ciel *CD*   2253 el] al *C*, en *G*   2257 Por quai en *C*
2258 Est en *RD*, En *C*; n. *not in RD*; p.] est p. *C*, dist p. *D*   2265 p. y ad *RD*;
lescrit *y*   2267 o. le s. *y*

Le Griu *climaz* les apellad:
L'un ad nun oriental,
2272   L'altre est dist solsticial,
La terce ad ñun occidental,
La quarte est apellé brumal.
Ces cunctrés sunt espuns   *207 a*
2276   En cel grezeis par altres nuns: [Cap. LXXXVI]
Anathole dist orient,
E *Disis* redist occident,
Aracon est septemtriun,
2280   *Messimbria* le su ad nun.
De ces quatre fu tresfurmé
Le nun Adam, e aurné;
La premere lettre pernez
2284   De chescun, e puis ensemblez,
Si bien espeudre le savez,
Le nun Adam i troverez.
Cest nun, ke del mund est estret,
2288   Mustre ke il pur home est fet,
E iço nun tres bien espunt
Ke home est droit le mendre mund.
Septemtriun iço nun a
2292   De .vii. esteiles que sunt la;
Trion, ke buf en griu ad nun,
Ot set, nume septemtriun.
Le suverain cel est firmament,   [Cap. LXXXVII]
2296   Kar entre eus mult fort s'estent;
I[l] reest tut rund en sa feture,
E si reest ewus par nature;
Il reest des ewes composté,
2300   Cum glace u cum cristal fermé.
Dous poles el firmament sunt,   *207 b*

2298 ews *C*, ewous *G*, en wus *D*, ewes *P*, ewe *R*

2276 cel *not in CD*   2279 Archon *C*, Archos *D*   2284 assembletz *Ry*   2291
S. de ceo non *y*   2297 r.] est *Ry*   2298 r. *not in C;* est *DG*   2299 Il est *y*   2300
f.] conferme *R*, formee *y*

Ke de polir numé sunt,   [Cap. LXXXVIII]
Kar il polisent si le ciel
2304   Ke il turne par eus tut uel.
En ces le cel turne sun vol,
Cum la ro fet en l'asol.

Le cel est trestut esteilé,   [Cap. LXXXIX]
2308   Me[s] pas ne veum la moité,
Kar del solail la grant luur,
Nus defent ver lur mireur;
Alsi fet la neire nue,
2312   Ke de[l] solail tot la vue.
Si li cel ruvist al serain,
Bel tens demustre a l'endemain;
E si al matin ruvist,
2316   Le jur sonz tempeste ne finist.

Tutes esteiles rundes sunt,   [Cap. XC]
E le nature de feu unt;
Mais sul Deu set lur pousté,
2320   Lur curs, lur nuns, lur qualité,
Lur signes, lur liu[s], lur tens;
Poi en set checun humein sens.
Li sages quis espigucerent,
2324   E tant cum l'um set, controverent,
Lur nun[s] de bestes lur donerent,
E de homes ke jadis erent,
Ke l'em puse le meus saver   207 c
2328   Lur lius, lur curs, lur poer.

Enz e[n] miliu del firmament   [Cap. XCI]
Sunt duze signes veroiement,

2305 vol RCDG] uoil P   2312 del RCDG; la RCDG] sa P   2321 lius CDGR
2322 set CDR] cest P, saueyr G; h. CDGR] hume P   2323 quis G] les P, qui les C,
qui R; e. CGR] espierent P, see note   2324 c. CR] cuntinerent P, trouerent G   2325
nons CGR

2302 n.] si n. C   2304 tut ouel Ry   2311 fet] cum f. DG, en f. R   2314 al
demain C, al matin D   2321 e lur t. DG   2322 checun not in y   2324 com bon
soit R, cum liun se C, homme set G   2326 des Ry   2327 Ke hom C; p. le] poeyt
puys G   2328 e lor p. y   2329 Eynz RG

Ke i sunt en travers tresposez,
2332 E uelement bien destinctez.
Iceste dispositiun
Le *sodiac* en griu numum;
Ço est *signifer* en latin,
2336 Kar les signes porte sanz fin.
Les signes de bestes unt nuns,
E nus *sodiun* bestes numuns;
Par fables furent cuntruvé
2340 Les nuns ke sunt a cls doné;
Mes jo voil les fables lesser,
Kar eles ne funt fors encumbrer;
E del nun ke je troverai,
2344 La signefiance vus dirai.
La premere signe Mutun est, [Cap. XCII]
Ke plusur esteilles revest;
E par ce est signefié,
2348 Si cum le mutun tut l'esté
Se cuche sur sun costé destre,
E tut l'iver sur sun senestre,
Si fet li solail quant la vient,
2352 E suz le Mutun sun curs tient
Del cel ver la destre partie, *207 d*
E sun curs a sa chalur guie.
Le secunde signe est Tor numé, [Cap. XCIII]
2356 E par tant est signifié
Ke quant li solail cel signe use,
Ses chauz alsi cum corns aguse,
E si refet le terre arable:
2360 Meus vaut cest cens ke fole fable.
Le terce signe Gimels ad nun, [Cap. XCIV]

2346 r. *RD*] renest *PC*   2349 Se *RCDG*] Si *P*

2331 i *not in Ry*   2337 des *RD*   2348 Ke si *CR*; Ke checum m. *G*   2349 destre
c. *RG*   2352 suz] sur *RC*, for *D*   2353 De *RCD*   2354 E *not in y*; a] et *Ry*
2357 Ke] Kar *C, not in DG*

Si ad significaciun,
Ke les jurs en lui plus luns sunt
2364   Ke es altre mes [que de]vant vunt.
         Le .iiii. signe Cancre ad nun   [Cap. XCV]
         Par tele significaciun:
         Si cum crabe vet a reburs,
2368   Si turne en li le solail sun curs.
         Le .v. signe a nun Liun   [Cap. XCVI]
         Par itele significatiun:
         Le leuns est en sa feture
2372   Par devant de chaude nature,
         E si est freide en sun derere;
         Li solail i est en tele manere
         En icel signe quant il [e]n ist,
2376   Primes enchaufe, pus ten[v]ist.
         Le sime signe Virgo ad nun   [Cap. XCVII]
         Par itele significatiun:
         La virgine ne consoit mie   208 a
2380   Ne terre adunc ne fructifie.
         Le .vii. est Libre veirement   [Cap. XCVIII]
         Par itele signefiement:
         Si cum la peisse uel balance,
2384   Ne l'un ne retret ne l'altre avance,
         Si sunt nuit e jur parigal,
         Kar il est equinoxial.
         Le .viii. [signe] est Scorpiun,   [Cap. XCIX]
2388   Beste mult puinant e felun,
         E signefie en sun tens
         Sunt grisil, pluies e turmens.
         Le .ix. signe est Capricorne,   [Cap. CI]

2364 que devant CGR] deuant D   2375 icel CG] itel P, cel RD; en RC] sen DG
2376 t. RC] tenist PG   2385 s. RCDG] cum P   2387 s. RCDG

2362 ad tele s. DG   2364 es] en RG, les CD; v.] unt D   2366 cele R, icele DG
2374 i est] reest R, est y   2375 il not in RC   2380 la t. y   2384 un r. RCD
2386 est] est donc CD, donqe est RG   2388 Sest C, Ceste D   2389 en] qe en
RC, ke a D, bien G

2392   Pur le solail ke dunt est borne,
        Kar dunc comence a monte[r],
        Si cum chevre [solt] mu[n]z haunte[r].
            Le .x. signe est Sagitrarie,   [Cap. C]
2396   Par pluie e grisil e gel fere.
            Le .xi. ad nun Aquarius,   [Cap. CII]
        Pur ce ke il est trestut pluius;
        Les nues sunt dunc desliés,
2400   Dunt les ewes sunt plus versés.
            Le .xii. signe est Pessuns,   [Cap. CIII]
        Feveres fet, ewes e glasçuns.
            Set esteilles autres resunt,   [Cap. CIV]
2404   Ke grant pluies e ewes funt;
        Pur ço sunt apellé Hiades,   208 b
        Kar en lur tens plut il adés.
            Ce ke il dient hii en gregés
2408   Nus apellum pluie en franceis.
            Pliades esteiles resunt,   [Cap. CV]
        Ke de pluralité lur nun unt;
        Kar ço ke est pliron en grezeis,
2412   Est plusurs en nostre franceis.
            Altres esteiles sunt plusurs,
        Dunt l'em set les lius e les curs,
        E les nuns e lur poustés,
2416   Mais jo m'en terrai de grez,
        Cel començail est fol e gref,
        Ke ne pout trere a nul bon chef;
        N'est merveille si a ennui turt
2420   Chose dunt sens ne pru surt,

2394 s. CGR] soleit D   2399 n. RCDG] nuns P   2405 H. CR] aidas P, pliatas
D, Iuades G   2419 a RC] est P, en D; t. RD] curt P, crut C

2392 d.] dunqe RCG, not in D; nest b. RG   2397 ad] signe ad RG   2400 plus]
plues R, pluies D, par lues C   2403 r.] sunt y   2406 il not in y   2407 il not in
RG; hii] hy Ry   2410 p.] plusurs D   2411 Ke tant dist plurin en g. D   2412
Tant cum p. en f. D   2414 l' not in y; lur c. RD   2415 lur] les CG   2418 a bon
RG   2420 pru ne curt D

E quel pru est oir la ren
Ke l'em ne put entendre bien!
Ke bien out sanz bien aprendre,
2424 Od le asne seit a l'arpe entendre.
Ke vaut de oir de astronomie
Ke l'astrologe nen ad mie!
Bel dire sanz tuz biens mustrer
2428 Fet le musard plus musarder;
Dunt li sages sun fiz chastie:
'Gardez ke vus ne prenge mie
De espigucer lé Dez secrez, 208 c
2432 Ne ke soit le cels esteillez.'
Suvent celi ke vult tut saver,
Tut pert quant voit sun nunpoer.
De chose ke pert tut a nue
2436 Put l'um dire resun sue?
Lessum a Deu sé privestez,
Tant [cum] il nus deigne mustre[r] assez.
　Galaras est une zone, [Cap. CXXXVI]
2440 Ke tant est cler, blanche e bone,
E tut parmi le cel s'en vad,
E il tel non de dux leit ad;
Leit est blanc e *galac* est leit,
2444 Dunt tele zone tel nun tret.
Les esteiles sa clarté funt,
Kar ele a checun respunt.
　En ceste zone par fiees [Cap. CXXXVII]
2448 Ver le nort perent cometes lees,
Unes esteilles mul[t] gremues,

2431 e. RC] cunter P, pincer D　2432 e. CDR] est celes P　2436 Put] Pur P,
Peut R, Pot C　2438 cum] *see note*　2447 C. RCDG] cestes P　2448 c. l. CDG]
cummectees P, cometeles R

2422 l' *not in y*; e.] atendre R, aprendre D　2424 s.] set RC; a. deit harpe aprendre D
2430 p.] pernez R, penez C, mesprenez D　2433 tot uolt y　2435 a veue RC
2439 Galaxas C　2441 tut] treis RD, dreit D　2442 Et cel R, E icel C, Icel D,
Itel G　2444 ceste z. R, cel z. y　2449 g.] cremues DGR, tenues C

E de mult flambans raiz kernues;
Change de regne signefient,
2452 U pestilence u guerre dient,
U granz vens u granz floz de mer:
Garniz est k'en set penser.
Set jurs perent, uitante al plus;
2456 De nus garnir est Deus gelus.
Amont iço grant firmament   *208 d*
E tut sun avironement,   [Cap. CXXXVIII]
Sunt unes ewes suspendues,
2460 Alci cum niule est en ces nues,
Ke le cel cloent tut envirun,
Si unt le cel ewin a nun.
Seur li est cel espirital,   [Cap. CXXXIX]
2464 Ke n'est coneu de home mortal;   o
Li angle sunt la enz maina[n]t,
Ke a tutdis unt joie grant;
La resunt les almes as seinz,
2468 Ke [a Deu] servir ne furent feinz.
Icel cel fu primes criez,
E ove la terre purtreitez.
Outre cesti, bien loinz de la,   [Cap. CXL]
2472 Est un grant cel ke fin nen a;
Il est numé cel des cels,
U maint li rai des angles, Deus.
La maint li rai trestut pussant,
2476 Liu nel tent, si est tut tenant,
[Tut feit, tut veit, tut governe,
Et liu ne tient ne liu ne cerne;
Il est par tut mes puissalment,

2450 k. *CDGR* (crinitae)] kerunes *P*   2455 u. al p.] *see note*   2460 nues *CGR*]
niules *P*, nwies *D*   2462 unt *RCG* (unde)] sunt *P*; Icel cel e. ad nun *D*   2468 a
Deu *GR*] deu *C*, en deu *D*   2477-80 *not in P, text from C*   2478 liu] *see note*

2450 E *not in RC*; raiz *not in y*   2460 est *not in y*   2461 clorent *C*   2466 B
begins   2467 r.] sunt *RD*   2468 s.] seruise *D*   2469 Icest *CBR*   2473 le
ciel *RCDB*; de cels *y*   2474 *Latin text ends*   2477 et tut g. *R*   2478 t. et l. *DB*
2479 mes *not in RDG*

G

2480 E nul liu nel tient nel comprent];
Par [tut] est tut e liu nel tient,
Rien nel tent e il tut maintent;
Dunt l'escripture [de lui dist,
2484 K'il escrit] par seinte espirit:
Il est plus haut ke le cel amunt,
E ke abisme plus parfunt;
Plus est lung ke la mer s'e[s]tent,   *209 a*
2488 E plus est lé ke terre ne tent,
Kar i[l] put tut, tut voit, tut o[t],
E tut le mund en sun poin clost;
Tut est el mund e tut est dehors,
2492 Mais ne[l] cumprent ne liu ne cors;
El mund est tut e tut ensus,
E tut a lez e tut dejus;
Il est desus tut pusant,
2496 Il est desuz [tut] sustenant,
Il est dedens pur tut tenir,
Il est dehors pur tut garnir;
Par les costés trestut cuntent,
2500 E par l'environ trestut maintent;
Mes i[l] n'e[st] pas confus deors,
Ne c[u]mpris enz en mundain cors,
Ne gre[vé] par sun sustenirs,
2504 Ne esquis par sun haut empirs,
Ne enhaucé par l'amunter,
Ne abessié par l'avaler.
Il n'ert ja plus haut ne plus bas,

2481 tut *RCDGB*   2483–4 *see note*   2487 s'estent *RCDGB*] se tent *P*   2489
tut ot *CDGBR*] o tut *preceding* tut uoit *P*   2492 nel *RCB*] ne *PG*, ne li *D*   2495
d. *RCDGB*] deus *P*   2496 d. *CDGBR*] deus *P*; tut *RCG*] trestut *DB*   2501 c.
CDGB] cum feu *P*, compris *R*   2502 enz *CB*] einz *PR*, *not in DG*   2503 grevé
RCDGB   2504 em.] *see note*

2480 nul liu] nuli *DG*, lui *R*; nul ne lui t. *G*   2484 par le s. *RCG*   2486 a.]
lab. *GB*   2491 e *not in DGB*   2494 a] de *CG*, as *B*   2495 d. trestut y   2500
t.] tut y   2505 l'a.] le m. *RC*, sun m. *DG*

2508 Kar il est tutdis en un cas;
Sanz labur est a governer,
E sanz travail a tut ovrer;
Tut fet, tut tent, tut aurne,

2512 E[n] peis est quant tut vait e turne;   *209 b*
Quanque fu e est e serat,
Tut a fet e tut defrat;
Quanque est ver lui ne est plus pussant

2516 Ke une gutette en raim pendant.
Que quide dunc li faucener!
Quei en ert quant il se vult venger!
Cum ert, quidez, l'alme anguisuse

2520 Ke tute creature encuse!
Kar tute ren l'encusera,
Ke al pecher einceis l'eida.
L'escrit dit ke tut le mund tendra

2524 O Deu, e ci cumbatera
Cuntre les pecheurs e les fous,
Ke le guerpirent pur lur avels.
La terre tute l'encusera,

2528 Ke la vitaile li trova;
E lé rechesses tut ensement,
Ke il despendi folement;
La mer, les ewes altresi

2532 L'e[n]cuserunt tut a un cri,
K'i[l] enbut [si s'en lava],
E pur plus pecher se ascema;
E l'eir par unt il espira,

2536 E le feu ke li treschaufa,

2510 al tut *RCB*] aut *P*, est *DG*   2516 r. *CDGB*] teim *PR*   2521 e. *CDBR*.
encurcera *P*, anuira *G*   2523 L'e.] *see note*   2533 si s'en l.] *see note*   2534 pe.
CDGBR] pechez *P*   2536 li *CGBR*] les *P*

2509 est al g. *RCB*, est gouernor *DG*   2510 tr. est oueror *DG*   2516 goute *RDG*
2517 Quai *RD*; quident *RCDGB*   2518 Ken ert *CDB*   2522 al] a *RCDG*   2523
ke *not in RCGB*   2524 e ci] si *R*, e se *C*, e *D*, si s'enc. *G*   2526 Ki deu g. *CD*   2527
tute] fort *y*   2530 d. si f. *CB*   2536 rechauffa *y*

E le solail ke l'aluma,
E la nout ke le mal cela,
Trestute dirrunt la vie fole,   *209 c*
2540   Kar tute ren a Deu parole.
Le cheitif pecheor ke fra
Quant tut le mund l'encusera?
Quant le mund [li] mut bataile,
2544   Ke fra dunc une ventaile?
Certes nent est home en verité,
Kar a nient tret par sun peché;
Nient est pur voir ke par folie
2548   Pert Deu e la durable vie;
Nient est a tutdis sonz resort,
Ke desert pardurable mort;
Nient est kar sur tute rien
2552   Tuz mauz averat ne ja nul bien.
Tute rien est pur home fet,
Ke il en face en Deu sun esplet.
Quant il ad tut sun estover,
2556   E ren est areré pur voir,
E idunc de celi retret,
Ke sanz deserte tut li fet,
Et sert [de] quer sun enemi
2560   O le tresor k'il ad de li,
N'est bien droit ke i[l] seit aneinti,
Robbé, perdu e tut peri?
Sertes si est il vereiment
2564   Si par tens ne se repent,
E la perte trestute rent   *209 d*
A li ke li dona bonement.

2543 li *RCDGB*   2559 de *RCB*   2560 k'il *BCGR*] ki il *P*   2561 N'est b. d. *RCB*] Ne croit *P*, Nest d. *G*

2539 la] sa *CDB*   2545 Certes *not in RG*   2547 ke] quant *RG*   2548 la pard. *CG*   2550 p.] la p. *CG*, la dur. *RB*   2552 ne] et *RGB*   2556 arere] a dire *RG*, dire *B*   2557 E i.] Et il donc *BR*, Cil d. *G*; de c. sa tret *R*, de li se treit *GB*   2564 Sil *CBR*   2566 li d.] le d. *RGB*

Ore seit ke tut leel rendu a,
2568   Soi memes coment rendra?
Home n'e[st] pas sa creature,
Mes Deu ymage e Deu feture.
Quant [Deu] ymage ad defurmé,
2572   E fet ymage al maluré,
Coment pora tut cest defere
E sei a sun fetur retrere?
Si li feturs tel [le] resceit,
2576   A maluré tort e force feit;
E Deu ne veut nule torture,
[Mes] justice, pes e dreiture.
Coment sera dunc raent
2580   Ke s'i ad vendu folement?
La rançun est fort e[n] voir,
  Mal[f]é vut tut le sen avoir,
Li faiters vut tut les sun prendre,
2584   Certes fort est tut a tuz rendre;
Chescun voudra aver le sen,
Ci[l] le pecheor, Deu le bon,
Kar tel l'estut a Deu venir
2588   Cum il le fit a sun pleisir;
E la seinte escripture dit:
'Les Deu overaines sunt parfit,
E Deu vit quantke il avoit fet,   *210 a*
2592   E tute rien tres bon estait.'
E le pecheur, s'il se retrait
Del malfé par alcun aguait,
Cument ja mes surdre pura
2596   Al grant bien ke Deu li duna?
Cument serra grant feu esteint!

2571 Deu *CGBR*   2574 r. *RCB*] recrere *P*   2575 le *CDBR*   2578 Mes
RCGB   2579 r. *CGR*] creant *P*, rent *B*   2581 en *RGB*] por *C*   2582
Malfé *RCGB*   2583 f. *RCG*] freres *P*, fautres *B*

2567 ke] qil *RB*; tut lui r. *RC*, tretut r. *G*   2572 lym. *CGB*   2573 p. il tut *CBR*
2576 Al malfe *Ry*   2580 si] se *C*, sei *G*, si li *B*   2582 Li m. *CR*, Car m. *G*   2583
les] le *Ry*

Poet fort pecheur estre bon seint!
Oil certes, se il se refraint,
2600   E sun cors de tuz maus restraint,
E sun quor a tuz biens enpaint,
E [ses] maus parfitement plaint,
E hunte par confession vaint,
2604   E en tuz biens estable maint.
    Deus est tant pius, tant dreiturer
Ke il le pecheur vult justifier,
Quant vult a merci repairer,
2608   E ses maus gehir e lesser,
E par tuz bienfez eslaver,
Par uveraines e par geuner,
Par afflictiuns, par esveiller,
2612   Par almones e par plurer.
E ne fet tort a l'adverser,
Quil trei par sun losenger,
Kar il le criat tut premer,
2616   E deigna en croiz achater;
En erres mist sun sanc tant clier.   *210 b*
Ki primes poeit rien enerrer,
Par asise le doit porter.
2620   Tut ce ne fit pas l'averser,
Einz trahit tuz par enticer;
Par bien promettre sanz rien doner,
Perdre deit quant[ke] il pout gainer:
2624   Tresun doit en soi repairer.
    Pur ce fet bien li pecheur,
Quant let sé mals e sa folur;
E reveint a sun creatur,
2628   Ke le sufre e atent checun jur,

2599 r. *CB*] restraint *P*, restraint *RG*   2602 ses *CB*] des *R*   2622 Par *RCGB*] Kar *P*   2623 quanqe *RCB*   2624 r. *RCB*] reperirer *P*, reperier *G*

2602 p. se pl. *R*   2606 iustiser *RCB*   2609 e.] resl. *C*, eux l. *R*, eshaucer *B*   2610 u.] oreisons *y*   2611 a. et par veiller *RCG*   2618 poeit] poit *RB*; pr. prist en arrer *G*   2619 le] lem *CB*   2622 Par bel p. *RG*; s.] e *CG*   2623 p. en doit *CB*

E rapele par grant doucur,
E puis receit par tel amur
Ke tut pardone sa haur,
2632 E defe[n]t ver le traitur,
E de cel li promet le sujur;
Mes k'il suffre ci un pou d'e[s]tur,
En repentonce, en doul, en plur,
2636 Pur eslaver sa grant pour,
E sei getter de la tristur,
Ke out apresté sun faus seinur.
E Deu! cum cil grant joie averunt,
2640 Quant il ad cel la sus serunt,
Ke si bien se repenterunt,
E par confesse se ellaverunt,
E par benfés se amenderunt,   *210 c*
2644 Establement se tendrunt,
E pus en maus ne recharrunt!
Les chais Deu het e confunt,
E les estables tent amunt,
2648 E tret de [cest] cecle parfunt,
E met la u ses angles sunt;
E ja mes pus mal ne sentirunt,
Mes en joie tutdis meinderunt,
2652 E ad duz chant respunderunt,
Ke li angle lur chanterunt;
Ke de salu mult lé serrunt,
Plus ke ne dirrait humme el mund,
2656 Kar tant plus lur ajoirunt
Cum de plus fort eschapé serrunt;

2632 t. CGBR] creatur P   2633 le s. CBR] li seinur P, le luur G   2634 k'il
CGBR] ki il P; d'estur CBR] de tur P   2636 e. sa RCGB] si auer si P   2638 Ke
CGBR] Ki P   2639 aueront CGBR, auera e amur P   2645 en mals ne recharront
CBR, tuz m. enchacerunt P, de m. se retrerunt G   2648 cest CB] ceo R

2630 puis] pus le CGB   2633 del CB   2634 ci s. CB   2635 d. et en RB
2640 ad] al R, el CB, v G   2642 se lauerent CB   2644 Et e. RCB   2650 E not
in y   2652 ad] al y   2656 lur] lui R, lees GB   2657 sunt Ry

E il meimes Deu plus loerunt
Ke enprés granz mals granz joies unt,
2660   E ke nul mal mes ne sumunt.
       Deu! cum cele alme ert ajoie,
E honuree et mult cherie,
Ke ci fu bien espenie,
2664   E de tuz pechez furbie!
Kar la averat la manauntie,
Dunt ja ne finerat la vie
En cele duce melodie,
2668   Ke li seint angle fort escrie,
Od sa tres chere cumpaignie,   210 d
Ke tant est bele e esclarie,
Ke nis penser ne put l'um mie.
2672   Dex! tant mar fet ke s'en ublie
Pur glorie ke tost est finie!
Ço est ceste tant feble vie,
Ki joie est de tuz mals emplie.
2676   Et ki de amer ad cuvaitie,
Dame u pucele eschevie,
La est la bele cumpainie,
Ke suit la mer Crist, Marie,
2680   De tutes buntez aducie,
De tutes beutez bien flurie;
La mains vaillante ke la se guie,
Valt plus ke terre d'or emplie.
2684   La purrez choisir bele amie,
Quele ke vodrez sanz envie;
Ja de altre ne avrez gelusie,
Kar tutes sunt cum une amie,
2688   E lur amur tuz mals defie,

2675 Ki CBR] Ke PG   2679 suit CR] fut P, sunt de G, fu B

2660 ne] nes R, les C   2663 tresbien CB   2664 de trestuz C; p. bien f. GB
2669 Od la t. GB   2670 esclarcie y   2671 nis] vis RCG, nul B; l' *not in* y   2672
fet] fu y   2674 tant *not in* CG   2677 escherie B, cherie C   2679 C.] ihesu CR
2685 La q. CG

Ke sa amur en teles enplie,
Bor nasquit, ja n'ert fenie.
E lur voiz par est tant serie,
2692   E tant duce lur melodie,
Ne dirrait humme ke seit en vie.
La est pucelage cherie,
Ke ci se tint sanz cuveitie, *211 a*
2696   Humblement, sanz surquiderie,
Plus bele e plus cliere en sa baillie
Ke n'est solail en sa maistrie;
E si chantent par tele baldie
2700   Ke altres lur chant ne dient mie;
Kar alme ki char n'est blemie,
Mult pres costeie al fiz Marie.
Deu! tant bor fut ci espenie
2704   Ke vient a tele cumpaignie!
Iloc reest espousaile asise,
Ke ci ne fu de mal esprise,
Ne ne mesprist e[n] nule guise
2708   Cuntre lai de seinte eglise,
Einz se tint en redde justice;
E se li fut unc de rien mesprise,
Sei memes juga par devise,
2712   E si en trait peine [e] juise,
Dunt tutdis est en joie mise;
Kar ele l'ad par droit conquise,
Quant ele en soi ad sa char ocise,
2716   E volenters de ses desporz demise.
Cil ke pur Deu ses avels debrise,
E nule vers li ne aime ne prise,

2701 ki *CR*] ki de *PG*, si *B*   2703 bor *RCB*] bon *P*, bien *G*   2712 e *RCGB*

2690 n. kar ia *CB*   2691 t. par est *Ry*   2693 Nel *G*; h. de ceste vie *GB*   2695
tient *Ry*   2697 b. e p. c. en] c. est *R*, bel e c. est en *C*, est b. *G*, b. est et c. *B*   2698
s.] li s. *CR*   2702 mult *not in y*; c.] se c. *B*, sacostaie *C*, se costez *G*   2704 cele *Ry*
2705 r.] est *RCG*   2708 C. la lei *RCB*   2709 tient *Ry*   2710 li] ele *y*   2711
iugera *CG*   2712 t.] prist *RCB*, fist *G*; t. e p. *CB*   2714 ele ad *RGB*   2715
Kant en *y*   2718 n. rien uers *y*

Sa glorie averat kar par drait l'ad conquise.

2720   Iloc resunt cil ke ja pecheor furent,   *211 b*
E lur pechez en repentant cunurent,
E la charge sulun le fet reçurent,
E en umble repentance se turent,
2724   E pus unc de bienfet ne se murent,
Ne de lur char pener unc ne recrurent,
E en oraisuns e en afflictiuns jurent,
Povres vestirent, herbergerent e purent,
2728   Herbe e gros pain mangerent, ewe burent,
Tut pardunerent quanke de mal reçure[n]t,
Parfitement la lai retindrent e crurent,
Dunt en glere sanz entrelais demurent.

2732   Iloc resunt les martirs honurez,
Ke tant furent pur Deu amur penez;
Ore sunt de glerie tuz vestuz e fefez,
Kar les paines suffrirent de grez,
2736   E de suffrir furent joius e lez,
Dunt ore sunt [de] Deu plus honurez
Cum plus furent detrait e defulez.
Plus unt joie quant al cel sunt levez,
2740   Quant d'enfer sunt par tant eschapez,
Kar ore sunt en itel liu posez,
De lur plaies tant docement armez,
De lur sanc curunez e helmez.

2744   Si feitement de tuz biens adobez,   *211 c*
Ne dutent mes tyranz ne malfez,
Kar il sunt tuz en enfer trebuchez.
Ke plus fit mal plus serra penez,
2748   Ke plus suffri pur Deu plus serra proisez.
Pur Deu! seignurs, vus ke terre tenez,

2737 de *RCGB*

2720 cil *not in* R*y*; ki p. *CG*   2725 ne retrurent *RB*   2726 E *not in* R*y*; e en] et R, en *G*; a. uirent *RCB*   2728 m. e ewe *CB*   2730 lei tiendrent *RGB*   2736 del s. *y*   2741 icel *C*, cel *R*; p.] luez *CB*   2743 lur cler s. *y*   2748 serra] iert *CB*, est *G*

E par suffrance Deu hummes [avez],
Estreitement de vus memes pensez,
2752 Ke as forz tyranz parigals ne seez,
Quant as altres lur aver ravisez,
E lur quor de ire, de dolur nafrez,
E par suffrance plusurs partuez,
2756 Ke lur martyre ne vus soit aloez,
Dunt en peine a tutdis mes seez.
Il sunt a vus en garde cumandez,
A vus e a els il sul est avuez,
2760 Bor le verrez si ben les governez;
N'estes pasturs mes lus quant les devorez,
Li ultre sire en ert graviz e irrez,
Par la ravine en enfer boillerez;
2764 E cil ke sunt par vus martirizez,
E apovriz e a grant mendivetez,
Quant par suffrance en Deu unt endurez,
De parfit glere serrunt tutdis chasez.
2768 Par les tiranz tut ço veer poez,   *211 d*
Ke as martyrs tuz mals firent de grez,
Dunt il sunt ja a tutdis dampnez,
E li martyr joiusement sauvez.
2772 Li povre Deu altresi martyrisez,
Quant terriens biens a sorfet avez,
Et poi ou nient a els pur Deu dunez,
Ne lur suffraite, quant poez, ne amendez.
2776 De tant serrez par devant Deu rettez,
Quant pestre, vestir, herberger ne volez,
E nel fetes de bones volentez,
Mes les choses ke Deu vus ad baillez,

2750 avez *RCGB.*

2750 s. de deu *CB*; h. sus vus a. *y*   2754 de d. e de ire *GB*; ire e de *C*   2755 s.]
suffaite *C,* surfeyte *D*   2757 peines *CB*   2759 a *not in Ry*; il] deu *CGR*   2761 les
mangez *y*   2762 g. e i.] grantment i. *RC,* granus e i. *B,* tres coraucez *G*   2765
e *not in Ry*   2772 a.] alsi *y,* ensi *R*   2775 ne *not in CB*   2777 Com *CB*; ne v.]
les poez *C,* poez *GB*; p .ne vestir ne les herbergez *R*

2780   Dunt il vus ad despensers ordenez,
    Ke a ses amis largement en donez,
    Estraitement u poi lur en paez,
    E as lechors les larges duns dunez,
2784   As povres poi, nient as ordenez,
    Ke de terres ne sunt pur ço fefez;
    Ke li riches lur doit doner asez,
    Dunt seint Pol dit as tuz cristienez:
2788   'De voz provoz—ces sunt prestres—enpensez
    Ke sunt pur vus penuz e esveillez
    Cum pur rendre resun pur voz pechez.'
    E Deu memes redit a ses privez:
2792   'Les ovrers sunt dignes ke gardez.'
    Mes ses cumandemenz ledement passez,   *212 a*
    Quant vus cloez voz mains as ordenez,
    E en poverte vilement aler lessez,
2796   De freit, de feim, de saif ledement turmentez.
    Sul cel refui ke ver Deu avez—
    Ço sunt povres, malades, ordenez—
    Cels despisez e lessez deshonurez,
2800   As lecheresces e as lechors donez,
    Pur accrestre les voz e lur pechez,
    Kar al peché sunt il tut turnez,
    Dunt estes fols, cheitif e asorbez.
2804   A un lechur pur folie donez
    Dunt vint povres sustenir pussez,
    E les fiz [Deu] lessez tut esgarrez,
    Par ki aie al cel munter deivez;
2808   La haute [es]chiele de vertu depescez,
    E l'enfernal chescun jor esforcez.

2781 d. *RCB*] donisez *P*, doygnez *G*   2806 Deu *CGBR*   2808 eschele *RCGB*
2782 en partez *CB*   2784 poy ou neint *Ry*   2787 crestiens *RC*   2788 pensez *y*
2789 penuz] peniz *CB*, pensis *G*   2790 pur] de *RCB*   2793 l. trespasez *y*   2796
l.] les *CB*, lesset *G*, *not in R*   2797 que vus vers *y*   2798 m. e o. *RC*   2799 e *not
in GB*   2805 s.] pestre v (et *B*) uestir *CB*, p. *G*   2807 deuez *RGB*, poez *C*

Pur Deu! seignurs, eez de vus pitez!
Voz murs, vos vies, voz duns adrescez,
2812　E pur mesfet Deu nel cel ne perdez;
Lessez orgoil si amez umbletez,
Ja surquidez de Deu n'ert privez,
Ne ramponuz ne gloiz ne malatechez;
2816　Ja lecherie el cel [ne] mettra piez;　　　　　*212 b*
Pernez la veie, le chemin, les degrez,
Ke al ciel meine, ou tutdis a plentez
De tutes joies, de honurs e de buntez.
2820　[De quantque vus en vos quers penserez,　*C, 143d, l. 9*
Uncore i ad del bien Deu plus ass[e]z;
Car unc oil ne vit n'en quer est montez,
Nen porra oir nes home nez,
2824　Les granz honurs que Deu ad aprestez
A ceu ke ci parfont sa volentez.
Trop sunt chaitifs ke pur fauses beautez,
Ou pur deliz ke tost sunt ci outreez,
2828　Perdent les joies, honurs e poustez,
Qe saunz terme ja ne serrunt finez,
Ou li seinz sunt plus lusant ass[e]z
Q'est li solail en ses greignur clartez;
2832　Ou plus ad bien en un an comblez
K'en cest mund cent mil anz anombrez.
Veez ke valent ces terres, ces regnez,
Ces burcs, ces viles, chasteals e citez,
2836　Ces noble dras, ces granz richetez,
E touz les biens ke vus ci tant prisez;
Tuz sunt umbre e tantost passez,
Tut deceivent par falses vanitez,

2816 ne *RBG*　　2819 h. *CB*] murs *PR; PR end*　　2820–2920 *text from C*

2810 de vous ayez *KB*　　2812 Ke pur *y*; ne son cel *CB*; ne *not in RC*　　2814 nen
ert *CB*　　2820 pensez *B*　　2821 de biens deu *B*,　　2823 Ne nc p. neis oir h. *B*
2825 ke si fount bien sez u. *B*　　2829 sanz termine *B*　　2830 reluisantz *B*　　2831
Ke li s. quant en este est esclarcez *B*　　2832 acomblez *B*　　2833 nombrez *B*
2835 b.] bures *B*; v. ces ch. cez c. *B*　　2838 e breuement p. *G*, tot sount t. p. *B*

2840 S'il ne seient pur l'amur de Deu donez.
E cil qui les donent par pure volentez,
Od Deu serrunt en son ciel coronez,
E od ses seinz cheriz e honurez
2844 Pur les honurs ke ci li firent de gre.
Cil qui sunt tenaunz e afolez,
Chinches, avers, orgoillous e sorquidez,
El puz d'enfer serrunt trebuchez,
2848 U tu[t]dis serrunt sanz fin dampnez;
Ci furent riches e de aver amassez,
La serrunt povres e de touz mals chargez;
Povres d'avoir e de peines chascez,
2852 Kar as povres ne firent largetez;   *C, 144 a*
Povres de amis, riches de malfez,
Kar il vers povres nul tindrent amistez.
Ne por eus n'ert nul ami escutez
2856 Del sage Deu que set tut lur foletez;
Ne deivent estre par amis rechatez,
Ne par aumoines ne par bons faiz salvez,
Ki sei meimes ublierent de grez;
2860 Dont l'escrit dit: 'Tant fetes cum poez
De quer, de bouche, de mains, de pez,
Kar en enfer n'est nul benfet presez;'
E si redist: 'Deu n'ert de mort loez,
2864 Ne cil del lai n'erent ja merciez.'
Les mors sunt cil qui morent en pechez,
E pur ceo sunt el lai d'enfer ruez.
Por nent serra Deus pur itels priez,
2868 Kar ja d'iloc ne istront a salvetez.
Ki son bien het, tant ert de Dé amez,
Mes li priant de Deu avera les grez

2869 Qui *B*] Kil *C*

2840 pur deu amor d. *B*   2841 par bone v. *B*   2843 h. et ch. *B*   2844 kil f. *B*
2846 o.] greynard *G*, graignus *B*   2847 s. tut t. *B*   2853 a. et r. *B*   2854 vers
nul ne t. *B*   2856 tot set *B*   2858 par f. *B*   2861 q. et de m. de b. et de p. *B*
2864 nert *B*   2869 h. com ert *B*   2870 p. aiunt de deu les *B*

Por ses benfaiz, por ses grant pitez;
2872 Dont David dist qui tant fu espirez:
'Mon [piu] urer en mon sein ert luez.'
Ceo est a dire, a li ert acuntez
Le grant benfait qu'il feit de volentez;
2876 Tut ne fet il autre, parfitement salvez.
Mes cil qui vot ben estre escutez,
Por sei le face tant cum ad poestez,
De quer parfit e de bone volentez;
2880 Dont le prendra Deu memes a grez,
Si lui serra al ciel a cent dublez.
E s'il se est en poi tresubliez,
Por ceo n'ert pas longement travaillez,
2884 Kar par amis ert tanttost deliverez,
Par oreisons e par bienfez alegez;
Si ert en bens que ja n'erent finez,
Od Jhesu Crist e od ses seinz feſſez.
2888 Ai! Deus de glorie! Com ert li bien dublez
Kant cors e alme se serrunt assemblez!
Kant ceste char que vus morir veez,
Cest cors cheitif de vermin percez,   C, 144 b
2892 Ke ci nasqui e vesqui en pechez,
Par un petit que serad espenez,
De quer parfit, de bone volentez,
Puis serra de sa alme restorez,
2896 Al grant juise a destre Deu posez,
Od lès beneiz joint e coronez,
Ou les pecheurs que ci furent haitez,
E ne vodreient ci espener lur pechez,
2900 Od les malfez serrunt tutdis dampnez!
E il serra en ciel halt menez,

2873 piu B   2874 est B] ert C
2872 D. saynt D. qui B   2876 Tut en sait a. B   2877 estre bien B; aseurez GB
2879 p. en b. B   2882 il est B   2884 .] tost B   2885 o. par B   2886 en] es B
2889 se not in GB   2895 P. resera B   2896 a] al BG   2897 j. e c.] choisez et c.
B, clers escor. G   2899 voudrent B; ci not in GB   2901 el c. hautement m. B

Od les angeles, princes e poestés,
De tant plus lez, plus joius, plus haitez,
2904 Ke de touz mals est tant bien eschapez,
E en touz bienz pur poi de paine entrez,
U ja mes puis n'ert dolent ne irrez,
Ne de nul mal enblemiz ne tuchez;
2908 Ainz se lusera com soleil en estez,
E plus assez que ja n'ert reconsez;
Ne de sa joie n'ert ja mes fastengez,
Kar ben celestre com vus plus en averez
2912 Plus le vodriez e plus le desirez,
Ne cel desir nen ert ja mes finez,
Kar mal n'en ist mes tut biens adurez.
Jhesu nos doint par sa seinte pitez,
2916 Si espenir nos mals e nos pechez
Ke ensemble od lui seon en ses regnez,
U li beneiz serront sanz [fin feffez;
E cil l'ottreye qui est saunz] nul degrez
2920 Treis en persones e un en majestez.]

AMEN

2904 Ke BG] Kar C   2916 e. GB] espenit C   2918-9 fin . . . saunz GB, see note
2908 A. reluira B   2909 p. dasez GB; r.] escunsez BG   2911 vus not in GB
2912 voudrez B   2913 Ne] E GB; mes definez GB   2914 t. b.] totdis bien B
2919 V cil B

APPENDIX

THE following Prologue of 40 lines occurs in MS *D*, and replaces ll. 1–166 of the present edition.

Ky vout saver del mapemund,   *128 c*
La forme de trestut le mund,
De terres e de regiuns,

4   E de citez les propre nuns,
         Ki les fist e edefia,
         E primes nuns lur dona,
         E des ewes ke portent navie,

8   Jeo en dirraie grant partie
         Si cum jeo ai en escrit truvé,
         Dunt jeo ai asez auctorité.
         Seint Luck li evangeliste dit

12   En le ewangeile k'il escrit,
         Ke Augustus Cesar l'empereer,
         En ki tens fud né li Sauver,
         Commanda par sun commandement

16   A tuz le mund communement
         Ke tut lui feisent a saver,
         E les escriz a lui enveer
         De teres e de regiuns,

20   E des hiles les propre nuns,
         E la manere de la gent,
         E des bestes ensement;
         E ke ren ne lui duissent celer

24   Que digne fut a remembrer;
         E quel servise chescun deveit
         A Rome ke lur chef esteit.
         Ceo fit il par le conseil

28   De un sage ke fud feel,
         Ke Cyrinus aveit a nun,

Esveske de Syre, sages hom.
Rome fud chef de tut le mund   *128 d*
32   Si cum le livre nus respund;
En tutes teres est ben seu,
A Rome rendirent treu.
Quant cest ban fud criez,
36   E par escriz partut enveez,
Tut issi e en teu manere
Cum out commandé l'emperere,
Par teres e par regiuns
40   A Rome aurent lur respuns.

CRITICAL NOTES

THE following spurious lines occur in MSS *CDG*. Preceding each are given the number of the line of text which it follows and the siglum of the MS in which it is found.

422 *C:* Austral le quint ad a non
        Ore ad chescun sun propre nun
449 *D:* Sachez de fi si deu me uaille (also in *V*)
450 *D:* Dunt nus en sumes plus baud
776 *C:* Ke dampnedeu li tramist (replaces 776)
876 *C:* Sachez grant biens en li tient (replaces 876)
1058 *D:* La fontene aon est clame (by later hand in space left by scribe; replaces 1058)
1116 *D:* Vnkes cel pais ne atucha
1178 *C:* Nul ne set auant la uoie (replaces 1178; cf. l. 1014)
1670 *D:* E quanke vit sur le firmement
1946 *D:* Sachez le pur ucrite
2069 *G:* Kar de peines ne veit termes
        De feu de puur sulferine
2172 *G:* Saunz le veir deu comandemenz
2224 *G:* Fore manger e beiuere a grant foisoun
2350 *G:* Solum nature ceo dist ly Mestre
2378 *G:* Ke nule femine en ceste vie
2379 *G:* E cel signe signefie
2381 *G:* Qen francoys est balaunce nome
2382 *G:* Ke li solail en owel setent
2572 *G:* E sey vendu par pecche (also in *B*)
        Ceo est ymage al maufee (also in *B*)
2637 *G:* E del feu saunz luur
2645 *G:* Puis au ciel mounte serrunt
2659 *G:* Issi deseruir pount
        La ioie de ciel lamount

The following lines are wanting in MSS *CDG:* MS *C*—174, 215–6, 264, 266, 669–70, 775, 823, 875, 951–2, 969–70, 1019–20, 1145–6, 1178, 1428–9, 1472, 1474, 1624–5, 1629–30, 2066–8, 2081–2, 2409–12, 2437–8, 2555–8, 2693, 2816; MS *D*—174, 215–6, 438–9, 505–8, 661–2, 669–70, 697–8, 705–10, 715–8, 741–4, 813–4, 874, 902, 913–4, 929–32, 969–70, 982–3, 1005–6, 1019–20, 1058, 1063–4,

1067–8, 1117–8, 1125–6, 1139–42, 1145–6, 1175–6, 1271–2, 1277, 1300, 1333–4, 1349–52, 1354–8, 1360–2, 1428–9, 1471–6, 1507–12, 1515–24, 1549–58, 1567–8, 1605–20, 1629–30, 1655–6, 1717–8, 1745–6, 1778, 1796, 1798, 1827–8, 1878, 1899–1902, 1991–2, 2095–8, 2101–2, 2117–8, 2149–54, 2168, 2177–8, 2187–2200, 2211–2, 2219, 2221, 2249–50, 2323–8, 2373, 2418, 2425–6, 2435–6, 2493–4, 2499–2500; MS G—215–6, 383–4, 473–6, 669–70, 725–8, 735–8, 751–2, 755–8, 791–2, 797–8, 803–6, 869–72, 950–3, 995–6, 1005–6, 1019–20, 1061–4, 1117–8, 1201–10, 1213–8, 1221–4, 1227–8, 1231–2, 1235–42, 1247–8, 1259–60, 1265–72, 1275–8, 1283–4, 1293–6, 1299–1308, 1311 –6, 1325–30, 1333–4, 1341–4, 1353–60, 1428–9, 1513–8, 1611–62, 1783–4, 1809–10, 1845–50, 1931–6, 2003–54, 2063–4, 2067–8, 2097–8, 2115–6, 2171, 2177–8, 2187–92, 2219, 2249–50, 2257–60, 2346, 2367–70, 2409–12, 2419–38, 2443–6, 2601–2, 2635, 2646–9, 2657–8, 2660, 2668, 2676–7, 2687, 2695–6, 2706, 2722, 2724–5, 2743–4, 2746–7, 2765, 2800–3, 2817–25, 2829–33, 2839–44, 2853–64, 2867–76, 2882–7, 2910, 2914.

4. 'Provided that I be suffered to discuss the good.' *Ki* (var. *ke*) is frequently used with conditional force, cf. ll. 152, 1900, 1901, 2676, and is normally followed by a singular verb. *Suffrir* may mean 'to permit' in OF, but the infinitive construction as found in this line is unusual in French. For *atendre* in the sense of 'direct attention to' or 'be attentive to' cf. l. 1901.

7–8. Cf. the discussion of the prologue in the Introduction, p. lvi.

10. **serpent venimuse.** *Serpent* is found as a feminine in early OF, but it is regularly masculine in the thirteenth century and *serpente* feminine. Another example of *serpent* feminine occurs in *Perlesvaus* 9784 (ed. Nitze and Jenkins). See also the *Image du Monde* (ed. Prior), p. 103, l. 3, and note. Elsewhere in the poem the word is apparently masculine, cf. *tuz serpens* 1350.

31. Cf. note to ll. 7–8.

40. **retraire.** Since the line has nine syllables the original form may have been *traire*, inasmuch as dropping of prefixes was frequent in Anglo-Norman, cf. Suchier *Vie de Seint Auban* p. 34, and Waters' *Brendan* 1789 note. Cf. also in our text *prendre* for *aprendre* 58 R and 140 R, *serre* 320 with *C*'s var. *aserre*, *tempree* for *atempree* 435, *numee* for *renumee* 834, *tenvist* for *atenvist* 2376, etc.

48. **motere.** An unattested adjective related to OF *muete* (<VL *movita*) which in Norman and Anglo-Norman has the form *mote*, cf. H. Moisy *Glossaire comparatif anglo-normand* (Caen 1895) p. 664; and Wace's *Rou* 9684 and 9689 (ed. Andresen). This form is found in the text l. 254, but is there based directly on the Latin *motu*. *Motere*

is formed on the radical *mot* by addition of the suffix *-aria* (cf. the noun *meuterie* cited by Godefroy); its meaning is 'subversive.'

55. 'Few there are in whom God inspires wisdom,' i.e. acquisition of knowledge depends on individual toil and mutual interchange of ideas. The idea is repeated in line 156; it may have been proverbial.

58. **ta.** *P*'s reading is either *sa* or *ca*. It seems preferable to accept *ta* from R, as confusion of *vus* (cf. *finez* in l. 57) and *tu* is frequent in Anglo-Norman, cf. Menger *Anglo-Norman Dialect* p. 115.

65–6. I have not identified the source of this quotation.

67. **marchandie.** Cf. Prov. 3, 14, 'Melior est acquisitio eius negotione argenti et auri,' which is rendered in English 'For the merchandise of it (wisdom) is better than the merchandise of silver, etc.' *Marchandie* may therefore be rendered 'acquisition.'

68. **curtaisie.** See also l. 73. The author considers cultivated manners and learning to be complementary accomplishments, which fact indicates that he was familiar with courtly society. Although certainly a churchman, he probably was not a monk.

69–71. Cf. Matt. 7, 14.

69. **la entree.** *P*'s reading *ladentree* suggests the possibility that the intrusive *d* served to indicate hiatus. Possibly the form *ad* (<*habet*), which usually retained in spelling its silent *d*, influenced the scribe's orthography in this case.

70. **L'aprise.** The MS has *La prise* but *aprise* occurs in l. 52. Such division is not infrequent in the MSS, cf. *sa reste* 676, *la luma* 2537, *sa corde* 338 C, *sa costeie* 2072 C, *et al. La prise* stands perhaps for *La aprise*, cf. note to l. 762.

89. **treslable.** The word *lable* occurs in the *Evangiles des domées* (ed. Aitken) 12201 and p. 100, and in *The Dialogues of Gregory the Great* (ed. T. Clotan) p. 12. Godefroy lists *labile* only.

95. **Scilbon.** The reference is to Stilpon, the philosopher of antiquity, who may have been known to the author from Seneca's ninth Epistle.

98. These words are attributed to Bias of Priene, one of the seven wise men of Greece; see *Nouvelle Bibliographie Littéraire* V, 930.

105–10. Solomon's choice is related in 1 Kings 3, 5–15.

111–12. The wise man, by choosing wisdom like Solomon, will also acquire wealth, for which the avaricious strive.

115. **jofne.** Cf. also *malvé* for *malfé* 1336, *briefiment* 1787 and possibly also *solivag* (<*solifugum*) 1337. *V* and *f* interchange frequently in Anglo-Norman; see the examples collected by Stimming, *Boeve de Haumtone* p. 220.

121. **mendive.** Cf. the rhyme with *vive*. Apparently a verb formed

from the adjective *mendif*, cf. also the noun *mendivetez* 'beggary', l. 2765. Neither word is listed by Godefroy. *Mendif* occurs frequently in Anglo-Norman texts, cf. *Le Lai d'Haveloc* (ed. Bell, Manchester 1925) 547; and Chardri's *Set Dormanz* 456. The meaning of our line seems to be 'He who is poor in (is mendicant of) all knowledge.'

130. Another form of this proverb is given in ll. 2111–2.

151–2. 'He who has the will and the power to do so, if he takes from everybody and is thereby the richer, deceives himself.' Understand 'whereas' before l. 153. The author wishes to contrast the pursuit of material wealth with the pursuit of knowledge.

153. **out.** *Out* and *ot* are interchangeable orthographies in *P* for the ind. pr. 3 of *oïr*, cf. ll. 155, 2423, and 2489.

153. **escute.** Prosthetic *e* apparently has no syllabic value after a fully pronounced vowel. Other examples from the text are ll. 758, 1934, 2265 and probably 116. On this point see Suchier *op. cit.* p. 31.

156. Cf. note to l. 55.

156. *Espire* is for *inspire*. The MSS of our text offer numerous examples of interchange or substitution of prefix, e.g. *entendre* 4 R, *asol* 2306, *ajoirunt* 2656, etc. Cf. also the list of examples collected by Stimming *op. cit.* p. xliv.

162. **pie.** The magpie was the symbol of vanity, conceit and boasting, cf. Neckham *De naturis rerum* II, Cap. CLXXXIX.

164. **Prie. . . . deigne.** Atonic *e* in hiatus after the tonic vowel tends to lose its syllabic value, cf. Suchier *op. cit.* p. 34. Other probable cases in the text are *geometrie* 378 and *crue* 562. It is possible of course that *prie* is scribal for *pri*, ind. pr. 1. *Deigne* may be scribal for *deint* the etymological form from *dignet*.

167. The passage beginning here and running to l. 252 serves to introduce the translation from the *Imago mundi*. MSS *CDVG* begin at this point, *D* after a unique prologue of 40 lines. In *C* at the top of the page is the rubric *Ici comence la petite philosophie. V* also has over the first line the rubric *Ci coṁce la petite philosophie.*

179. *il* has been added in *x* to replace the lost syllable *poinz*.

188. **Mustre.** Final atonic *e* appears to retain syllabic value before a vowel when it is preceded by a consonant combination consisting of mute plus liquid. Other cases are ll. 663, 1228, 1700, 2188 and perhaps 50.

189–90. 'By something he has created which waxes or wanes in its measure.'

194. The MSS all offer confused readings but it is clear that all four elements must be mentioned, cf. l. 319 below. This line occurs

in the *Vie de St. Georges* (ed. Matzke) 1403 as *Tere, ewe, fu e eir*.
205-6. Except for *afebleie* in C the orthography of the MSS points
to a rhyme in *-ie*. *Afebliee* is attested in l. 1508 by the rhyme with *bee*,
but the reduced form might stand here nevertheless; in any case it
could be the past participle of *afeblir* not *afebleier*. The context
indicates that *devie* is from *desveier* 'to lead astray' and not from
devier 'to kill.' The original rhyme may thus have been *afebleiee:
desveiee* which gives a regular octosyllabic line. An alternative would
be to read *afeblïë:devïë* without agreement.

212. **feu sur glace.** Doubtless a popular phrase to indicate
insecure or precarious position.

215-6. This couplet, found only in *x*, may be an addition, as l.
217 could follow directly after l. 214.

224. This line cannot be read as octosyllabic in its present form.
Del is a contraction of *de+le* for *de+la*, but it is probably scribal
and the articles may be intrusive, cf. *D'enfer* in l. 223. Secondly, it
appears that atonic *e* final after *l, m, n*, or *r* may lose syllabic value in
our text, cf. ll. 614, 663, 888, 1228, 1289, 1414, 1482, 2188 and 2234.
Cf. Suchier *op. cit.* p. 37. Finally *sol* may be read for *soleil*. MS *P*
offers the monosyllabic form in ll. 415, 443 and 1558, all of which
are octosyllabic whereas ll. 1379, 1832, and 2368 which offer the
disyllabic form contain nine syllables. It seems assured, therefore,
that the author used whichever form his line required. *Sol* occurs in
the MSS of Philippe de Thaün, see Mall *Li Cumpoz* p. 52.

229-30. MSS *DV* transpose these lines and offer the rhyme
brisile (brisele V):aubegele. The form *brisile* cannot be the word cited
by Godefroy and connected by him with *brasier*. Antoine Thomas
has suggested that the rhyme is *drisile[e]:aubegele[e]* and that *drisile[e]*
means 'drizzle,' (see Langlois *Connaissance du monde* p. 163, n. 2),
but this seems most doubtful.

245. 'He who composes it gives to the book the title,' etc. For
the sake of clarity I have in this case indicated by an apostrophe the
suppressed final *e* of *don* which is in all the other MSS. The author is
speaking of himself in the third person but changes to the first in
ll. 248 ff.

251. **Aturt.** Cf. the explanation of this emendation given in the
Introduction, p. xxi.

252. **frai certain.** This turn of phrase is probably modelled on
the Latin *certum facere*, consequently *certain* may be taken to mean
'well-informed.'

254. **en mote.** Cf. note to l. 48.

258. **ver.** Scribal for *veer* or *veeir* since the disyllabic form is

needed in every case to make octosyllabic lines, cf. ll. 60, 928, 1348 and 2768 (decasyllabic).

263. **escale.** Prosthetic *e* appears to be elided here after nasal consonant. Perhaps however *est* loses its vowel following a tonic vowel.

265–6. Line 265 is found in P after 246 and is followed by the line *Le pur eir envirune bel* written in a different hand. After 264, l. 265 is wanting and 266 reads *Le purs eir envirune bel*. In R after 246 is written *L'esthre com album fet muel,* after which is a space. After 264 R writes *Le pur ayr enviroune bel Si com le album le muel* (note the reversed order). The error resulted from the repetition of the couplet in question in the common ancestor of P and R.

266. **espés eir.** *Pur eir (purus aer)* is a synonym for ether (cf. l. 1791) and *espés eir (turbidus aer)* refers to the ordinary air. It is clear from the context that *espés eir* is required in this line.

267. **Muel.** This word is apparently disyllabic, cf. the rhyme with *bel* 265–6. Perhaps the author wrote *clost* rather than *enclost,* cf. ll. 380, 934, 2461 and 2490.

268. **purceint.** The scribe occasionally confuses *t* and *c*. He writes this word with *t* here and in ll. 492 and 540, whereas in ll. 380, 873 and 1624 he writes *c,* which latter I have generalised.

273. **ren nule.** This order is peculiar to MS P, all the others placing the adjective first. The same situation is found in ll. 1651 and 1935.

281. An example of a line in which it is necessary to replace the short demonstratives by the longer forms in order to get an octosyllabic line. MS C wrote *cesti* and *itel.* Such cases are frequent in our text and in nearly every case at least one MS gives the form required.

287–8. Eccles. 18, 1, 'Qui vivit in aeternum creavit omnia simul.' Migne cites the passage as 'Qui manet,' etc. but does not identify it.

293 ff. cf. Gen. 1.

295. **quarte.** Final atonic *e* after *t* began to lose syllabic value in the late twelfth century, cf. Suchier *op. cit.* p. 37. Other examples from the text are ll. 290, 1867 and 1905.

301–2. This couplet is apparently corrupt and the variant readings do not indicate clearly what emendations should be made. I have therefore printed unaltered the text of P with full variants. The Latin original is 'unumquodque de semine sui generis nascitur', which makes it plain that the meaning is 'There is nothing in the world which God does not reproduce according to its seed." Perhaps the original reading was *N'est chose sulunc sa semence Ke Deu el mund ne recomence.*

303. The original is cited by Migne without identification, 'Pater meus usque modo operatur.' cf. John 5, 17.

304. **Uncore.** Several examples of overflow lines occur in the text, cf. ll. 1310, 1492, 1494, 1800, and 1806.

308. **nuvelerie.** The second *e* is apparently to be elided in scansion. Similar cases of *e* losing its syllabic value in the body of polysyllabic words are found in ll. 1061 and 1103.

310. Rev. 21, 5, 'Ecce nova facio omnia.'

331. The Migne text (Cap. III) reads incorrectly 'acqua in terram' instead of 'acqua in aerem.'

336. The idea is that of four people standing in a circle each with an arm around his neighbour.

337-8. The rhyme is *descord:acord* R*G*. *Acord* is found in rhyme with *mort* 1993.

341. **muistie.** Apparently a pp. adj. from *muistir*, v. n. 'be moist,' cf. *moitir* cited by Godefroy.

343-4. The rhyme is *chaud:baud* R*DVG*.

347. The reading of *y*, *ces quatre cum plus*, is to be preferred to that of P*R*.

351. **milluiens.** This form is to be interpreted as *miliueins*, cf. the rhyme with *veins*, and also *miluein* 399 of which Godefroy cites a second Anglo-Norman example. The etymon is *medium + locum + anum*.

363. **surverreit.** Note the parallel use of a past subjunctive, *fust* in l. 362, and a conditional in the protasis of a conditional sentence. This equivalence existed in the apodosis (cf. the example cited by Foulet *Petite Syntaxe* p. 213), but it is exceptional in the protasis.

367-74. cf. Ps. 103, 5.

377. The variants of the line result from confusion between the two Latin forms of the computation, in leagues (12,052) and in stades (180,000). *Cent* has crept into the text of R*DV* from marginal glosses giving the quotation in stades (such a gloss actually existing in MS *D*). Finally *miler* (< *milliariu*) is a synonym for *liue*, which accounts for the variants of *DV*.

382. Ps. 103, 6.

384. **put amirer.** P reads *puramirer* (the scribe used the abbreviation for *ur*), R has *purra muer*, and *y* reads *poet amirer*. The corrector in P, noticing that the context required a verb in the present, wrote a *t* over the *a* and after the abbreviation for *ur*. The reading of *x* results from confusion of *r* and *t*.

388. **truverez.** The *e* following the stem in the future and conditional may not have syllabic value, cf. also ll. 2, 141, 142 and

2658, but this elision appears to be optional, cf. ll. 310, 2521, 2653 and 2820.

422. By reading *E* with *RCDG* and *ad a nun* with *C* the line becomes regular metrically. *Aveir nun* and *aveir a nun* are both frequent in our text.

425–60. Cf. the 'Introduction,' p. lxv. It is of interest to note that there are strong verbal resemblances between certain ll. in this passage and other passages in the text. Compare ll. 425–8 with ll. 1188–94, ll. 439–40 with ll. 2385–6, ll. 441–4 with ll. 1263–6 and ll. 458–60 with l. 1695. The only part of this passage which seems original is that on the zone called *brumal*, 445–52.

441. It is preferable to read *si* after *zone* with *y* and interpret *Ke* in l. 442 as 'that'. The atonic *e* of *zone*, following an *n*, may be dropped in scansion.

461. *ke*. The form was written by the scribes of both *P* and *R*, but the corrector of *P* rejected it and wrote *ou* above, which form is also found in *y*. A transitive use of *maneir* is not recorded and it is altogether probable that the author wrote *ou*, but it seems certain that *ke* in *P* was not a scribal error, else it would not occur also in *R*; consequently I have left it in the text.

464. **Mediterraine.** Cf. *Mediteraine* 784, but the form in rhyme is *Mediterin*, cf. ll. 523, 862 and 1027 and in the line 1016. Both forms probably belong to the author as other proper names in the text are dimorphic, cf. notes to ll. 855, 745 and 967.

470. **Asie.** Final *e* representing a Latin *a* appears to stand in hiatus, cf. ll. 315, 789 and 1007.

481. **occean.** Apparently the Mediterranean Sea is meant, as the route to Paradise was overland via India; cf. the *Iter ad Paradisum* and the Alexander legend.

483. **Ke. . . . ke.** This correlative use of *ke* occurs three times in our text, cf. ll. 1303 and 1747–9.

484. **trespassast.** The original form was probably *trespast* as found in *CDV*, which gives an octosyllabic line.

487. **deluje.** Cf. also ll. 926 and 1115. The regular form in the other MSS is *-uvie*.

495. **fust.** *Fust*, found in *P* alone, reproduces the Latin *lignum* which proves its authenticity. This word does not normally mean tree, but is used in our poem with this meaning again in l. 1374

506. **Orcoban.** The *Imago mundi* writes this name as *Orcobares* which is the *Oscobares* range in which the Ganges rises according to Orosius' map. On Isidore's map the Ganges rises in the Caucasus

range, see the reproductions of these maps by K. Miller *Mappae-mundi* VI (Stuttgart 1895).

506. **munt.** This word is to be understood frequently as 'mountain range' in our text.

506. In MS *G* this line has been crossed out, and in the margin, written in another hand, is the line *Dekes mount auban en ynde vyent.*

515. **set.** Cf. l. 1986 where *P* again omits the final *t* of this word. To avoid misinterpretation of the text I have restored the consonant in both cases.

519. **Eufrates e Tygre.** Both words have two forms, cf. *Eufrates* 764 against *Eufrate:late* 745 and in the line 783; *Tygre* 745 and *Tygrin:veisin* 721.

520. **Caucas.** Cf. also ll. 533 and 893. The form *Tankas* of PR is an evident corruption of *Caucas* given by *V*, i.e. the Caucasus range, which name has been introduced erroneously in place of *Parchoatrus*, cf. 'mons Parchoatros' in Orosius' *Historiarum libri septem* (Migne *Pat. Lat.* XXXI) I, 2. This form reappears in manuscript Cleop. B iv in the British Museum and in the editions of 1497 and 1544. The Migne edition has 'de monte Barchoatro funduntur.' Since the Tigris and Euphrates rise in the mountains of Armenia the substitution of names was probably deliberate, but we cannot attribute it with certainty to our author as it may have stood in the Latin MS he was using.

533. **Caucas.** On the form see note to l. 520. The range of mountains here referred to is the *Caucasus Indicus*, so-called by the soldiers of Alexander the Great, now commonly referred to as the Hindu Kush. The Indus river rises in Thibet and breaks through the mountain barrier into India at the eastern extremity of the range.

536. **Mer Ruge.** On Isidore's map the Red Sea is called the *Sinus Adriaticus* and the *Mare Rubicum* is placed below India, hence the Indus river was said to flow into it.

537–9. In the *Imago mundi* the Red Sea is made identical with the Indian Ocean which is said to be cut off by India from the west: 'Hoc (mare Rubicum) India ab occidente clauditur et ab hoc Indicus oceanus dicitur.' Since the various oceans which were distinguished by the ancients all formed part of the great ocean which flowed around the earth, it results that the terms *Mer Ruge* 536, *grant occean* 538 and *occean l'Indien* 539 of our text all refer to the same body of water. *Grant occean* in l. 538 is of course subject of the verb *enclost* l. 537.

552. **grips.** This form as acc. pl. is found in rhyme with *pais* in l. 585.

555. **Caspy.** cf. *Caspin:chemin* 893, here referring to the sea, not the mountain range; but there is no such distinction in form in the Latin, cf. 'mons Caspius' and 'a Caspio mare,' hence our author must be held responsible for the variant forms in his poem.

559. **Gog e Magog.** Referred to in Ezek. 38 and 39. For the most recent discussion of the tradition concerning these tribes, see A. R. Anderson *Alexander's Gate, Gog and Magog, and the Inclosed Nations* Cambridge, Mass. 1932, and the review by P. Barry in *Speculum* VIII (1933) 264.

562. **crue beste.** For *crue* cf. note to l. 164. The Migne text at this point has the ludicrous error of 'caudis bestiis' for the correct 'crudis bestiis' found in Cleop. B iv and the edition of 1544.

563–4. **bandun:regiun.** The original rhyme was *banduns:regiuns* as found in *y*, cf. l. 1317.

569. **Pigneos un munt.** This error resulted from misinterpretation of the Latin 'In montibus Pygmaeos,' in which Pygmaeos was taken for an adjective.

575. **utime an.** Since *an* stands in l. 574 it may be omitted in 575 (*D* omits) and the final *e* of *utime* may be elided (cf. note to l. 224). An alternative to elision would be to read the disyllabic form *utme* which is known in Anglo-Norman, cf. *uitme* in the *Cumpoz* 1387 and 3205 and in the *Brendan* 769. This form does not occur in our MSS.

578. **Si.** P's form *sil* may be for *cil* as *s* and *c* frequently interchange in *P*. More probably it is merely scribal for *si* because final *l* appears to have been silent for our scribe in certain forms, cf. *i* for *il* ll. 110, 775, etc., *de* for *del* l. 2312, *ma* for *mal* l. 2538, and the form *ad* for *al* in ll. 2640 and 2652. Conversely the scribe writes *del* occasionally where we should expect *de*, cf. ll. 16 and 410; cf. also *kil* for *ki* in l. 2869 *C*. It seems probable consequently that *sil* merely represents an inverse spelling for *si* in the case in question.

586. **defendunt.** A similar case of *-unt* for *-ent* is *ount* 1543, and MS *G* furnishes a third example in *perdunt* 2828. *Mangunt* in l. 598 is rather a reduction of *manguent*, cf. the syllable count and the rhyme *malostrue:mangue* 561. These forms are of course scribal.

597–600. These lines follow l. 628 in *P* and *R*, which is opposed both to *y* and to the Latin.

602. 'Some call them men, others beasts.' Note the correlative use of *tels*.

604. This line is corrupt in all the MSS, the form printed, apparently representing the original line. The passage is clear in the Latin, 'et octonos simul sedecim in pedibus digitos.' Either the

author misunderstood his Latin text or he was using a MS which was corrupt at this point.

618. The line becomes octosyllabic by reading *durer CDG*, omitting *an* (not in *D*) and eliding the *e* of *utime* (cf. l. 575). Here again the form *utme* would serve, but it does not appear in any MS.

623. **Cynope.** The Latin form *Scinopodae* proves that a syllable *od* has disappeared and that we should read *Cynopode*. In *CDR* appears the form *Ciclope* by contamination from l. 622.

627. **sarcu.** This detail is not in the Latin which reads 'et in terram positi umbram sibi planta pedis erecta faciunt.' I do not know where the author found it; possibly the idea was furnished to him by an illustration in which the upturned foot suggested the lid of a sarcophagus.

648. **orrille.** *ei* tonic is written *i* several times in *P*, cf. *ortilz* 604, *orille* 668, *nis* 487, 824 and 2671, and *Marsille* 1330 (perhaps by analogy with the Latin form). For other examples of this relatively infrequent development see Stimming *Boeve de Haumtone* p. 200, and Waters' *Brendan* p. 154.

650. **purpostement.** This word translates the Latin *pene*. Godefroy does not list such a form, but since *purpost* is a possible variant for *propos* our form is perhaps to be identified as a variant of *proposeement*. If so, the word might be more precisely defined as 'intentionally.'

656. **cornes.** A feminine form from the neuter plural *cornua*; cf. also *braces* (< *bracchia*) 706 R. This is the favourite form in our text, cf. ll. 657, 669, 693, etc., but the masculine *cors* is also found, cf. l. 645.

661. **rebukee.** The Latin reads *illo obtuso*, consequently I have defined the word as 'blunted.' However the verb *rebuker* is found in the *Set Dormans* 1589 with the meaning of 'repulse' or 'defeat,' and it may be that this meaning 'pushed back' was intended in our text.

683. For 'fugiens descrimina volat' in Migne's text read 'fingens descrimina vocum.'

712. **paisanz.** Cf. *paisant* 938, *tyranz* 2745 and *tiranz* 2768. For a discussion of these forms with added *t* see Walberg *Bestiaire* p. lxiii.

721–28. In *CDG* (*G* lacks 725–8) these lines are placed after l. 734, which is manifestly incorrect as shown by the order of the Latin and by the fact that the correct sequence of the description is thereby disrupted.

722. **Parchie procain veisin.** For the form *Parchie* see note to l. 767.

724. **la.** The definite article regularly stands in this formula, cf. ll. 729, 753, 879, etc.

733. **ki.** The dative *ki* for *cui* is required in this construction. This form is written *ki* nine times in our MS, ll. 743, 802, 856, 947, 1115, 1272, 1693, 2260 and 2807, against twice as *ke*, here and in l. 2675. I have therefore generalized *ki*.

741. **pyride.** Modern English and French *pyrite* or native disulphide of iron. Godefroy defines it as metallic sulphur. On this stone see Marbode's *Lapidary* p. 909, and Studer and Evans *Anglo-Norman Lapidaries* p. 402.

742. **li quil.** Since *pyride* is generally feminine the original reading was doubtless *ki la* as given by *CG*.

743. **senilite.** Selenite or sulphate of lime or gypsum, cf. Marbode *op. cit.* p. 567, and Studer and Evans *op. cit.* p. 403.

746. **late.** So written in *G*; the scribe of *P* wrote *lace* but the rhyme proves the form. *Late* is an evident Latinism for *lee* (< *lata*) to provide a rhyme for *Eufrate*. *RCD* rejected this unusual form and inserted *cité*. Since this word occurs frequently in our text the substitution could have been made independently. These three scribes probably read *Eufrate* as *Eufraté* thus giving a rhyme with *cité*.

757. **reine.** *R* reads *regne*, and the scribe of *P*, after writing *reine*, placed a *g* above *i* but did not expunctuate. He probably had *regne* in his original.

760. **Ad.** Note that the verb is placed by *CG* in l. 759 in which case the final *e* of *Cinquante* could elide, cf. note to l. 295. An alternative explanation is that *d* of *ad* being silent, *a* + *le* give by enclisis a phonetic *al*.

762. **cité e.** Two like vowels may coalesce when in contact within a word or in adjacent words, cf. ll. 788, 829, 1574, 1786 and 2567. See on this point Suchier *op. cit.* p. 29.

763. **portes de.** The atonic ending *-es* may lose syllabic value when the following word begins with a consonant, cf. ll. 657 (unless we should read *corns* with *RDG*) and 1903. See Suchier *op. cit.* p. 33.

767. **Parthie.** *P*'s reading *Perchie* (cf. *Parchie* in ll. 722 and 728) resulted from misinterpretation of the abbreviation for *er* or *ar*. The poem is in error at this point as the Latin 'In ea quoque est Chaldaea,' refers to Mesopotamia and not to Parthia. This error extends to Arabia in l. 769 which is also in Mesopotamia according to the Latin. In *P* the scribe was apparently puzzled as he introduced an illumination in l. 769 but not in l. 767. A more logical division is at l. 767 which begins a new paragraph in Migne. Both *C* and *D* have illuminations here but not in l. 769.

LA PETITE PHILOSOPHIE III

777–8. These lines refer to Jethro, father-in-law of Moses, who was a priest in the land of Madian, a district in Arabia Petraea, bordering the Red Sea, and close to Mount Sinai. The people of this land were the Midianites of Biblical history, and were supposed to be the descendants of Midian, fourth son of Abraham by Keturah. See the passage in Exod. 3, 1, 'Moyses autem pascebat oves Jethro soceri sui sacerdotis Madian,' and also Exod. 18.

782. **despite.** This form from *despecta* is the past participle of the verb *despire* (<*despicere*) 'to despise,' and means 'unloved' or 'rejected.' The agreement of past participles in our text is quite irregular, but the singular may be explained by the fact that *gent* seems to permit either singular or plural agreement.

787–792. The Migne text reads as follows: 'in qua est Damascus, a Damasco Abraae liberto constructa et dicta, olim Reblata vocata.' This is incorrect, the following words found in all the early editions having dropped out between *dicta* and *olim*, 'Ibi et Antiochia ab Antiochio rege cognominata.' Our text is therefore correct.

798. **par sun tresor.** I have found no explanation of this statement which is not based on anything in the Latin. We should expect *pur* (not *par*), but no MS offers this reading.

800. **a priser funt.** The construction *faire*+*a*+*inf.* instead of *estre*+*a*+*inf.* is quite common in OF and numerous examples occur with the verb *preisier*, see G. Gougenheim *Etudes sur les périphrases verbales de la langue française* (Paris 1929) pp. 212 ff.

804. A line of ten syllables in Continental French. MS *C* introduces the doubtful *del* for *de la* (cf. note to line 224). More probably the *e* of *de* elides by enclisis and the *es* of *Palestin* has lost its vowel, although this reduction usually occurs only when the syllable is final, cf. note to l. 763.

814. **mist.** The Latin is 'inhabitavit,' which proves the OF form means 'dwelt' and not 'placed.'

814. **Jebusen.** Jebus, the son of Canaan, is not specifically named in the Bible, but his name may be inferred from Gen. 10, 16, where the Jebusites are given as descendants of Canaan. On these forms and on Jebus as a name for Jerusalem see Hastings *Dictionary of the Bible* s. v. 'Jebus.'

817. This line could be reduced to octosyllabic form by omitting *Dunt*, which is unnecessary. Possibly *dous est* counts as one syllable, cf. note to l. 263. The line presents an awkward combination of *d*'s and *s*'s.

831. **Samarie.** The rhyme with *afeire* in l. 830 establishes the form as *Samaire* of which the final *e* after *r* may elide, cf. note to l. 224.

834. **numee.** For the dropping of a prefix see note to l. 40.

837. **Pentapolis.** Cf. Isidore *Etym.* XIV, iii, 24, 'Pentapolis regio in confinio Arabiae et Palaestinae sita.' The province of Cyrenaica is also called Pentapolis in our text, cf. l. 1211.

839. **furent.** According to Suchier *op. cit.* p. 34 this word may count as one syllable.

839–40. The context shows that the transposed order of *P* and *R* is incorrect as the words *trois altres* in l. 840 refer necessarily to *Sodome e Gomorre* and not to *Cinq citez* in l. 838.

844. The *palu noir* is not mentioned in the Latin.

846. This line, an addition by our author, is probably corrupt in *x* for it is incorrect to say that the Dead Sea does not drink any pure water inasmuch as the Jordan empties into it. The variants of *y* indicate that the correct reading is *Mes de cel ewe hom ne beit*, i.e. no one drinks the water of the Dead Sea.

858. **mult grant tens.** We have to choose between this reading and that of *par geant teus* in PR. Since the line is added by the author to provide the rhyme and is not based on the Latin, it is difficult to prove which reading is the original; but there is no record of these people, the Nabathaei of Roman history, ever having been considered giants, whereas for centuries they were the most powerful people of Arabia; see Pauly-Wissowa *Real Encyclopädie der classischen Altertumswissenschaft* XVI 1453, s. v. 'Nabataioi.' The reading adopted not only fits the facts of history but has the advantage of being irreproachable metrically. Possibly the original was *par grant tens.* The tradition of the twelve nations (*duze genz*, l. 857) descended from Ishmael is based on Genesis 25, 16.

865. **Del su de ces Egypte gist.** This reading is unsatisfactory not only because of the unusual *Del su* but because there is no mention of south in the Latin, which reads 'Quibus (the regions of Asia) usque ad Austrum Aegyptus connectitur.' Moreover Egypt cannot be said to lie south of Asia. *El su* of *C* and *Al su* of *D* appear to represent attempts to correct the reading *Del su.* The key to the puzzle is furnished by the reading of MS *G Iuste cele*, the *cele* referring in this case to the Mediterranean Sea in l. 862. The original reading was probably *Dejuste ces* which fits the Latin and which, being corrupted into *Del su de ces*, explains the readings of the other MSS.

869. **Eurize.** This name is a corruption of *Euxia*, cf. *Eurie* in *C*. The name was apparently treated as trisyllabic.

870–1. These lines refer to the twin brothers Aegyptus and Danaus, the sons of Belus, king of Egypt, according to Grecian legend. I have not discovered where the name *Acelé* originated.

872. **remembrer.** Perhaps the initial syllable is to be suppressed, cf. note to l. 40.

893. **Caucas.** See note to l. 520.

907. **Baarie.** This form is a corruption of *Bactria*, in Migne *Bactra*, MS *G* has *Bactrie*, the original OF form.

907. **acosté.** Note that *G* offers the variant *costee* without prefix. The verb is *s'acoster* as proved by the variant of *DG* in l. 945. The usual form of this verb is *s'acostoier* as listed by Godefroy, and which appears regularly in MS *C*, cf. *C*'s variant for this line, for 945 and for 2702. In l. 2702 *P* uses *costeier* in the same sense, whereas *B* makes it reflexive and *G* again offers a corrupt form of *se coster*. Godefroy lists the verb *costeier* only in the sense of Mod. Fr. *côtoyer*.

913. **Ciht e Hunnie.** *Ciht* is for Scythia, the original OF form probably being *Sithie* or *Sithe*. The Migne text reads 'Scythia et Hirnia,' but this is an error for *Hunnia* which is the form in Cleop. B iv and the editions of 1497 and 1544. O. H. Prior suggested that *Hirnia* is a reduction of *Hircania* (cf. *Cambridge Anglo-Norman Texts* p. 64), but it is clearly a misreading for *Hunnia*.

924. **Ararath.** This is the correct form as found in the editions of 1497 and 1544. Migne's form *Arat* is corrupt.

930. **vermie.** This form cannot be from *vermir* 'to fill with worms.' Perhaps it represents *fermie* by interchange of *f* and *v*, cf. note to l. 115. More probably it is a corruption of *guarnie C* or *urnie G*.

931. 'Where the winds make the mares fecund.' The scribe of *G* alone understood this line as he wrote *ywes* 'mares,' whereas all the others wrote *ewes* the regular form in our text for waters and which is not attested as a spelling for Latin *equas*. The misinterpretation of this key word led the scribes to make further alterations as the variants show. For a similar confusion in OF of this same Latin passage see Langlois *Connaissance du monde* p. 132, n. 1.

932. **sul.** *P*'s form *sur* is explained by confusion of final *l* and *r* which occurred very early in Anglo-Norman, cf. Walberg *Bestiaire* p. lv.

939-40. This couplet should follow l. 936 according to the Migne text, but the passage is confused in the various editions.

946. **Chalie.** A mistake for *Carie*, Latin *Caria*. All the MSS offer forms with *l*.

947. **Hermes.** This form occurs in Cleop. B iv. Migne reads 'Hirnus' an error for 'Hermus.'

949. **Libie.** This form, found in all the MSS, is an error for *Lydie*, Latin *Lydia*. The author probably used a MS which read *Lybia*.

964. **ki n'est Lide.** The latter part of this line represents an

I

obvious cheville to give a rhyme. It appears that the scribes did not understand what was meant as the MSS are all different. The reading I have adopted is conjectural, meaning 'which is not Lydia,' and which was suggested by the forms ending in -**ide** in l. 963. No such adjective as *lide* exists and the reading *n'eslide*, though possible, is equally unintelligible.

983. **Grant Mer.** See note to l. 1028.

990. The correct reading for the Latin is 'Alania, Dacia, Gothia.' Migne's *Dania* is an error for *Dacia*. From the foregoing it results that our author has translated *Gothia* by *Germanie*.

991. **munt Giu.** This term is used to translate *Alpes* in our text. Cf. note to ll. 1131-4.

994. **occean.** All the MSS have this reading which is an error for *occident*, Latin *occasum*, i.e. Germany is bounded on the west by the Rhine.

1005. **regné.** The form is proved here by rhyme as also in ll. 2834 and 2917. Within the line I have not used the accent as there is no proof that the author did not also use *regne*.

1006. The mention of Ratisbon in the *Imago mundi*, which city is nowhere mentioned in its sources, is accepted by many as proof that the author was German, see Introduction, p. liii.

1010. **finant.** The readings of the MSS are confused, but the Latin for l. 1011, 'Ab Albia fluvio est Germania inferior,' proves that the Elbe was considered the boundary between Saxony and Lower Germany, consequently *finant* must stand.

1019. **Pennine.** Refers to *Pannonia inferior* lying north of *Bulgaria*. In l. 1075 *Pannonie* refers to *Pannonia superior* lying north of *Dalmatia*.

1021. **Tyras.** This form is correct, appearing in Cleop. B iv. Migne reads 'a tras.'

1024-6. Migne's text reads, 'et civitatem Hebron, ibi constructa,' an error for 'et civitatem Constantinopolim a Constantino constructa,' as found in all the early editions.

1028. **Grant Mer.** The text of the *Imago mundi* reads 'A Mediterraneo mari est Graecia, . . . et versus austrum Magno mari terminatur.' This passage is not clear owing to the use of the term *Magnum mare* in the Latin text. In Cap. XXII the marshes called Meotides were said to join the *Magnum mare* near the city of Theodosia; cf. the text, ll. 981-4. In Cap. XXIV the Danube is said to flow into the *Ponticum mare*; cf. the text l. 1001. Thus the *Magnum mare* is in this case equivalent to the Black Sea. However, the Nile also flows into the *mare Magnum*; cf. the text, l. 516. This apparent confusion arises from the fact that *mare Magnum* was an inclusive term used to refer to all the expanse of water from Gibraltar to and including the Black Sea, the various parts of which each bore individual names, cf. Isidore of Seville *Etym.* XIII xvi 1. Our author has translated literally, and the passage means that Greece extends from the Ionian Sea on the east to the Adriatic Sea on the west.

1032. **mer Illico.** The Illyricum mare or Adriatic Sea is meant. This is the same body of water referred to as *Grant Mer* in l. 1028. There appears to have been confusion between Illyricum and Illyria, cf. R's variant *Ylirie*. The syllable count favors a trisyllabic form.

1043. **Elen fiz Hector.** The Latin text reads 'Helenus frater Hectoris.' Probably our author's MS read *filius* instead of *frater*. The scribes of *C* and *D* substituted the reading *Eleine fille Hector* doubtless because of the fact that Helen of Troy was well-known from the *Roman de Troie*, whereas the name Helenus was quite unfamiliar to them.

1061. **Pelopenens.** The second *e* is probably elided in pronunciation, cf. note to l. 308.

1067-8. These lines are found after l. 1072 in *P* and *R*, which is clearly incorrect. The Migne text does not mention Corinth, but the following statement is found in Cleop. B iv and in the early editions, 'In hac (Achaia) est Chorinthus a Chorintho filio Horestes dicta.' The words *el est* in l. 1068 have no support whatever in the Latin and appear to exist in the line solely to provide a rhyme. Corinthus, the legendary founder of Corinth, was not the son of Orestes, but of Zeus, or according to another legend, of Marathon.

1075-6. 'Deinde et Pannonia superior usque ad Peninum montem.' Cf. the note to l. 1019 where *Pennine* referred to *Pannonia inferior*. The form *Appenin* in l. 1076 is an error owing to confusion with the Apennines, cf. l. 1123 below. MS *C* reads *Pennin* and *D* reads *perin*.

1079. **Ceste.** This should refer to Italy; cf. the Latin, 'Italia olim magna Graecia est dicta.'

1085-6. The author derives Latium from *latere* which in French means *tapir* 'to hide.' He probably intended a pun in l. 1086 on *la terre*.

1093-6. 'Cities possess in ancient representation the forms of the noblest beasts. The ancients, following their beliefs, gave them forms according to their symbolical meaning.' *Vels* in l. 1093 without agreement (cf. *veil* 116, *velz* 575), for which G gives *veille* showing agreement, may have been influenced by *viez* (< *vetus*), normally indeclinable in OF, cf. Pope *From Latin to Modern French* sec. 795. This form is apparently explained by depalatalization of *l*-mouillé before consonant as in the form *solalz*, see Phonology, paragraph 3. Suchier (*Voyelles toniques* sec. 69) cites *veuz* from Benoit de Sainte-Maure.

1113. **Ymbrie.** This form prevails in the editions, *Umbria* occurring in that of 1544 only.

1125. **Bene.** The Latin is 'a Beneco rege,' the trisyllabic form occurring in all editions. The original reading of our text seems to be *Bene*, which indicates that our author sometimes took liberties with the forms of names.

1131–2. This statement is out of order in Migne's text. It should appear at the end of Cap. XXVIII instead of in Cap. XXIX. *Munt Goie* in l. 1131 renders *mons Jovis* and stands in contrast to *munt Giu* in l. 1128 which translates *Alpes*; cf. also ll. 991 and 1089. *Mons Jovis* is Mount Saint-Bernard.

1136. **Belgis.** Cf. Isid. *Etym.* XIV iv 21, 'Belgis autem civitas est Galliae, a qua Belgica nominata est.' The site of this city was near the modern Tolbiac.

1143–4. The term *occident* (the reading of *y* is *orient*) is correct in that the line refers to Gallia Lugdunensis (which included all Northwestern France) as opposed to Gallia Belgica (cf. l. 1136) and Gallia Narbonensis (cf. l. 1148). Since Gallia Lugdunensis had its capital at Lugdunum (Lyons), which was in the Southeastern part of the province, the substitution of *orient* for *occident* is easily explained. There is also the possibility of confusion between Lugdunum Segusianorum (Lyons) and Lugdunum Batavorum (Leyden). The term *munt Leun* in l. 1144 results apparently from the fact that the name Lugundum contains the Celtic root *dun*, which means hill, and was in fact built on the hill now known as La Fourvière, which overlooks the present city. Strabo referred to Lyons as situated at the foot of a hill; see Harper's *Dictionary of Classical Literature and Antiquities*, s.v. 'Lugdunum.'

1145. **Cumee.** This form is derived from the Latin term *Comata* 'long haired' which Migne has incorrectly written 'Comaga.'

1147. **Leunais.** Gallia Lugdunensis (*le Lyonnais*) is meant.

1154. **Lengres.** All the MSS have this form which stands for the Latin 'Liger,' the Loire. The Roman province of Narbonensis Gallia lay south of the Loire and west of the Rhone.

1157–9. The Latin reads 'prius Iberia ab Ibero flumini, et Hesperia ab Hespero rege nominata.' The OF text appears to have been based on a Latin MS in which this passage was corrupt.

1160. **la fu neé.** The form *né* of *P* is clearly an error for *neé*

(< *necatu*). This detail is not in the Latin and I have found no source for it.

1163. **Cinq.** Cf. also *cinq* in l. 1164. The Latin reads 'sex,' and both the Latin and the poem proceed to enumerate six provinces. The error arises from the inclusion in the list of Tinguitane (Mauritania Tingitana) which was in Africa, and is mentioned later as the most western of the North African provinces, cf. l. 1241. Isidore of Seville (*Etym.* XIV iv 29) refers to this province as follows, 'et transfreta in regione Africae Tingitania; cf. also *ibid.* XIV v 3.

1169. **grant mer.** The Latin text reads 'versus occasum sunt in oceano,' hence the term *grant mer* is here used to mean the Atlantic ocean; cf. note to l. 1028.

1171. **Bretaigne.** In ll. 1173 and 1177 *Engleterre* and *Escoce* are mentioned as separate islands. The author has followed his Latin original, but, since he lived in England, he must have been aware that all three names referred to one island. He was probably familiar with the use of the word *ydle* in the sense of country or region.

1178. **furnie.** This form cannot be read as the past participle of *furnir* 'to offer' or 'to provide' unless *Ke* be emended to *De*, for which there is little support, the *Ke de* of *D* resulting from the *sunt fermés* at the end of the line. It seems necessary to admit *furnie* as a variant of *furnist* introduced by the author to provide a rhyme with *Orkenie*.

1190. **lee.** The variants prove that this word represents *liée* (< *ligata*) meaning here ice-bound.

1195. **Afe.** The Migne text reads 'Apher uno ex posteris Abrahae,' which refers to Epher, son of Midian and grandson of Abraham, cf. Gen. 25, 4.

1196. **Abrahé.** This name occurs in l. 788 as *Abraham*.

1205. **Cathabathinon.** This is an error for *Cathabathmon* the form found in the early editions, and which gives an octosyllabic line.

1209. **Carmarike.** An error for Cyrenaica, but found in all the MSS.

1219. **Censis.** So written in all the MSS. Migne has 'Heusis,' but the correct form is Zeugis, cf. Isidore *Etym.* XIV v 9.

1222. **Edisse.** Agrees with the edition of 1497. Migne has 'Elisa,' the correct form.

1223. **retint.** The variants and the context show that this form is present, i.e. stands for *retient*. *Tint* in 2695 may also be present, RCB reading *tient*, but the past could stand.

1231. **Genilie e Indie.** *D* reads *Genule* and *CD Medie*. These forms represent Getulia and Numidia. Our original may have read *Getulie e Numidie*. *Numide* appears in the text l. 1334.

1232. **Jugnice.** *CD* writes *Gogrite*. The Latin is 'Jugurtha' for which we can postulate an original *Jugurte* in the poem.

1238. The OF corresponds to Migne's reading 'Stiffensis a Stiffi oppido.' Cleop. B iv and the early editions read correctly 'Sitifensis a Sitifi oppido.'

1241–2. Cf. note to l. 1163.

1259. **Utre.** The 'Intra' of Migne's text is an error for 'Ultra.'

1268. This line has nine syllables and no emendation seems possible unless the author used the form *cit* instead of *cité*.

1269. **Gabes.** The modern Cadiz, the Latin form being Gades. All the MSS have the *b* instead of *d*. The location of this city seems to have been a matter of uncertainty. On the maps of Orosius and Isidore it is on an island facing the Straits of Gibraltar. In the *Divisiones mundi* edited by O. H. Prior, ll. 925–7 it is mentioned as being surrounded by the sea.

1272. **plan.** The rhyme is *Gaditain:plain*. For a similar form in rhyme of a Latin name in *-an* see Waters' *Brendan*, l. 13 and note to same.

1283–4. *C* and *D* incorrectly insert these lines after l. 1266. The couplet is wanting in *G*.

1287. **Taphe.** This form appears to have stood in the original OF text. The *Imago mundi* states that Cyprus was called Paphos from the city of the same name. Perhaps there has been confusion with the name Thapsus, a city and peninsula of Sicily. On Isidore's map an island called Tapsus is found just east of Sicily. Cf. also *Etym.* XIV vi 35.

1292. **Adrien.** Latin 'adriaticum.' The OF form is explained by the necessity of a rhyme for *Libien* 1291.

1293. **Anidos.** The only variant is *Aniclos* in *D*, consequently *Anidos* must represent the original OF form. The author's Latin MS must have read *Anidos* for *Abydos* the form given by Migne. No island called 'Anidos' is recorded and Abydos was a town on the Hellespont. However an island Avidos is mentioned in the *Image du Monde* (ed. *Prior*, p. 130).

1296. **Elle.** Helle was not the name of a city, but of the daughter of Athamas and Nephele who was drowned in the Hellespont, from which incident this body of water derived its name.

1297–8. No mention of Jason and the golden fleece is found in any of the versions of the *Imago mundi* which I have examined. Jason found the golden fleece of Colchis, which was not an island but a country on the east shore of the Black Sea. Colcos is referred to as an island in the *Image du Monde* (ed. Prior, p. 130). It is doubtful, however, that the author added this detail himself.

1309–12. The Migne text, 'Sicilia a Siculo rege dicitur. Italia dicta,' should read ' rege fratre Itali dicta.'

1322. **comedia.** MSS *CDG* have the variant *comedie*. The Latin form in *PR* suggests that the word had not become French at the date of composition.

1326. **Coile.** The Latin is 'ab Eolo rege;' *C*'s variant *Olle* and *D*'s *Elle* indicate that the original OF form was *Eole* or *Eolle*.

1342. **Cum riant mort si bel reschine.** The Latin for this couplet is 'quae comedentibus rictus contrahit et quasi ridentes interimit.' This poisonous plant causes contraction of the facial muscles which creates a sort of grin giving the impression of laughter.

1346. **sancté.** Cf. the forms *cunctrés* 2275, *cummectees* 2448 *P* and *equinocte* 1469. Perhaps it was from such forms as the latter, which were undoubtedly influenced by the Latin spelling, that the use of *ct* elsewhere developed.

1351. **Colubrie.** Colubria (Migne) or Colubraria (Isidore and Pliny). O. H. Prior in his edition of the *Image du Monde*, p. 43, argues for the identification of this island with the modern Iviza, one of the Balearic group. This interpretation is assured by the term *Aparmemes* 'alongside' of our text.

1353. **Gorgoines.** The reading of all the MSS; an error for *Gorgodes* which goes back to the original OF text.

1359. **s'entresemblerent.** This form is a reduction by haplography of the regular form *s'entreresemblerent*, which would give a seven syllable feminine line.

1371. **Menee.** The reading of all the MSS; an error for *Meroe*.

1374. **iban.** The orthography of R is *Eban*. This word is normally trisyllabic in OF, cf. forms such as *ibanus*, *ebaine*, *ebenus*, etc., cited by Godefroy, who, however, cites *eban* defined as the 'pocke tree' from Du Guez, p. 914. Tobler-Lommatzsch also cite *eban* from the *Entree d'Espagne*.

1375. **Syrine.** All the MSS have forms with *r*, which is an error, the Latin form being *Syene*. There has been confusion with the name *Cyrene*, a city of Cyrenaica in Northern Africa; cf. l. 1215.

1379. **soleil.** Cf. note to l. 224.

1401. **terre foreigne.** Translates the Latin 'novissima terra.'

1415. **terre de obliviun.** The Hades of the Greeks was similarly a land of forgetting, cf. the river Lethe, which meant 'oblivion,' The explanation offered in our poem, ll. 1416–8, represents the christianizing of a concept borrowed from pagan antiquity. 1423–4. Cf. ll. 2071–2, where this idea is repeated with *ymage* replacing *umbre*.

1427. **Sa buche.** The Migne text reads 'Hic patens os dicitur et barathrum,' which should read 'Hujus p. os d. b.'

1429–30. This couplet translates the Latin 'Hujus loca fetorem exhalantia dicuntur Acheronta, id est spiracula immundos spiritus emittentia.' The couplet thus means 'Its regions which are overhung with foul exhalations are called Acheron.'

1435–6. This detail is added by our author at this point. For the idea of alternate heat and cold in Hell, see note to ll. 2075–82.

1439–40. Cf. ll. 2103–4 which repeat this idea.

1465–6. The Latin reads 'cujus (the moon's) aspiratione retro trahitur, ejus impulsu refunditur.' The text may be rendered 'by its attraction on the earth it draws back the waters and (by its repulsion) pours them back again.' *Refunt* is therefore from *refundre* and not from *refaire*.

1471. **En solstice ses salz reprent.** This line refers to the fact that the rise and fall of the tide is less at the solstice than at the equinox. The Latin text reads 'cum in solstitio minores (fluctus).' It is thus evident that *salz* means 'rising and falling' and *reprent* stands presumably for *reprient* from *repreindre*, unattested derivative of *preindre* (for *priembre* < *premere*).

1487. **tru[v]um.** Cf. l. 1952 where the *v* has likewise been restored and l. 272 where the scribe puts it in. Dropping of the *v(u)* may have been merely negligence, but it is possible that the scribe equated *u* in this case with *w* which in Anglo-Norman had the value of two *u*'s, cf. *wnt=vunt* 1554.

1488. Cf. Gen. 7, 11, 'Rupti sunt omnes fontes abyssi magnae.'

1492–3. **esperit De tempest.** Cf. 'spiritus procellarum,' Ps. 148, 8.

1499. **floz.** Cf. l. 2453. See Godefroy *Supplement*, s. v. 'fluet.' The context proves that the meaning is 'high-tide' as opposed to *retreanz* 'low-tide' in l. 1450. *Flot* may still mean 'tide' or 'high-tide' in Mod. Fr., see Larousse *Dictionnaire*, s. v. 'flot.'

1502. **les crus.** The scribes of *PRD* interpret the invariable word *crus* as a plural and so write *les*.

1507. **se avent.** The reflexive is probably scribal, cf. the variant of *y* and *avient* in l. 387. *Avenir* reflexive meaning 'to happen' is unusual in OF, Tobler-Lommatzsch citing one case only, and Godefroy none.

1510. **sa tenvesse.** The reading in Migne's text is 'loca cava, et continuis aquis frigida, ventis conclusa rumpuntur,' which is to be corrected to 'loca cava continuis aquis fragilia (cf. *tenvesse*) ventis concussa (cf. 1509) rumpuntur.' *Sa* could refer to *terre* in l. 1507 but it may refer to *les crus* in 1509 for such cases of confusion between *sun*(*sa*) and *lur* are found; cf. ll. 1717 and 2669, possibly also l. 58 (cf. note). The Latin indicates that *sa* in the above case does refer to *les crus* in l. 1509.

1512. **aoverir.** The Latin verb is 'aperiuntur,' which supports *aoverir*, of which *P*'s reading *anurrir* appears to be a corruption. The objection to *amireer:chayer* in R is that *chair* is the usual Anglo-Norman form of this infinitive and that a rhyme such as *chaer* (< *chaeir*):*amirer* (cf. ll. 394) does not occur elsewhere in the text.

1515. The Latin reads 'Inde tellus Siciliae, quia cavernosa.' Evidently the author's MS lacked the word 'Siciliae.'

1516. **espoigne.** An early example of this word, of which Godefroy's earliest example is from 1402.

1522. **destempree.** The Latin reads 'fumam, vel vapores, vel flammas eructat.' Since the flames and smoke are mentioned in 1521, it is necessary to equate *vapores* and *destempree* if we assume a literal translation. It appears that this word is connected in meaning with the English 'distemper,' a disease of dogs and horses, a sort of catarrh accompanied by foul breath and nasal discharge. An alternative is to accept it as a pp. subs. meaning 'disturbance.'

1529–30. The Latin on which this couplet is based reads 'dum aquarum concursus spiritum in imum profundum secum rapiens.' The OF is not an exact rendering, the Latin stating that the waters suck the air down into their depths by their movements rather than that they create winds. Further we should expect *les ewes* instead of *des ewes*, but *les* is found in *G* only. As it stands we may translate the couplet 'For waters which are below are always creating winds by their agitation.' The reading of *PR* in l. 1530 *E en muant* might perhaps be read as *E enmuant* for *E esmuant*, the participle functioning as an adjective meaning 'agitated.'

1543. **ount.** cf. note to l. 586.

1544. **marinail.** *P* alone gives this form, but the adjective *marinail* occurs elsewhere as a substantive, for instance in the *Roman de Horn*.

1560. The Latin is 'quia fluenta dulcia partem salsis vadis consumuntur.' The text thus means that the brine does not allow the ocean to increase in volume because it consumes part of the fresh water of the rivers. For *Ke* = *Kar* cf. note to l. 2087.

1563. **venz privez.** Translates the Latin 'occultos meatus,' which proves that the meaning is 'secret or hidden passages;' cf. the Mod. Eng. 'vent.'

1572. The meaning of the line is 'whereas it is bitter in its depths.' The readings are confused owing to the scribes having interpreted *parfund* as an adjective. The scribe of *P* wrote *ele ē parfund ē amere*. The original reading may have been *ele est par fund amere,*' in which *par fund*, 'at the bottom,' stands opposite *en sum*, 'on the surface,' in l. 1571.

1578. **demoist.** The variant of *RDG* is *demoiste*, which gives an octosyllabic line. Godefroy lists *enmoistir* in this sense, which suggests a form *demoistir*, but this infinitive seems uncertain in view of the variant *demoiste*.

1591–2. All the MSS place this couplet here, but it is clearly out of its context. Its correct position is not certain as it does not reproduce any Latin phrase, but it surely belongs to the passage 1609–24 (cf. note to same). I suggest that it be read after l. 1612.

1597. **parfunt.** *Curs* having dropped out in *y*, the scribes confused the verb *parfunt* with the adjective *parfund* and replaced the adverb *enterinement* by the substantive *enterrement*. *P* apparently understood his line but wrote *parfund*. Since *d* final in this word is not used elsewhere in the MS I have altered it to *t*. The line refers to the rivers of Paradise which must complete their course by flowing back underground to the point at which they rose to the surface.

1601–4. See Eccles. 1, 7, 'ad locum unde exeunt flumina revertuntur ut iterum fluant.' In the Latin text this is found at the end of Cap. XLVI and not in Cap. XLVII, but the lines fit their context perfectly and were doubtless placed here deliberately by the author.

1602. Hiatus appears to have been introduced in the text after the fourth syllable of a line in which there is a well-marked pause or caesura, cf. ll. 2088 and 2203.

1609–24. This passage is not based on anything in the Latin text. Of the ideas developed, the first, evaporation of sea-water as a cause of the ocean being salty is found already in the text, cf. ll. 1561 and 1567 ff.; the second and the third, the dissolving of salt from the earth and evaporation taking place mainly in the tropics are too obvious to need sources.   They could also have been suggested by ll. 1263–6 of the text.

1616. **sal gemme.** Native chloride of sodium or rock-salt, cf. the Mod. Fr. *sel gemme* and the English *sal-gem*. See Studer and Evans *Anglo-Norman Lapidaries* p. 402.

1618. **la quit.** *La* refers to *ewe* in l. 1617 and *quit* is the ind. pr. 3 of *cuire* 'to cook' or 'to boil.'

1629–30. This couplet is probably an addition in *x* as it is found neither in *y* nor in the Latin, and the text reads better without it.

1639–40. The Migne text, 'qui viciniam veneno inficiunt,' should read 'qui vicinam aquam veneno inficiunt.'

1662. **niules.** The Latin is 'nubes,' consequently *C*'s reading *nues* is probably correct as *niule* (< *nebula*) means 'mists' not 'clouds.' In the Latin text of Migne for this line, 'et inde nubes undis excussae coelum aperiunt,' the word *undis* should be omitted.

1677. **commu.** As written in *P* the line is heptasyllabic, which raises the question whether we should read *comměu* with RCG. Unfortunately the author of our text appears to have introduced heptasyllabic lines, both masculine and feminine, into his poem. Further, the orthography *eu* for *u*, which developed as a consequence of the disappearance of atonic vowel in hiatus before the tonic vowel, is attested in our MSS, cf. *Seur* 2463, and the Introduction, pp. xxxviii and xliii. Lines such as 2137 indicate that the atonic *e* in hiatus was elided or at least could be in the author's scansion, but the uncertainty of the metre makes it difficult to determine precisely his practice. It may be that he could count or elide such vowels at will, as Suchier suggests, cf. *Vie de Seint Auban* p. 27. Such a conclusion is supported by comparing l. 1677 with l. 2175. On the other hand certain words seem to be used consistently with the *e* retained, cf. *rançun* in ll. 1416, 2221 and 2581, all lines of seven syllables unless we read *rěançun*, which spelling is, however, never found in the MSS. A similar case is *veer*, cf. note to l. 258, but in this case the orthography of the scribes varies.

1679. **multes remuvemenz.** All the other MSS read *remuemenz* which is the usual form. *P*'s form may represent a scribal error. *Multes* before a masculine (R alone has *moltz*) seems to have been introduced merely to avoid a seven syllable line. It is not possible to affirm whether it is scribal or belongs to the author.

1680. **meut.** The subject is *il* in l. 1676, which refers to *eir* in l. 1675.

1682. Migne offers the reading 'illorum collaterales,' which should read 'octo illorum c.' as the context shows. The early editions read 'alii' instead of 'octo.'

1688. **mult.** The Latin text reads 'faciens frigora et nubes,' which supports the reading of R in which *froiz* is a substantive translating *frigora*.

1689. **diu.** The form is clearly so written in both *P* and *C*, the other MSS having *deus*. The regular forms in the MSS are *deus* and *dous*. On the question of metathesis of vowels in OF see the article by J. Vising in *Medium Aevum* VI (1937) pp. 210–2. Vising lists a number of cases of *iu* passing to *ui* but none of the passage of *ui* to *iu* as in the above example.

1701–2. The Latin text reads 'Australes venti faciunt majores tempestates, quia ex humili flant in mari.' The adjective *umbles* thus translates the words *ex humili*. A variant for 'ex humili' is 'ex humido,' but *umbles* derives certainly from *humiles*. *Humilis* is defined by Forcellini as follows, 'Humilis proprie est humo proprior, humi declivis, ab humo non alte se extollens.' The words *ex humili* must therefore mean 'blowing close to the ground,' whence 'heavy and humid.' Winds from the south were regularly thought to bring rain; cf. Neckam *De laudibus divinae sapientiae, distinctio secunda*, 85–88. *Umbles* may then be defined as 'low blowing' and 'rain bringing.'

1711. **Kanz.** A prepositional use of *quant* in the sense of 'along with' or 'at the same time as.' Analogy of adverbial expressions involving *quand*, cf. *quand e quand* meaning *en même temps*, may have led to the addition of an adverbial *s* to *quant*. However it is quite possible that the *s* is merely scribal, reflecting the confusion of *t* and *ʒ* final which is evident in MS P. The prepositional use of *quant* was particularly common in Normandy, cf. the examples cited by Littré.

1717–9. All the MSS read *est* and *lur* in l. 1717, *unt* in l. 1718 and *pulse* in l. 1719 except *D* which rewrites the line. These forms do not necessarily belong to the author, as *sunt* may have stood in l. 1717, and *pulsent* could be read in 1719 if the atonic *e* were not counted, cf. note to l. 839.

1719. **pulse.** Gamillscheg gives this verb as fifteenth century from Provençal *polsar* and states that it apparently did not belong to the North. It is possible of course that the word was borrowed by Anglo-Norman directly from Provençal.

1745. The scribes were puzzled by this line which seems to mean 'The winds separate the rain from the air.' The Latin reads simply 'Imber ex nubibus descendit.'

1748–9. The text of Migne reads 'non vento impellente, non sole dissolvente,' which is to be corrected to 'nunc vento impellenti, nunc sole d.'

1760. **offes.** From *offas* 'particles,' cf. *REW* 6041a. Du Cange cites the form *ofella*.

1763. **chaut.** So all MSS. The Latin has 'rigore noctis,' which gives the meaning required by the context. *Chaud* is either a mis-reading for *froid* or else our author's Latin MS read *calore* instead of *rigore*.

1770. **od.** Here used in the meaning of 'near' or 'close to,' cf. the Latin *apud*. *Funt* of PR does not make sense, whereas *sunt es eines* of *y* is a common phrase, cf. Waters in *Mod. Lang. Rev.* XXI (1926) p. 395 and XXII (1927) pp. 199 ff.

1775. **sunt.** The scribe of *P* carelessly repeated *sunt* instead of writing *feus*.

1781–2. The rhyme is *tempest:vest*, cf. *tempest:arbest* 1072 and *est* in ll. 1432 and 1754.

1783. 'He who inhales the polluted air.'

1787–8. The Migne text omits this statement which reads as follows, 'Aerem transvolavimus iam etheris ignem conscendamus.'

1828. Migne's text 'licet tota sit' should read 'lucet tota.'

1829. Migne's text 'tamen crescit nec minuitur' should read 'non enim crescit,' etc.

1832. **soleil.** Cf. note to l. 224.

1835. **ke le.** In combinations of monosyllabic pronominal forms ending in atonic *e* the second vowel may lose its syllabic value, cf. Suchier *Vie de Seint Auban* p. 31. Other examples from the text are ll. 1829 and 2823.

1887–8. **dite:escrite.** The rhyme is *dit:escrit* as given by *y*. Agreement of the past participle is very erratic in our text and cannot be used to prove *dite*.

1892. Migne's text omits the words 'qui et Phenon.'

1899–1902. 'After these thirty years, when it (Saturn) is beginning its course again, if someone makes an image of shining brass, and listens attentively after he has cast it, it will talk like a man.' For *ki* with conditional force and for the verb *atendre* meaning 'be attentive,' see note to l. 4.

1903. This line may be read as octosyllabic if the atonic *e* in the ending *-es* before consonant be not counted, cf. note to l. 763.

1929–30. R first wrote this couplet after l. 1924, and then re-copied it in the correct position, substituting *dolcor* for *melodie*. In P after l. 1924 is an erased line which can still be deciphered as l. 1929. Following this is a space. It is clear, therefore, that *P*'s original repeated the couplet just as it occurs in R and that *P* merely avoided an obvious repetition.

1939. **Ceste.** The *Celeste* of *y* is undoubtedly the original reading, cf. the Latin 'coelestia musica.'

1941. Migne's text omits the word 'gamma,' the correct reading being 'In terra namque si gamma,' etc.

1943. **Mercurie.** Cf. *Mercur:aseur* 1955 and within the lines 1851 and 1957. The Latin form is also used, cf. *Mercurius:curs* 2007, unless we should read *Mercurs* in this case.

1979. **consonances.** Translates the Latin *consonantias*, and means 'musical note' in this case. Each of the seven spaces containing the respective planets gives forth its own characteristic note as it turns.

1986. **set.** See note to l. 515.

1990. The three *forces* (*vires*) of the soul are described as follows in Lib. III of the *Elucidarium* of Honorius Augustodunensis, 'anima etiam habet tres vires, quae sunt rationalis, irascibilis, concupiscibilis,' cf. Migne *Pat. Lat.* CLXXII, col. 1158. This may be compared with the passage from William of Conches, 'Hujus animae diversae sunt potentiae, scilicet *Intelligentia, ratio, memoria,*' cf. *De philosophia mundi libri quatuor* (Migne *Pat. Lat.* CLXXII 98D).

2006. **pinc.** The word is still used in English to mean a small hole made in a garment for decorative purposes. The verb is 'to pink,' in Middle English *pinken*.

2011–3. The distance from Venus to the sun is given in l. 1960 as three half tones and the half tone measures 7812.5 leagues according to ll. 1975–6; consequently the distance in leagues would be 23,437.5 as given by the *Imago mundi*. However MS Cleop. B iv. and the editions of 1477, 1497 and 1544 all read 36 for 37.5 as does the OF save for MS R, which has corrected this figure to 37.5, thereby making the line hypermetrical, cf. variants. Precisely the same situation is found again for the distance from Saturn to the firmament, cf. the text ll. 2023–5. Further, in the distance from Mars to Jupiter, given in the *Imago mundi* as 7812.5 leagues (a half tone), the same relationship is repeated, Cleop. B iv, the editions and the OF dropping the half, cf. the text ll. 2019–21, with MS R again correcting at the expense of the metre.   It is clear therefore that our text is based on a MS which had at this point readings similar to those of Cleop. B iv. Someone in the tradition of R discovered the discrepancies in the calculations and undertook to rectify them. This fact probably explains the appearance of *Cent* for *Duze* in R 377. The corrections were probably first made as marginal glosses and later were incorporated into the text. It does not follow that the source of these corrections was a MS of the *Imago mundi* as numerous other sources existed. Since elsewhere in the poem R follows P consistently in error against the Latin, it is clear that only the numerical computations were checked, which indicates that another MS of the *Imago mundi* was not the source of the corrections in R.

2013. To get an octosyllabic line *altresi* could be replaced by *alsi*.

2017. The Migne text reads 'et triginta,' which is an error for twenty-five, the number found consistently elsewhere.

2026. *Ne* is perhaps enclitic after *mesura*, but more probably *pas* should be omitted.

2028-30. The correct computation of the distance from the earth to the firmament is 109,375 miles as given in the Migne text. The OF reads 130,365, which is incorrect even for the sum of the distances as given in the poem, which would be 109,371. R and G lack this passage, and the three remaining MSS agree on the sum as given, except for *P*'s error of *cent* for *cinc* in l. 2029. Consequently the original text must have read 130,365, which indicates either that the author misread his Latin MS, or that it was incorrect itself.

2030. **en eslink.** The form *eslink* is not attested elsewhere. It is apparently the OF words *eslingue* 'a sling,' in Norman *élingue*, and Middle English *slinge*. Final atonic *e* has a tendency to fall in Anglo-Norman, and *g* final would unvoice to *c* or *k* as in the word *sanc*. The word 'sling' is used to denote a rope or chain used in hoisting or lowering, and more specifically in nautical terminology it signifies the chain attached to the bow and stern of a boat when it is being lowered overboard. Thus by an extension of meaning *en eslink* could mean 'suspended perpendicularly' or 'straight up.'

2035-6. Cf. Matt. 19, 24, 'Facilius est camelum per foramen acus transire, quam divitem intrare in regnum caelorum.' See also Luke 18, 25 and Mark 10, 25. The article in l. 2035 may be intrusive, which would correct the syllable count. For *i* used redundantly as here, cf. l. 146.

2039-40. Line 2039 as given in *D* (see variants) may be read as eight syllables by counting *de* as enclitic after *Ki* (cf. l. 2410), which would make *lui* in l. 2040 refer back to *ren* rather than to *Ki*, in which case we should expect *soi*.

2045-6. 'He who carries only a small burden and tries to mount aloft falters and perishes.'

2057-8. 'There the fire without end burns him who, etc.'

2064. **paine ne quit.** 'does not pain or burn,' cf. *D*.

2069. **Ke totdis.** Cf. l. 2066. The omission of ll. 2066-8 in *C* is clearly a case of haplography.

2072. Cf. Mark 9, 45, 'ubi vermis eorum non moritur, et ignis non extinguitur.'

2072. **desist.** An early example of this verb; Gamillscheg dates it as fourteenth century.

2073–4. Cf. note to ll. 1423–4.

2075–82. The alternation of extreme heat and cold in hell is not prominent in Holy Writ, although we can cite Job 24, 19, 'Transibunt ab aquis nivium ad calorem nimium.' It is rather in mediaeval vision literature that this idea prevails, cf. the punishment of Judas as described in the *Voyage of Saint Brendan* (ed. Waters), 1397 ff. However these two forms of punishment had become standard in the orthodox Christian hell, cf. the *Elucidarium* of Honorius, *Pat. Lat.* CLXXII, col. 1159. It is of interest to note also that the list of punishments given by Honorius corresponds closely to the description of the infernal tortures found in our poem, except that the last, the fiery chains, is not mentioned. Cf. the references given by K. Warnke in his edition of the *Espurgatoire* (Halle 1938), p. xvi, n. 4.

2087. **Ke.** *C* reads *Kar*, which form occurs occasionally in this MS for *ke*, cf. l. 2904.

2094. **Ke.** *C* has the form *Ki*. The substitution of *ki* for *ke* occurs also in *P*, twice when a word beginning with *i* follows, cf. ll. 2560 and 2634 and once before *out* when elision occurs. Forms such as *ki il* are presumably scribal for *k'il* as elided vowels are frequently written by the scribes. *Ki* for *ke* arises doubtless from the fact that *ki* is so frequently written *ke* in the MSS. A similar use of *qui* for *que* occurs in the MS of *Gui de Warewic*, cf. Ewert's edition, I p. xxx. As these cases are exceptional in our text I have emended them consistently.

2097–8. The elect in heaven and the damned in hell can see each other. The suffering of the lost is intensified at the sight of the joys they have missed and the joy of the saved augmented by the sight of the torments they have escaped.   The idea that heaven and hell are visible one to the other is illustrated by the parable of the rich man in hell, see Luke 16, 19–31. A passage similar to that in our text is found in the *Elucidarium* of Honorius, *Pat. Lat.* CLXXII, col. 1161, in which case the rich man is said to have been in the limbus.

2104. **deist.** The reading *deit* of *D* must be for *deist* since the subjunctive would necessarily follow the negative in l. 2103. *C*'s reading *nissist une* is unintelligible.

2105. Although *averont* counts as two syllables only, the line still has nine syllables. Possibly the article *li* is intrusive, but l. 2106 makes this appear improbable.

2109-10. Morawski does not list this proverb, but has collected several others with the same moral; cf. J. Morawski *Proverbes français antérieurs au XVe siècle* (Paris 1925) p. 6.

2111-2. Cf. ll. 129-30.

2115. **nul.** Means 'anybody' or 'somebody,' cf. l. 2115.

2118. 'Who relies entirely on another's action for his salvation.'

2119-20. Cf. Morawski *op. cit.* p. 2.

2125-6. I do not find this statement in the Epistle of St. James but in I John 3, 14 we read 'qui non diligit, manet in morte,' and in 15 'Omnia qui odit fratrem suum, homicida est.'

2152. **leiez.** Scribal for *leiz* or *laiz C.* The second *e* is inorganic.

2166. *Volt* is a preterite, cf. also l. 2200.

2176-9. Cf. Matt. 10, 32-33, 'Omnis ergo qui confitebitur me coram hominibus, confitebor et ego eum coram Patre meo qui in caelis est. Qui autem negaverit me coram hominibus, negabo et ego eum coram Patre meo qui in caelis est.' The author is using the verb *cunoistre* in two senses: first, 'to recognize or admit a fault,' hence 'to confess;' secondly, 'to acknowledge or accept the sinner's repentance.'

2199-2200. 'Whatever confession and repentance, expressed in good works, were not willing to cover up here.' *Volt* is a preterite and is singular agreeing with its nearest subject.

2249-50. 'As the point (centre) is of little value to the circle (*cumpas*), so is the earth insignificant in relation to the sky above.'

2257-8. 'Wherefore [it is called] *celature* in Latin and in our French tongue *peinture.*'

2262. **en chambre.** *Chambre* (dial. *cambre*, Mod. Engl. *camber*) is the OF adjective derived from *camurus*, 'arched', 'vaulted'.

2265. See note to l. 153.

2279. **Aracon.** The correct form is *Arctos*, cf. *Archos* in *D*.

2305. **sun vol.** The reading *sun voil* of *P* cannot be accepted as the orthography *oi* does not occur for open *o*. The scribe doubtless had in mind the phrase *sun voil* 'at will.'

2305-6. **vol:asol.** Cf. the rhyme *fous:avels* 2525. On these rhymes see Phonology, paragraphs 1 and 14.

2316. **sonz.** Cf. the same form in l. 2549 and *repentonce* in l. 2635. Prior claims that this orthography for *an^e* is Kentish and represents the pronunciation *on*. He likewise considers as Kentish the orthography *ie* for *e*, of which several examples occur in MS *P*, cf. *clier* 1543, 2617 and 2697, and *fieble* 147 (see O. H. Prior *Cambridge Anglo-Norman Texts* pp. xxiii and 2). Since *P* is a Canterbury MS, Prior's opinion on this point seems justified.

K

2322. **set.** The rejected form *cest* of *P* may be for *sest* with intrusive *s* before consonant, cf. M. K. Pope *From Latin to Modern French* sec. 1282.

2323. **espigucerent.** Cf. *espigucer* 2431 RC. The scribe of *P* wrote this form but the corrector struck out *-gucerent* and wrote *-erent* above, i.e. *espierent*. The only other known example of this verb is in the *Resurrection Play*, cf. the edition by Jean G. Wright (Paris 1931) 323. The etymon of the word is unknown, but its form and meaning suggest that it belongs to the same word family as the English ' spigot,' ' spike,' etc.

2338. **sodiun.** The reading of R*G* is *ʒodyn(s)* and of *C* *ʒodin*, which is apparently the OF original. The form *ʒodin* occurs in the earliest edition, that of 1477. Migne gives the Greek form ζῷον.

2339-44. The author rejects the legendary origins of the signs of the zodiac as recorded in the *Imago mundi* on the ground that fables are a useless encumbrance and announces that he is going to substitute his own explanations. Nevertheless the explanations are all taken from the *Imago mundi*, where they follow the mention of the classical legends which served as sources of the names.

2349. *P*'s reading *Si* may be merely a scribal slip caused by the *Si* in l. 2348, or it may be for *S'i*, but it is also possible that the scribe of *P* wrote *si* for *se*, cf. l. 2580 where I have read *s'i* but where *se* would be expected, and *ci* in l. 2524 which could represent *si* < *sic*, but also *si* for *se*. Since *ki* occurs for *ke* (cf. note to l. 2094), *si* may stand for *se*, and perhaps also *ni* for *ne*, cf. *n'i* in ll. 146 and 2035. Another possibility is that *si* stands for *sei*. Reduction of tonic *ei* to *i* is attested in *P*, cf. note to l. 648, but no examples occur in final position.

2363-4. It appears that the author misunderstood the Latin text which reads 'quia sol sub hoc signo duobus diebus amplius quam sub aliis moratur.'

2368. **solail.** Cf. note to l. 224.

2383-4. 'Just as the balance swings evenly, and neither side is above or below the other, so . . .'

2391-6. The OF reverses the correct order of the ninth and tenth signs: Sagittarius should come first, then Capricornus, as in the *Imago mundi*.

2399. For Migne's 'solutis nivibus' read 'solutis nubibus'.

2424. Compare *Li Cumpoʒ* 143-4, 'Si i pot esculter Cum l'asnes al harper.' See also *Romania* XXXVII (1908) 220 f.

2430. 'Beware that the desire does not seize you to, etc.' The construction is impersonal but the *vus* has led the scribes to change the verb form. The impersonal construction is regularly followed by *de* (cf. l. 2431), whereas if the construction were *se prendre* meaning 'to begin' it should be followed by *a*.

2435. **a nue.** *P* alone reads *nue* against *veue RC* which is probably correct inasmuch as *P*'s reading, being adverbial, should be *a nu*, an attested phrase.

2438. **cum.** Written in the margin by corrector. The scansion of the line indicates that *qu'il* (R has *qe il*, *D* rewrites, and the line is wanting in *CG*) is the correct reading and that *deigne* is scribal for *deint* (< *dignet*), cf. note to l. 164.

2443. **galac est leit.** This information is in the *Imago mundi* (Cap. XXVIII) in another connection: 'Gallia a candore populi dicitur, *gala* enim lac dicitur;' cf. the edition l. 1127.

2446. **respunt.** The Latin text reads 'quia omnes stellae fundunt in eam sua lumina,' consequently the verb *respunt* must mean 'responds to' or 'reflects the light of' the stars. In the *Divisiones mundi* 506 *respunt* translates the Latin *reflectit* 'turns back (of a horn)', cf. Prior *op. cit.* p. 50.

2448. **cometes lees.** *Cummectees* of *P* is an unattested form invented apparently by the scribe to give a rhyme with *fiees*. R's reading *cometeles* would have to be interpreted as *cometelees* to give a rhyme, which is also inadmissible. These forms seem to be corruptions of *cometes lees*, the reading of *CDG*. The adjective *lees* 'broad' (referring to the tails of the comets?) appears in the line solely in order to provide the rhyme with *fiees*, but it seems preferable to admit the reading rather than accept the doubtful forms of *P* or R. The syllable count is no objection since *cometes* may be read as disyllabic before *lees* if we do not count the atonic *e* of *-es*; cf. note to l. 763.

2449. **gremues.** The normal form is *cremues* as given by *DGR*. Conversely *grasse* in l. 267 was written *crasse* in MS *C*.

2455, **uitante.** The Latin text reads 'cernuntur autem septem diebus, si diutius, octoginta.' The readings of the MSS are *de tante P*, *de tant* R, *ou .viij. C*, *ou vint D*, *v vyt G*. *P* has preserved the *-tante* and *C* has *.viij.* supported by *vyt* in G. I have therefore restored the word *uitante* which must have stood in the original.

2462. **unt.** The Latin reads 'unde et aqueum coelum dicitur.' Thus it appears that *Si unt* translates *unde et*. The scribes seem to have understood *unt* as a verb despite the fact that *cel* is necessarily singular, since they all write *a nun* except *D* who wrote *ad nun*. This mistake is facilitated by the fact that *aveir a nun* is used alongside *aveir nun* in our text.

2478. **liu . . . . liu.** The reading of *C* (the text is based on *C* at this point) in both cases is *lui*, but I have altered it to *liu* to conform to the orthography of *P* which is consistent for this word. The MSS offer both *liu* and *lui*, none of them being entirely consistent except *P*. For a discussion of *lui* for *liu* see Menger *Anglo-Norman Dialect* p. 77.

2484–5. *P* has but one line, the words in square brackets having been lost by internal haplography. *P*, noticing the missing rhyme, left a space, which proves that the error was already in his original. The text has been restored from *RC*.

2504. *esquis* cannot be the past participle of *esquerre*, which would not make sense, but is rather a variant of *eschius* (cf. ll. 526 and 1260) or *eschis* (see Godefroy under *eschif*). The line thus means that God is not haughty or difficult of approach because of his exalted power. Godefroy cites several instances of the spelling *esquis* for this word.

2504. **empirs.** The form *empris* of *P* is an evident metathesis for *empirs* as shown by the rhyme; cf. *brucs* for *burcs* 1099. Since *sustenirs* is the infinitive used as a noun in the oblique case, it should have no *s* (*P* is the only MS which offers *s*); consequently the rhyme is *sustenir:empir*, the latter for *empire* with final atonic *e* dropped in rhyme after a liquid; cf. note to l. 224.

2523. **L'escrit.** The scribe of *P* wrote *Hele crist* and the corrector struck out *Hele. L'escrit* is found in all the other MSS.

2523–5. Cf. Job 20, 27, 'Revelabunt coeli iniquitatem illorum, et terra adversus eos consurget,' cf. also Sap. 5, 21.

2525–6. **fous:avels.** Cf. note to ll. 2305–6.

2533. **si s'en lava.** The end of the line is blank in *P*. The readings of the MSS are: *et bust aussi* R, *si lui lava* C, *e sa seif estancha* D, *si sen leua* G, *et il sen laua* B.

2544. **ventaille.** Cf. the variant *nentaille* of B. The meaning is a light object which cannot resist the wind, the ending *-aille* serving to indicate something of little value. *Ventaille* is probably the same word as *ventail* cited by Cotsgrave meaning a childish toy or whirligig of paper on the end of a stick.

2556. **areré.** The verb *arerer* for *arrierer* is attested for England only, where it became a legal term, cf. the Modern English 'arrears.' We could also read *arere*, but the verb is stronger in meaning and fits the context perfectly.

2590–2. Cf. Gen. 1, 31 and Ecclus. 39, 21.

2613. The subject of *fet* is *Deus* from l. 2605; also in l. 2615 *il* refers to God. In l. 2614 *quil trei* means 'who betrayed him (the sinner).'

2623. **pout.** Perhaps a preterite, but the other MSS have present forms.

2656. **lur ajoirunt.** 'Will rejoice over them.' *Ajoirunt* (cf. also *ajoie* 2661) is for *esjoirunt*. This construction with the dative is cited by Godefroy from the Cambridge Psalter.

2660. **ne.** *nes* of R is the correct reading, cf. *les* in C.

2676–93. On this idea of heavenly mistresses see the discussion in the 'Introduction,' pp. lv, lvi.

2695. **tint.** Perhaps for *tient* the present, which is found in all the other MSS; cf. note to l. 1223.

2701. **ki char.** PG read *ki de char*. The passage is devoted to extolling virginity, which proves that this line must mean 'For the soul whose flesh is not blemished,' i.e. 'is virgin.'

2702. **costeie.** See note to l. 907.

2705–19. For the re-establishment of marriage in heaven see the Introduction, p. lvi.

2705. 'Marriages are there renewed which here, etc.'

2710. The line is difficult, but as written in PR *meprise* appears to be a substantive and the line would mean 'and if ever a misdeed of any sort were [imputed] to it.' In *y ele* replaces *li*, in which case we should have to translate 'If ever it (*espousaile*) were guilty of any transgression.' In either case the line appears to be hypermetrical.

2715. **ele.** *y* omits. It is intrusive from l. 2714.

2731. **glere.** R reads *glerie*. In l. 2734 both P and R read *glerie*, while in ll. 165 and 2719 P reads *glorie* and R *glerie*. In l. 2767 P reads *glere* and R *glerie*. The form *glorie* is apparently scribal for *gloire* as this word may be monosyllabic before a following vowel, cf. l. 2719. *Glere* is an inverse spelling for *gloire*. The diphthong *ei* < tonic free *e* gives *e* in Anglo-Norman, not *oi;* but the orthography *oi* occurs, doubtless through Continental influence; cf. Phonology, paragraph 4. Thus *oi* was a possible spelling for *ei* and *e*, and inversely *e* may stand for *oi*. Similarly C writes *aver* (*aveir*) 2849, and *avoir* 2851.

2762. **ultre sire.** Clearly means the 'Most High.' The reading is guaranteed by the agreement of PRCB. *Sire* is used of God and Christ with adjectives such as *grant*, but I know of no other case of *ultre*. Moreover this word, being normally an adverb, is used with adjectives to express a high degree of some quality, cf. *outrepreux*, *outrecuidant*, etc.

2762. **graviz.** This form occurs in P alone and is probably a variant of *grevez* from *grever* for which the meaning 'aggrieved' is possible.

2765. **mendivetez.** Cf. note to l. 121.

2777. The correct reading is *herberger poez* as found in *GB*.

2788–90. I do not find an exact original for these lines in the writings of St. Paul, but passages abound urging generosity towards the saints who are in need; e.g. Rom. 12, 13.

2792. Cf. Luke 10, 7 and I Tim. 5, 18.

2796. **ledement.** Error for *les* as given by *CB*.

2799. **e.** Omit with *GB*.

2815. **gloiz.** All the other MSS have either *ou* or *u*. After *oi* and *ui* had coalesced the two orthographies were interchangeable, and after *ui* was reduced to *u* both *ui* and *oi* could be used for *u*, which in its turn was interchangeable with *ou* and *o*. This gives a series *oi*, *ui*, *u*, *o* and *ou* as possible orthographies for the vowel in question.

2815. **malatechez.** Cf. the form *maltechez* of B which gives a decasyllabic line by suppression of the prefix.

2817. **degrez.** A reference to the *eschiele de vertu* in l. 2808. The Christian's life was frequently represented as a ladder, cf. the *Scala coeli major* and the *Scala coeli minor* as described by Honorius Augustodunensis in *Pat. Lat.* CLXXII, coll. 1229 ff., and 1239 ff.

2822–5. Cf. I Cor. 2, 9.

2823. **Nen.** Represents *Ne ne* (B); cf. note to l. 1835.

2853. **malfez.** From *malefatos* 'devils'. The line means that (in Hell) they will have few friends and many devils.

2863–4. Cf. Isa. 38, 18.

2876. 'Saved wholly, although he does no other.'

2888–9. Cf. the *Elucidarium* of Honorius Augustodunensis, *Pat. Lat.* CLXXII, col. 1162.

2891. **vermin.** Read *vermine* with B; cf. the rhyme *gastine:vermine* 1261.

2910. **fastengez.** One other example of this word occurs in the *Miroir des Domées* (ed. Aitken), l. 10875 and p. 98. Godefroy defines it as meaning 'dégoûter.' See *REW* 3215 where it is derived from *fastidiare* on the model of *laidengier*.

Appendix, 11 ff. Cf. Luke 2, 1, 'Factum est autem in diebus illis, exiit edictum a Caesare Augusto, ut describeretur universus orbis.'

Appendix, 29. Cf. Luke 2, 2. 'Haec descriptio primo facta est a praeside Syriae Cyrino.'

Appendix, 40. **aurent.** Apparently a variant of *eurent* or *ourent* 'received.'

GLOSSARY

THE glossary is selective; it is intended to include those words, forms and phrases which are peculiar to the text or to Anglo-Norman in form or meaning, and likewise those which are relatively rare in Old French. Words are not included which are in common use in Old French, or which exist in Modern French unaltered in form or meaning except for standard and easily recognized variations. Line-references are complete unless followed by the sign etc. Verbs are listed under the infinitive form, this being followed immediately by a line-reference if it occurs in the text, otherwise by a semi-colon. Unless otherwise stated, nouns are given under the accusative singular with the gender indicated only when it can be determined from the text, and adjectives under the accusative singular masculine. When orthographical variants occur for a word to be glossed, these are usually indicated within round brackets immediately following the entry. Attention is drawn to explanatory notes by the letter *n* immediately after the line-reference. It should be noted that the orthography of forms occurring between lines 2031–2144 and 2820–2920 is that of MS *C*. Elsewhere the orthography is that of MS *P* unless the line-reference is followed by the siglum of another MS.

acerter 2210, *v. a.* certify 180, render evident 2210

ache, *s.* parsley 1344

acorder; *v. a.* harmonize, bring into agreement 176

acoster; *v. refl.* (+*dat.*) lie beside, be adjacent to 907n, 945 *DG*

acostoier (-aier); *v. refl.* (+*dat.*) lie beside, be adjacent to 907 *C*, 945 *C*, 2702 *C*; cf. note to l. 907

acreis, *s.*; *de acrés* besides 2025 ; *en a. de* with augmentation of 2097

acumbler; *v. a.* accumulate, magnify 2151

acunter (acon-); *v. a.* reckon 376 *C*; credit, count 2874

acurt v. **sure**

adés, *adv.* without pause 2406

adobez, *pp.* of **adober,** *v.* (+*de*) endow with 2744

aducie, *pp.* of **aducir,** *v.* (+ *de*) sweeten 2680

adurez, *pp. adj.* enduring, eternal 2914

afeire, *s.*; *prendre a.* take form, exist 314; *de noble a.* great, very important 830; *de naturel a.* by nature, naturally 1647

afermer; *v. a.* found 1052

afoler; *v. a.* harm 17; *pp. adj.* unwise, foolish 2845

afumer; *v. a.* extinguish, damp down 1039

agoille, *s.* needle 2036

agreer; *v. n.* (+*dat.*) please, be popular 733, 1146

aguait, *sm.* ruse, deception 2594

ahan, *s.* torment, distress 1552

ajoir; *fut.* 6 -runt 2656, *pp.* -ie 2661: *v. n.* be joyful 2661; (+ *dat.*) rejoice over 2656n

ajuster; *v. a.* place alongside 2081 D; *v. refl.* (+*dat.*) be alongside 945

aleines, *sf. pl.* vapours 1769

alier; *v. refl.* (+*dat.*) combine with 334

aloer; *v. a.* charge against 2756

amassez, *pp.* of **amasser,** *v.* (+*de*) endow with 2849

amendement, *sm.* reformation, change in way of living 2102

amender, *inf. subs.* reformation 2178

amener; *ind. pr.* 3 **ameine** 405: *v. refl.* (+*dat.*) blend into, mingle with

amerté, *s.* bitterness 1584, 1610

amertume, *sf.* bitterness 1579, 1591, 1614, 1621

amirer (-reer) 384, *v. a.* behold 384n, gaze upon with astonishment 1512n R

amistez, *s.* friendship 2854

amunter, *inf. subs.* rising, exaltation 2505

aneinti, *pp.* of **anentir** *v. a.* annihilate 2561

antif, *adj. subs. nom. pl.* ancients 1095

aparisant (app-) *pres. p. adj.* apparent, visible 290, 1739

aparmemes, *adv.* alongside 1351

apendre; *v. n.* (+*dat.*) appertain to 40, be connected with 905

apernement, *s.* learning 114

apert, *adj.* plain, disclosed 2099; *en a.* plainly, clearly 1601

apresture, *s.* preparation, learning 148

aprise, *sf.* apprenticeship, period of learning 52, 70n

apuail, *s.* base, foundation 369

arbest, *s.* asbestos 1071n

architipes, *sm. nom.* archetype 277

arerer; *v. a.* retard, hold back 2556n

arester; *v. refl.* stay, dwell 676

arpent, *s.* unit of linear measure 2015

arsun, *s.* burning, fire 582, 1318, 1631

ascemer; *v. refl.* prepare 2534

asenee, *pp. adj,* richly endowed 949

aseoir; *pret.* 3 **assist** 926; *pp.* **asis** 794, **assis** 1077, **asise** 2705: *v. a.* establish 2705n; *pp.* situated, located 794, 1077n; *v. refl.* come to rest 926

aserrer; *v. refl.* be limited 1954; (+*dat.*) combine with 320 C; cf. **serrer**

aseur, *adj.* assured, certain 1956

asise, *sf.* arrangement, ordering 393

asol, *s.* axle 2306n

asorbez, *pp. adj.* blind 2803

assens, *s.; de a.* by common accord 2019

asseurer; *v. refl.* rely on, depend on for safety 2115

assis, assist v. **aseoir**

assumer; *v. a.* add up 2027

ataindre; *pp.* -nt 2132: *v. a.* accuse, charge

atemprer (att-), *v. a.* temper, moderate 352, etc.; *pp. adj.* temperate 451, etc.; *v. refl.* regulate one's actions 202

atemprure (att-), *sf.* temperature, weather 406, 414

atendre (att-) 4, *v. a.* await 685 *CG,* 2628; *v. n.* be attentive 1901; (+*a*) direct attention to, discourse on 4

atenvir; *v. n.* become vaporous, 1458, 1634

aturner; *subj. pr.* 3 aturt 251: *v. a.* turn toward 251; arrange, set 1966

aubun 259, 260, 264; **al-** 265: *s.* albumen, white of egg

auner; *v. a.* assemble 1357

aurner; *v. a.* arrange, dispose 2282, 2511

avaler, *inf. subs.* abasement 2506

avels v. **avols**

avenir; *ind. pr.* 3 avent 1507n: *v. refl. impers.* happen

aventer; *v. a.* fan 954, 1528

aventure, *sf.* coming event 183, 186, 203; fortune 1108

avesprer, *inf. subs.* evening 1161

avironement, *sm.* surroundings 2458

aviruns, *s. pl.* oars (by metonymy oarsmen, sailors) 1656n

avols (avels), *sm.; nom. sg.* will 240; *pl.* desires 2131, 2717; pleasures 2526n

avuez, *sm. nom.* advocate, defender 2759

baees, *s. pl.* chasms 1512

baer; *ind. pr.* 3 **bee** 1507: *v. n.* yawn, crack open: *pres. p.* **baant** agape 668; (of dogs) with mouths wide-open 1540; *pres. p. adj.* gaping 647, yawning, deep 1486

baillie (-ilie), *sf.* possession, power 111, 1314; high estate 2697

baldie, *sf.* joy, transport 2699

baraigne (-ingne), *adj.* (+*de*) barren of 1134, 1172; deprived of 1348; free from 1350

bandun, *sm.* jurisdiction 563, 1317; *aveir en b.* hold sway over 966; *a b.* in abundance 134, 598, 1524

bee v. **baer**

bevee, *sf.* drink 600

baud(e), *adj.* (+*dat.*) well disposed towards 344

besturnez, *pp. adj.* turned backwards 603

betum, *s.* bitumen, mineral pitch 1647, 1650

betumee, *s.* deposit of bitumen 1517

betumeis, *s. pl.* deposit of bitumen 1645

blemie, *pp.* of **blemir,** *v. a.* blemish 2701n

borne, *adj.* squint-eyed, shining obliquely 2392

boves, *sf. pl.* caverns 1490

brai, *sm.* outcry, tumult 2086

bruir; *pres. p.* **bruant** 441 : *v.* burn, be hot

burc 2835, **bruc** 1099; *sm.* town, city

carké, *pp.* of **carker,** *v. a.* load 2033

cas, *sm.; en itel cas* in such a situation 1830; *en un cas* without change, constant 2508

cervin, *adj.* of a deer 643

chais, *pp. subs. pl.* sinners, fallen 2646

chambre, *s.* trellis, arch; *en c.* arched 2262

chanuz, *adj. pl.* grey-haired, white-haired 611

chaser; *v. a.* endow with domains; *pp.* -sez 2767, -scez 2851, **casee** 542, rich in, endowed with, possessing

cheitifvesce, *s.* pettiness, meanness 25

chinche, *adj.* stingy, mean 2846

clore; *ind. pr.* 3 **clot** 380, **clost** 2490; 5 **cloez** 2794; 6 **cloent** 2461; *pp.* **clos** 924: *v. a.* hold, envelop, enclose

clos, *s.* prison, enclosure 1717

començail, *sm.* beginning 1474, 2417

compasser; *v. a.* design, plan 396

composter; *v. a.* create, set up 1585, 2299

conceivre; *pret.* 3 -çut 274: *v.* conceive a plan, decide; *pres. p.* -cevanz fertile, fecund 931n

confermer; *v. a.* confirm 178, establish securely 2300 R

confesse (cun-), *s.* confession 2100, 2199, 2642

confus, *adj.* confounded, in confusion 1420, 2501 C

consonance, *s.* harmonious sound 1979n

content, *s.* pleasure, satisfaction 1918

corupture, *s.* corruption 1782

costé, *sm.* side, flank 643, 1102, 2349, 2499

costeier; *v. n.* (+*dat.*) be close to 2702n

coveitie (cuv-, cuvai-) *s.* covetousness 2060, 2676, 2695

creatur, 214, 2627; *nom.* **crieres** 238: *sm.* creator

creature, *sf.* creation (collective) 213; creation (result of creative act) 2569; creature 2201; thing created 2204, 2520

cressant, *sm.* growth 1344

criees, *sf. pl.* things created 294

crier; *v. a.* create 284, 288, 296, etc.

crieres v. **creatur**

crouller; *v. n.* rock, totter 360

crus, *sm.* hollow space, cavern 1502, 1509, 1511

crusesce, *s.* vein, narrow opening 1531

cumparer; *fut.* 3 -rra 2116: *v. a.* pay for, expiate

cumpas (co-), *sm.* circle 395, 1909, etc.

cunceler 86, *v. a.* dissimulate, conceal

cunoistre; *v.* know, be acquainted with 38, 2464; acknowledge, confess, witness 2176, 2177, 2178, 2721; *v. refl.* recognize one's sins 2179

cuntenanz, *en vint e set jurs c.* within the space of twenty-seven days 1841

cuntruver (con-); *v. a.* invent, discover, conceive 1940, 2324, 2339

curbs, *adj. pl.* curved 606

cursage (cor-), *s.* body 587; *prendre c.* take on bodily form 1673, 1793

curteis, *adj. subs.* person with polished manners; *fol. c.* empty-headed dandy 74

danter, *inf. subs.* taming 674

danture, *s.*; *metre en d.* tame, domesticate 702

deboneire, *adj.* generous, noble 289

debriser; *v. a.* crush 2717

dechacer 579, *v. a.* drive out

decrest v. **descreistre**

decurt, *ind. pr.* 3 of **decurre,** *v. n.* flow down 500

defalt, *ind. pr.* 3 of **defailir,** *v. n.* (+*de*) falter in 243

defalture, *s.*; *sans d.* without error 216

defenderunt, *fut.* 6 of **defendre,** *v. refl.* part, open 1662

defendre 126, *v. a.* and *refl.* defend, protect 126, 164, 553, 586n, 2632; (+*inf.*) prevent from 2310

defere 2573, *v. a.* kill 1175; spoil, render unusable 1254; end 1705; undo 2573

defie, *ind. pr.* 3 of **desfier,** *v. a.* reject 160, defy 2688

defire; *v. n.* dissolve 1617; vanish, cease 1786

defrait, *pp. adj.* decrepit, broken down 575

defulez, *pp.* of **defuler,** *v. a.* downtrodden 2738

delit, *sm.*; *par bon d.* gladly 143; *a d.* merrily 1122

delivre, *adj.* quick, ready 19; swift, nimble 1257; free from 2240

deluje, *sm.* deluge, flood 487, 926, 1115

demenez, *pp.* of **demener,** *v. a.* agitate 1676

demier; *v. refl.* crumble, dissolve 328

demise, *pp.* of **demetre,** *v. a.* separate, part 2716

demoist(e), *ind. pr.* 3 of ?, *v. a.* wet, soften 1578n

demurer; *v. n.* dwell 2731

demustrer; *v. a.* indicate, show 2314

departir; *v. a.* divide, separate 1459, 1757, 1986

depescer 1651, *v. a.* dissolve 1651; break into pieces 2808

depraver; *v. a.* decry, vilify 31

deruter; *v. a.* rupture, break open 1510

descreistre; *ind. pr.* 3 **descret** 1467, **decrest** 1829: *v. n.* fall (of sea) 1467, become smaller 1829

deserrer; *v. a.* scatter 1749

deserte, *sf.* merited punishment 2054; *sanz d.* without having merited it 2558

deservir; *v. a.* deserve, merit 1438, 2070, 2550

desheriter; *v. a.* render uninhabitable 398

desist, *ind. pr.* 3 of **desister,** *v. n.* cease, desist 2072n

deslier; *v. a.* loose 2399

desment, *ind. pr.* 3 of **desmentir,** *v. refl.* lose intensity, be moderated, cease 1436

despenser, *sm.* dispenser, distributor 2780

despite; *pp.* of **despire,** *v. a.* scorn, reject 782n

desport, *s.* pleasure 2716

destempree, *sf.* discharge 1522n

destincter; *v. a.* distinguish, differentiate, separate, characterize 257, 469, 1983, 2332

destreit (-**roit**), *s.* distress, embarrassment, difficulty 2165, 2196

destresces, *s. pl.* narrow and confined cavities 1532

desturber 2143, *v.* perturb, trouble

detrait, *pp.* of **detraire,** *v. a.* rack, torture 2738

detrier; *v. a.* hamper, delay, resist 28

deverie, *s.* folly 74

devie, *pp.* of **devier,** *v. a.* lead astray 206n; see Tob.-Lom. s. v. 'desvoiier'

devise, *sf.* plan, design 192; *par d.* strictly 2711

deviser (div-); *v. a.* and *refl.* expound, plan, devise, distinguish, separate, divide 173, 188, 394, 1358, 1587, 1911

devurement, *sm.* bottomless pit 1428, immense opening 1477, 1537

diu, two 1689n.

dreiturer, *adj.* equitable, just 2605

droiture (drei-), *sf.* uprightness, justice 209, 2578

durer, *v. n.* be resistant 1630

efforcer; *v. refl.* (+*de*) struggle, strive 1534

eines, *s. pl.; es e.* in suspense 1770n

el, *pron.* anything else 2147

electiun, *s.* choice 106

elident, *ind. pr.* 6 of **eslider,** *v. n.* glide, slip 1773

enblemiz, *pp.* of **enblemir,** *v. a.* mar, sully 2907

enchaufer; *v.* heat, warm 2376

encumbrer 2342, *v.* hinder, confuse

encumbrers, *sm. pl.* encumbrance 2240; *faire ses e.* encumber 1186

encuntrement, *s.* meeting, contact 1927

encuser; *v. a.* accuse 2520, etc.

enditer; *v. a.* set forth, edit, write 2, 245

endroit, *prep.; e. soi* in one's own right 472

endurci, *pp. adj. subs. pl.* hardened sinners 2106

endurer; *v. n.* live 618, endure 2766

enerrer 2618, *v. a.* secure by bond, engage to purchase by paying a deposit

enercir (enn-); *v. n.* become black 581, 612

enfantomer 2144, *v. a.* bewitch, bewilder

enfundrer; *v. n.* sink 1369, *v. a.* engulf 1514

englutir; *ind. pr.* 3 -tist and -te: *v. a.* swallow up 502, 511

enhabiter; *v. a.* inhabit 397, 428

enhaucer; *v. a.* exalt 2505

enmaler; *v. a.* enclose 264; *v. refl.* be enclosed 260

enpeindre; *ind. pr.* 3 -eint and -aint, 6 -eignent: *v. a.* smite, clash against 1504; drive, force 1726, 1777; fix, set (one's heart on) 2601; *v. refl.* push, exert pressure 1519

enpeinte, *pp.* of **enpeindre,** *v. a.* portray, reproduce 874

enpenser; *v. n.* (+*de*) remember, think of 2788

enplie, *ind. pr.* 3 of **enplier,** *v a.* employ 2689

enprendre; *v. a.* undertake to acquire 132; take possession of 1385; kindle 2058

enprist v. **enprendre**

enserrer; *v. refl.* penetrate, work into 389

entendre 24, *v. a.* understand 2264, 2422; *v.* listen 407; (+*a*) fix attention on, listen to attentively 24, 235, 2147, 2424

enterinement, *adv.* entirely 1597

enticer 2621, *v. a.* entice, tempt 2092, 2621

entredous, *adv.* between 1831

entrelacer; *v. a,* bind together 336

entrelais, *s.* break, interruption 2731

enturner; *v. refl* (+*en*) change into 325

envers, *adj.* growing inward 666

envirun (**-on**), *sm.* circumference 761, 2500; everything round-about 1929; *en ses enviruns* within its boundaries 723

enviruner; *v. a.* surround, encircle 266, 513

erree, *s.* course, route 1916

erres, *s. pl.; metre en e.* pledge, place in bond 2617

escale, *sf.* shell (of an egg or snail) 259, 263, 713

eschaloine, *sf.* shallot 806

eschars, *adj. nom.* (+*de*) poor in 1396; *nent e.* full measure 1962

eschevi, *adj.* slender, svelte, elegant 2677

eschius (**esquis**), *adj. nom.* (+ *de*) deprived of 526, 1260; inaccessible, unapproachable 2504n

eschole, *sf.; de bone e.* sound, scholarly 30

esclarie, *pp. adj.* brilliant, shining 2670

esclarcie, *pp. adj.* brilliant 2670 CGB

escrier; *v. a.* intone 2668

esforcer; *v. a.* re-enforce, strengthen 2809

esgarrez, *pp. adj.* abandoned 2806

eslaver (**ell-**) 2609, *v. a.* cleanse, wash away 2609, 2636; *v. refl.* cleanse from sin 2642

eslink, *s.; en e.* perpendicularly 2030n

espanir; *v. refl.* spread, expand 1457

esparnie, *ind. pr.* 3 of **esparnier,** *v. a.* hoard 112

espars, *adj. nom.* extended, scattered 1395

espeise, *s.* density, heaviness 1934

espenir 2182, 2916, **-ner** 2899; *pp.* **-ie** 2198, 2663, 2703, **-nez** 2893n: *v. a.* expiate, redeem

espeudre 2285, *v. a.* explain, interpret

espigucer 2431 RC, *perf.* 6 **-cerent** 2323n: *v.a.* investigate, pry into

espirer; *v. a.* inspire 156, 2872; *v. n.* breathe 2535

espirement, *sm.* attraction 1465; blowing, drawing, suction 1491, 1495, 1713; breath 1669

espirit (**-per-**) sm. exhalation 1430n; breath 1493n; spirit 2484

esploit (**-eit, -et**), *sm.* rapid course 535, 1464; *en face en Deu sun e.* should use it to strive toward God 2554

espoigne, *s.* sponge 1516n

esprendre 1536, *v. n.* break out (of fire) 1536; *v. refl.* catch fire 1520, 1628, 1630; *espris de feu* on fire, ablaze 1073, 1403

espundre; *ind. pr.* 3 **-nt** 2289, *pp.* **-ns** 2275: *v. a.* explain, interpret

esquis v. **eschius**

essoin, *sm.* obstacle, difficulty 1380

estage, *sm.* arrangement, ordering, outline 250

estal, *sm.* location, position, abode 417, 454; *faire e.* be situated 1008

estanc, *s.* pool, small stagnant lake 1409

estant, *pres. p.* of **ester,** still, standing, stagnant 1304, 1646, 1740; *pres. p. adj.* viscous 1650.

esté, *s.* extent, size 750

ester 350, *ind. pr.* 3 **esta** 755, 789, 2136, **estat** 367, 801, 1235, **estait** 1609, **esteit** 811, 1707, **estet** 803; 6 **estunt** 318, 1741; *fut.* 3 **esterra** 119; *pres. p.* **estant** 1304, etc.: *v. n.* exist, be located, be placed, stand; **li esterra bien** will stand him in good stead 119

estover, *inf. subs.* that which is necessary 2555

estraine, *s.*; **aveir e. de** have store of, display 1846

estree, *s.* way, path, course 1876

estreindre; *v. a.* harass, beset 2140

estreitement, *adv.* diligently 169, 2751; niggardly 2782

estrus, *adj.*; **a e.** certainly 1100, purposefully, without hesitation 1809

estuné, *pp. adj.* thoughtless, indifferent 2227

estunt v. **ester**

estur, *s.* struggle, combat 572, 2634

esturmir; *v. a.* shake, move, dislodge 374

ewus, *adj.* watery 2298

ewin, *adj.* watery, of water 2462

fableant, *sm. pl.* storytellers, storywriters 1539

facunde, *sf.* eloquence, facility of speech 683

faitement (fei-), *adv.* in such a manner, 553, 2744

faitres (-ters) v. **fetur**

faiture (feit-, fet-), *sf.* creation, thing created 189, 2570; creation, created universe 215, formation, fashion, nature 250, 1999, 2246, 2297, 2371

falture (faul-), *sf.* error, mistake 2017, 2116

fanc, *s.* mud 1578

fastengez, *pp.* of **fastengier,** *v.* (+*de*) be surfeited with 2910n

faucener, *sm.* liar, deceiver, falsifier 2517

feindre; *ind. pr.* 3 **-nt,** *pret.* 6 **-ntrent:** *v. refl.* pretend 976, 2150

feint, *pp. adj.* half-hearted, faint 475, 2468

feintise, *s.* pretence 85

felun 1224, 2388; *nom. pl.* **fel** 596: *adj.* treacherous, disloyal

fermer; *v. a.* found, establish 731, 756, 1099; make solid, cement 1653, 2300

fes, *sm.* weight, burden 2045

fetur 2574, 2575; *nom.* **faitres** 215, **faiters** 2583: *sm.* creator

ficher; *v. refl.* (+*dat.*) attach to, adhere to 1992

figure, *sf.* type, pattern 280; shape, form, likeness 1094, 1107, 1853, 2203; symbol, representation 2000

figurer; *v. a.* portray, represent 204; conceive in the mind 282

finement, adv. certainly 1848

finer 890, *v.* end, finish 868, etc.

finir; *v.* end, finish 1162, 1206, etc.

flambe, *s.* flame 1521, 1536

flat, *adj.* word borrowed from English 660

flestrir; *v. n.* wither 582

floter; *v. n.* move without resistance, float 360

floz, *s. pl.* tide, flood-tide, high tide 1499n, 2453

fluie, *s.* river 500

flum (-un), *sm.* river 721, 745, etc.

fluvie, *sm.* river 532, 634

folage, *sm.* folly 52

foletez, *s.* folly, foolishness 2856

folif, *adj.* erratic 1798

folur, *sf.* folly 2626

forein (-ren, -reigne), *adj.* outer, outermost, outlying, distant 397, 402, 1267, 1551; (of hell) strange 1401

fort, *adj.* severe, bitter, strong, large 426, 456, 904, etc.; difficult 2134, 2137, 2584; *adj. subs.* difficulty, danger 2657; *a f. adv.* vigorously 1124, 1129

franchement, *adv.* freely 1503

freint, *ind. pr.* 3 of **freindre,** *v. a.* break 718

frestelement, *sm.* music (of flutes) 1928

frivole, *sf.* idle chatter 18

fruis, *s.* tumult, uproar, din 1535

fuin, *adj.* fiery 1729, 1812, 1854, 1863, 2245

fuir; *v. a.* and *n.* dig 387, 1377

fundement, *s.* foundation 824

funder 1666, *v. a.* found 737, etc.; place, set 1666

fundez, *pp. adj.* learned, well-informed 36

funt, *ind. pr.* 3 of **fundre,** *v. n.* fall, sink 1760

furbie, *pp.* of **furbir,** cleansed 2664; *pp. adj.* smooth, glib 45

furnie, *ind. pr.* 3(?) of **furnir,** furnish, present 1178n

fust, *sm.* tree 495, 1374; beam, timber 927

gamme, sf. musical scale 1950

garant, *s.* protection 494

garir 128, *v. a.* and *refl.* protect, save 128, 475

garnir 199, *v. a.* warn, forewarn, counsel, prepare, fortify, provide, protect 130, 182, etc.

garnissement, *s.* protection, provision, preparation 131

gehir 2608, *ind. pr.* 3 **geist** 2158: *v. a.* confess, avow

gel, *sm.* cold, frost 410, etc.

gelee, *sf.* hoarfrost 229, 1768; cold, frost 456, etc.

(1) **gelus,** *adj.* frosty, cold 1897

(2) **gelus,** *adj.* desirous, zealous 2456

geometrie, *s.* geometry 378

glasçun, *s.* piece of ice 2402

gloiz, *s.* glutton 2815

graignus (granus), *adj. nom.* irritated 2762 B, 2846 B

grant, *sm.* size 1353

graviz, *pp.* aggrieved, annoyed 2762n

gre(z), *s.* favor, goodwill 2870; *de g.* gladly, willingly, with pleasure 510, 2416, etc.; *venir a g.* suit, please 1788; *prendre a g.* take into favor, be well-disposed towards 2880

gref, *adj.* harmful 2417

gremues, *pp.* feared 2449n

gresil 230, 1690, **grisil** 1754, 2390, 2396: *s.* sleet

grevance, *s.* grievance, nuisance 322; *en g.* in danger, in distress 2174; *a g.* overburdened to saturation point 1762

grever 2188, *v. a.* burden, weigh down, distress 2188, 2503; lie heavily on, oppress 2268

greynard, *adj. nom.* irritated 2846 G
guast, *s.* uncultivated land, wilderness 483
guastés, *pp. adj. pl.* waste, desolate 529
guastine, *s.* desert, waste land 881
guerpir; *v. a.* abandon 2526
guez, *s. pl.* source, spring, fountain 1564
guier; *v. a.* turn, direct 21, 2354; guide 2092; *a vielesce lur tens guient* they approach old age 594; *v. refl.* direct its course 522, 1012, 1556, 2682
gutette, *sf.* little drop 2516

habitacle, *sm.* dwelling-place, abode 2241
habitement, *sm.* inhabitation 424
haitez, *adj. pl.* merry 2898, 2903
han, *s.* pain, suffering 590
haschees, *s. pl.* catastrophe, upheaval 1513
haunter (han-) 2394, *v. a.* associate with 354; frequent 2394
haur, *sf.* spite, hate 2086, 2631
helmez, *pp.* of **helmer,** (+*de*) armed with, protected by 2743
herberger 2777, *v. a.* lodge 2727, 2777; *v. n.* dwell 771
heriter; *v. n.* enjoy possession 792, 1091; dwell 1239
humur, *s.* humidity, wet weather 1697

iban, *s.* ebony tree 1374n
idle 540, etc., **ydle** 1284, etc.: *sf.* island
ignel, *adj.* quick 20; swift 519, 1927
ignelement, *adv.* swiftly 1802, 1924, 2263

ignelesce, *s.* speed 1799

jofne, *adj.* young 115n
jointure, *sf.* structure, composition 2001
jurent, *perf.* 6 of **gesir,** *v. n.* lie 2726

kanz, *prep.* along with 1711n
kernu, *adj.* (of comet) possessing a tail 2450

(1) **lai,** *sm.* lake 998; lake of fire 2864, 2866
(2) **lai** 2730, 2708, **ley** 776: *sf.* law
largetez, *s. pl.* alms, generous gifts 2852
late, *adj.* broad 746n
laur, *sf.* width, breadth 759, 1229, 1912
lé=les, *def. art. pl.* 602, 623, 989, 1360, 2431, 2529
lé 2488, *f. pl.* **lees** 713, 1489, 2448: *adj.* broad
lé 2654, **lez** 2736, 2903, *adj.* joyful
ledement, *adv.* wickedly, basely, shamefully 2792, 2796
lee, *adj. f.* ice-bound 1190n
leel, *adj.* according to law, full, honest 2567
leiez, *adj. pl.* ugly 2152n
leis, *adv.* yonder 478
lettrure, *s.* writing, literary work 198
(1) **lez,** *prep.* beside 633, etc.
(2) **lez,** *s.* side; *a lez* beside, alongside 2494
liement, *s.* combination 312
liquur, *sf.* liquid 1568, liquid form 1756
lisant, *pres. p.* of **lire;** *en escrit l.* on reading the Scriptures 1487; *sm.* book, writing 1366

losenger, *inf. subs.* flattery, entice-
ment, deception 2614
(1) **luer** (**lo-**); *v. a.* praise 117,
2658, 2863
(2) **luer**, *inf. subs.* praise 163
luez, *pp.* of **luer**, *v. a.* reward, pay
2873
luur, *sf.* light 1832, 1834, 1874,
2083; brilliance, glow 744, 2309

maen, *adj.* medium sized 1303
maistrie, *sf.* power, brilliance 2698
malatechez, *s. nom.* person of
evil characteristics 2815
maleurez, *adj. pl.* ill-fated, unfor-
tunate 2225
malfé, *sm.* devil 2143, 2186, 2192,
2853n; **malvé**, evil creature, 1336
(*cf. note on* 115).
malostru, *adj.* ugly, deformed,
uncouth 561
maluré, *sm.* devil 2572, 2576; cf.
maleurez
manauntie, *sf.* habitation, abode
2665
maneir 444, *v. n.* dwell, remain
444, etc.; *v. a.* inhabit 461n
mansiun, *s.* habitation, inhabitable
country 1460
marchandie, *sf.* acquisition 67n
marchent, *ind. pr.* 6 of **marchir** *v.
n.* lie beside, be contiguous 892
marinail, *sm.* pl. sailors 1544
marine, *s.* saltwater, sea 1595
medlee, *s.* confusion 324
medler (**mell-**) ; *v.* mix, mingle 16,
948, 1813, 1815; *v. refl.* (+*a*)
mingle with 405 CG
melz v. **meus**
mendive, *ind. pr.* 3 of **mendiver**, *v. n.*
be poor, be mendicant 121n
mendivetez, *s.* indigence, state of

beggary 2765; cf. note to l. 121
menur 933, 986; *nom.* **mendre**
1997, 2187, 2290: *adj.* lesser,
smaller
merciez, *pp.* of **mercier**, *v. a.* pardon
2864
mesmes, *adv.*; *a m. de* as far as 896
mesprendre, *v. n.* transgress 2707
mesprise, *s.* transgression, fault,
sin 2710n
meus (**melz**), *adv.* better 1734, 2094,
2113, 2360; *le meus* the better
2327
meut v. **mut**
milluien 351, **miluein** 399: *adj.*
middle, central, intermediary
mireur, *s.* glimmer, faint light 2310
(1) **mist**, *pret.* 3 of **metre**, 348, 872,
2018; *pret.* 6 **mistrent** 198, 1978
(2) **mist**, *pret.* 3 of **maneir**, 814, 819,
1279; *pret.* 6 **mistrent** 1321
moble, *adj.* mobile, in motion 258
mote, *s.*; *en m.* in motion 254n
motere, *adj.* subversive 48n
muel, *sm.* yoke of an egg 260,
261, 265, 267
muist, *ind. pr.* 3 of **mugir**, *v. n.*
bellow 698
muiste, *adj.* moist, damp 342, 343,
1769, 1778
muistie, *adj.* moist 341n
muit v. **mut**
muncel, *s.* heap, pile 1524
murs, *s. pl.* customs, habits 2811,
2819 PR
musard, *sm.* trifler, giddy person
2428
musarder 2428, *v. n.* act irrespon-
sibly
mut 1643, 2543; **muit** 360n; **meut**
1680n R; *ind. pr.* 3 of **muveir**,
v. n. move

L

muvable, *adj.* restless, mobile 1718

natre, *adj.* strange, odd 565

naturelment, *sm.* natural state, nature 1629

navie, *s.* ship, Appendix 7

neer (noier); *v. a.* destroy, kill, drown 488, 710, 840, 1116, 1160n

neiresce, *s.* black colour 1236

neis 149, **nes** 2187, 2823; **nis** 487, 824, 2671: *adv.* even; **neis un** no one 617;

niule, *s.* mist, fog 230, 1769; water vapour 2460; cloud 1414, 1662

nurir (nurr-); *v. a.* produce 715; nourish, sustain 864, 1573

of, *sm.* egg 258, 1858

offe, *s.* particle, pellet, flake 1760n

or, *s.* air, wind 954

ord, *adj. pl.* vile, filthy 1430

oree, *s.* wind 625

orin, *adj.* golden 1298

orine, *sf.* origin 316, etc.

os, *sm.* profit, use 1305

ost, *s.* host, army 821, 823

overaines (uv-), *s. pl.* works, acts 2590, 2610

(1) ovrer (uv-) 2510, *v. n.* work, labour 303, 2510

(2) ovrer, *s.* worker 2792

palu(z), *sm. nom.* marsh 844, 981

parfin, *s.*; *a la p.* finally 1087

parigneler, *adj.*, exceedingly swift 1257

paringal 440; **-igal** 2385, 2752: *adj.* equal, similar

parhonir; *v. a.* ruin, destroy 2111

parreindre 2208; *v. a.* redeem

passer; *v.a.* transgress, disregard 2793

pece, *sf.*; *une p.* awhile 1080; *bone p.* rich district 1168

peisse, *sf.* balance, scales 2383

pelote, *s.* small ball 253, 359

penus (-uz), *adj.* afflicted, full of pain 1426, 2789

perir; *v. a.* ruin, undo 2562

pinc, *s.* small hole (re-enforcing negation) 2006n.

pius, *adj. nom.* merciful 2605

plan, *adj. pl.* clear, plain 1272

plede, *ind. pr.* 3 of **plaidier,** *v. n.* (+*a*) quarrel with 340

plener, *adj.* complete, full 1962

plenté, *s.* plenty 1626, 2818; *a p. adv.* immensely 981

plentif, *adj.* plenteous, productive 1173, 1387; (+*de*) abounding in 1276

plet, *s.*; *tenir p.* remember, take into account 2222

plier; *v. n.* turn, wind 327; *v. refl.* (+*vers*) turn toward 1824

pluius, *adj.* rainy 1848, 2398

(1) point (pui-), *sm.* point, part 179, 1988; spot 1814, 1849; instant, moment 2115; centre (of circle) 2248, 2249, 2253; *adv.* a little 497; (re-enforcing negation) 148, 846, 2006, 2164

(2) point (pui-), *ind. pr.* 3 of **poindre,** *v.* goad, sting 2066, 2067

porpeis, *sm.* porpoise 1657, 1660

pour v. **puur**

poverte, *s.* poverty 84, 2051, 2795

prendre; *v. refl.*; *se p. a* adhere to, cleave to 109; *se p.* begin 1667; *v. impers.* (+*dat.*) be seized by desire 2430n

pris, *sm.*; *de p.* worthy, excellent 838, etc.; *aveir en p.* hold dearly 1948

priser (pre- proi-) 800, *v. a.* prize, esteem 800n, etc.

privestez, *s. pl.* secrets 2437

(1) **privez,** *adj.* secret, hidden 1563n

(2) **privez,** *s. pl.* elect (of God) 2791, 2814

pulentie, *sf.* vileness 307

pulser; *v. a.* drive, press, impel, 1627n, 1719

purent v. **pestre**

purpostement, *adv.* intentionally (?) 650n

purpre, *sm.* cloth of royal purple 1364n

purquant, *adv.* wherefore 2257

purseisir; *v. a.* seize upon 1758

purtreire 275; *v. a.* portray

purtreiter (-tret-); *v. a.* represent 1106; plan, arrange 2470

purtreture, *sf.* portrayal, description 218, 1093

purvertir (per- RG); *v. a.* upset, overthrow, defeat 209

purvoir; *v. a.* foresee 203, 211; ordain 278, 286; *v. refl.* examine, judge 2191

puur (pour), *sf.* stench 1414, 1434; vileness 2636

puz, *sm.* well 1376; pit (of hell) 2847

pyride, *s.* fire-stone, pyrite 741n

quite, *adj.* free from hommage, without overlordship 736, 1048, 1112; (+*de*) free from 485, 1580

raent v. **rendre** (2)

rai, *sm.* ray, beam 1735, etc.

raim, *s.* branch 2516

ramponuz, *adj. subs. nom.* reviler 2815

rebukee, *pp. adj. f.*, blunted, dulled 661n

rebundir; *v. n.* re-echo, vibrate 1929

reburs, *adj.*; a r. in opposite direction 1804; backwards 2367

reclos, *s.* prison, enclosure 1717 RC

recomencer; *v. a.* reproduce 302

reconsez *pp.* of **reconser,** *v. a.*, conceal, hide 2909

recrurent, *pret.* 6 of **recreire,** *v. n.* become weary, renounce 2725

(1) **recuvrer,** *sm.* recovery, escape, salvation 1412

(2) **recuvrer;** *v.* (+*a*) recover 103

refraindre; *v. a.* hold in check, repress 2131; *v. refl.* restrain oneself 2599

refui, *sm.* refuge, asylum 2797

refunt, *ind. pr.* 6 of **refundre,** *v. a.* pour back, make to flow back (of tide) 1466n

regeir 2181, *v. a.* confess, avow

reguier; *v. a.* turn back, direct back 434; cf. **guier**

remuable, *adj.* changeable 256

remuvement, *s.* stirring, movement 1679n

(1) **rendre** 66; *v. a.* return, restore 2236, etc.; return, reciprocate 163; emit, pour forth again 1478, 1481, 1538; *r. cunfessiun* confess 2148; *r. raisun de* answer for 2790; *le travail r.* expend the effort 66

(2) **rendre** 166; *pp.* **raent** 2579 C: *v. a.* redeem

repairer (-pei-) 2607, *v. n.* return 1564, 1603; *r. a merci* turn back to mercy 2607; *r. en soi* fall back on itself 2624

repentement, *sm.* repentance 2101

repentir 2043, *ind. pr.* 3 **-nt**, *fut.* 6 **-terunt**, *pres. p.* **-tant**: *v. n.* repent 2043, 2199, 2721; *v. refl.* 2564, 2641

reprendre 62; *v. a.* resume 1474, 1878, 1906; belittle, deride 113; *r. od grace* receive back generously 62

reprent 1471, cf. note.

reprover, *sm.* reproof, correction 2093

reschiner; *v. n.* grimace, show the teeth 1342

resort, *sm.* succor, remedy, 1408 2549

resplendir 1738; *ind. pr.* 3 **-nt**, 1764, **-ndit**, 1792: *v. n.* shine

resplendisant, *pres. p. adj.* shining 695; *adj. subs. pl.* creatures of fiery nature 358

respundre; *v. n.* answer, reply 97, 2120, 2652; (+*dat.*) reflect the light of 2446n; *v. a.* set forth, Appendix 32

respuns, *s.* reply, Appendix 40

retraire (**-rei-**) 41, *v. a.* withdraw 658, 1466, 2110; (+*de*) lead away from 41: *v. n.* retreat 1463, 1476; (+*de*) renounce 2557: *v. refl.* (+*de*) escape from 2593; (+*a*) come back to 2574

retreanz, *s. nom. pl.* ebb-tide, ebbing 1500

rettez, *pp.* of **retter**, call to account 2776

returner; *v. a.* change, transform 1896; *sercle returnee* fully described circle 323

revalent, *ind. pr.* 6 of **revaleir**, *v. n.* (+*dat.*) be useful to 124

revert, *ind. pr.* 3 of **revertir**, *v. n.* (+*en*) turn into 1768; *en sei r.* returns to its source 1602n

revest, *ind. pr.* 3 of **revestir**, *v. a.* take the form of 2346

richetez, *s. pl.* riches 2836

rober (**-bb-**); *v. a.* pillage 821, rob 2562

rubes, *s. pl.* pillage, robbery 483

rundesce, *sf.* disc 1819, sphere 1913

ruver; *v. a.* order 1588

ruvir; *v. n.* be ruddy, glow 1843, 2313, 2315

sabelun, *s.* pile of sand 1523

sal gemme, *s.* rock salt 1616n

salce, *adj.* salt 1623

salse (**sause**), *sf.* salt water, brine 1560, 1580

salvetez, *s.* salvation 2868

salz, *s. pl.* rising and falling (of tide) 1471n

sarcu, *sm.* sarcophagus 627

sauner, *sm.* evaporating bed for salt 1620

seant, *sm.* location, position 348

seisine (**sai-**), *sf.* possession 996, 1316; nature, character 1596

senilite, *s.* moon stone, selenite 743n

serain, *sm.* evening, dusk 409, 2313

seri, *adj.* harmonious, serene 2691

serpent, *sf.* serpent 10n, 11; *sm.* 527, etc.

serré, *pp. adj.* thick, impenetrable 671

serrer; *v. refl.* (+*a*) cling to, adhere to, combine with 320

set, *ind. pr.* 3 of **seoir**, *v. n.* be situated, be located 620, etc.; *v. refl. do.* 1294

seurement, *adv.* with assurance 37

severer; *v. a.* separate 463

signefiement, *s.* significance, meaning 2382

signifer, *sm.* zodiac 1907, etc.

signifiance (-nef-), *sf.* significance 2344; *par s.* symbolically 1095

sime, sixth 2377

soleil 401, etc.; **solail** 432, etc.; **solalz** 449: *sm.* sun

solivag, *s.* small poisonous creature 1337; see Du Cange s. v. 'solifugum'

sols 415, 443; **solz** 1558: *sm.* sun

suduiant, *sm. pl.* seducers, deceivers 2105

suef, *adv.* leisurely 1193

suffraite, *s.* indigence, privation 2775

suffrance, *s.* permission, suffrance 2750; suffering 2755

suffrir 1533, 2108; *v. a.* endure 1108, 2634, 2736; await 2628; permit (+*inf. constr.*) 4n: *v. n.* endure, suffer 1533, 2108, 2735; *v. refl.* (+*inf.*) allow oneself to be 2206

sumunt, *ind. pr.* 3 of **sumundre,** *v. a.* warn against, predict 1658; remind, point out 1998; harass, press 2660

suratendre; *v. n.* wait too long 2138

sure, *adv.; acurt s.* comes to in abundance 137

surquiderie, *s.* presumption 2059, 2696

surquidez (sor-) *s. nom.* presumptuous person 2814, 2836

surunder; *v. n.* overflow 877, cover the land 1115

susprisement, *adv.* unexpectedly 2139

sustenement, *s.* means of support 367

sutil, *adj.* rare 2246

suverain, *adj.* upper 1845, highest, uppermost 2295

tapir 1086, *v. n.* hide 1084, 1086

taster 2151, *v. a.* try, taste

tempree, *pp. adj.* temperate 435

tenant (-aunt), *adj.* viscous 1650, avaricious 2845

tencer; *v. a.* maintain 64; *v. n.* argue, nag, dispute 2066, 2069

tendre; *v. n.* extend 1076 R, 1144, 1148, 2488; direct one's course 1923;

tenir; *fut.* 3 **tendra** 2523: *v. a.* hold; (+*o*) hold with 2523

tendrement, *adv.* moderately 448

tenve, *adj. f.* thin, diluted (of liquid) 1568; rarefied (of star) 2449 C

tenvesse (-sce), *sf.* thinness, weakness 1510; volatile portion 1612

terremute, *s.* earthquake 1501

tessun, *s.* badger 32

tirer; *v. a.* draw, attract 1714; *v. n.* (+*a*) hold to, lean toward 13

torture, *sf.* injustice 2577

trebble, *adj.* triple-rowed (of teeth) 678; *a t.* threefold 116

tref, *sm.* sail, craft, boat 1194

trere 2418, *v. a.* derive, draw, attract, inhale, absorb, pursue (a course), bring 507, etc.: *v. n.* draw, exert suction 1481; (+*a*) lead to 80, 2418, 2546; *v. refl.* extend 1144

treschaufer; *v. a.* warm up 2536

trescurt, *ind. pr.* 3 of **trescurre,** *v. a.* traverse 1839, 1858

tresfurmer; *v. a.* arrange, set up 2281

treslable, *adj.* most unstable 89n

tresnoer; *v. a.* cross (of water) 1663; *v. n.* cross the sea 1284

trespercer; *v. a.* transfix, pass through 699, 1725

tresposer; *v. a.* place at intervals, arrange 2331

tressuer, *v.* sweat 332

tresublier; *v. refl.* fall into error 2882

tresveient, *ind. pr.*6 of **tresveeir,** *v. a.* see yonder 2096

tresvoler; *v. a.* traverse (of air) 1787

tricher; *v. refl.* deceive oneself 151

trier; *v. a.* choose 1158

tristur, *sf.* harm, injury 672; affliction, despair 2637

truveure, *s.* discovery 197

uel, *adv.* evenly, equally 2304, 2383

uelement, *adv.* equally 2332

ultre, *adj.* most high 2762n

umble, *adj.* heavy, humid 1701n

umbletez, *s.* humility 2813

unt, *adv.* whence 2462n; *par unt* by which 2535

urer, *inf. subs.* prayer 2873

user; *v. a.* frequent, be in, traverse 2357

utime, eighth 575, 618

uvrer v. **ovrer**

uveraines v. **overaines**

veil 116, **velz** 575, **vels** 1093n: *adj.* old

vein, *adj.* empty, transparent 1665; weak, imperfect, poor 1922

ventaile, *sf.* whirligig 2544n

venz, *sm. nom.* passage, outlet 1563n

verms 705, **verm** 2072, **verme** 2065: *sm.* reptile 705, worm (of conscience or torment) 2065, 2072

vermie, *adj.*? 930n

vertu, *s.*; *a v.* vigorously 1872

viel, *adj.* vital, life-giving 1669

vitaile, *sf.* food 2528

voil, *s.* will 289

voillance, *sf.* purpose 157

wai, *adj.* erratic, wandering 1798

ywes, *sf.* mares 931n G

INDEX OF PROPER NAMES

PROPER names are identified by their English equivalents when these exist, otherwise by the Latin forms which they represent. Occasionally both the English and Latin forms are given when these differ widely. For names which remain unchanged in English line-references only are added. Attention to notes is indicated by the letter n following the line-reference.

Cesariene, Mauritania Caesariensis 1239

Chaldee, Chaldaea 767

Chalie, Caria, a country of Asia Minor 946n

Cham, Ham, son of Noah 810, 816

Chambises, Cambyses 883

Champaine, Campania 1109

Chanaan, Canaan, son of Ham 810, 816

Chananee, the land of Canaan 809

Chao, brother of Helenus and Hector 1045

Chaonie, Chaonia, a district of Greece 1041, 1046

Cheo, Achaeus, king of Achaia 1066

Chipre, Cyprus 1285

Choatres, Coatres, a nation of India 566

Ciclopes, a nation of India 622

Ciht v. Sithie

Cilice, Cilicia 955

Clement (seint), Saint Clement 969

Coile, Aeolus, god of the wind 1326n

Colchi, a nation living in the Caucasus Mountains 900

Colcos, Colchis 1297n

Colubrie, island of Formentera 1351n

Comagent, Commagene, a country bordering on Phoenicia 793

Constentin, the Emperor Constantine 1025n

Constentinoble, Constantinople 1024n

(1) Corinthe, Corinthus 1067n

(2) Corinthe, city of Corinth 1068n

Crete, island of Crete 1288

Crise, a city of Taprobanes (Ceylon) 547

Crist, 2679, Jhesu Crist 2887; Christ

Cumee, Gallia Comata, Gallia Lugdunensis 1145n

Cus, Cush, son of Ham 771

Cyclades, a group of islands in the Ionian Sea 1299

Cyclope, the Cyclops 1321

Cynope, the Scinopodae, a nation of India 623n

Cyrene, a city of Cyrenaica 1215

Cyrinus, bishop of Syria, Appendix 29

Dacie, Dacia 990

Dalmathie, Dalmatia 1034

Damas, city of Damascus 787

Danemarche, Denmark 1013

Danubie, the Danube 988, 991, 999, 1015

David, King David 813, 2872

Didon, Queen Dido 1221

Deu 55, etc.; Deus 350, 1450, 2474; Dez 2431 (corrector in P): God

Disis, δύσις, Western quarter of sky 2278

Eale, an animal of India 653

Ebosus, Iviza, one of the Balearic islands 1349

Edisse, error for Elissa, Dido 1222n

Egipte 514, 886; Egypte 863, 883: Egypt

Egipteis Acelé, Aegyptus, king of Egypt 870n

Elen, Helenus, son of Priam 1043n

Elle, Helle 1296n

Ellespont, the Hellespont 1294, 1295

Enee, Aeneas 1139

Engleterre, England 1173

Hector, son of Priam 1043
Hely Adrian(e), Aelius Adrianus, emperor of Rome 825
Helyam, Jerusalem 828
Herculis, Hercules 1333
Herebus, the pit of Hell 1425
Hermes, the Hermus river in Asia Minor 947
Hesperus, the Evening Star 1860
Hiades, the constellation Hyades 2405
Horeb, Mount Horeb 775
Horest, Orestes 1067n
Hunnie, Hunnia 913
Hyberie, Iberia (modern Georgia) 929
Hystre, the Danube (Ister) 1078
Hystrie, Istria 1077

Illico (mer), the Adriatic Sea 1032n
(1) Inde, India 506, 531, 537, 563, 565, 569, 715, 720, 1710
(2) Inde, the Indus river 532, 721, 1198
Indie, Numidia 1231n
Indien (mer), The Indian Ocean 711

Jacob 808
Jake (seint), Saint James the Apostle 2125
Japheth, son of Noah (Gen. 10, 1) 1021
Jason, 1298
Jebusen, Jebus, son of Canaan 814n
Jebuz-Salem, Jerusalem 818
Jehenne, Gehenna 1421
Jerusalem 811, 813, 817
Jetro, Jethro 778n
Jhesu, Jesus 2121, 2679 RC, 2887
Johan (seint), Saint John the Apostle 936

Jordan 802, 845
Jove 1947, Jovem 2019, Jovis 1891, 1963, 1965: the planet Jupiter
Juda, Judah, son of Jacob 818
Judee, Judea 807
Jugnice, Jugurtha 1232n
Jupiter, King of the Gods 976

Karibde, Charybdis 1320

Laciun, Latium 1085
Lateranes, the Lateran buildings at Rome 1103
Lengres, the Loire river (Liger) 1154
Leun, Lyons 1144n
Leunais, Gallia Lugdunensis 1147n
Liban, Mount Lebanon 801
Libe 868, Libie 1201; Libya
Libie, Lydia 949n
Libien (mer) the Libyan Sea 1208, 1291
Libre, Libra, seventh sign of the zodiac 2381
Licie, Lycia 963
Liconie, Lycaonia 945
(1) Lide, ? 964n
(2) Lide, King Lydius or Lydus 950
Liun, Leo, fifth sign of the zodiac 2369
Lucifer, the Morning Star 1861
Lumbardie, Lombardy 1119; Italy 1324
Lusitane, Lusitania, a province of Spain 1166

Macrobins, the Macrobios, a nation of India 583
Madian, the land of Midian 777
Madianite, the Midianites 781

Magog, a nation east of the Caspian Sea 559n

Manticora, an animal of India 675

Marie, the Virgin Mary 2679, 2702

Mars, the planet Mars 1887, 1946, 1961, 2015

Marsille, the city of Marseilles 1330

Mede, King Medus 730

Medie, Media 729

Mediterraine 464n, **-teraine** 784; **-terin** 862, 1016, 1027: the Mediterranean Sea

Menee, the Island of Meroe 1371n

Meodides, the Maeotides Marshes (Lake Maeotis or Sea of Azov) 982

Mercur 1851, 1955, 1957; **Mercurie** 1943n; **Mercurius** 2007: the planet Mercury

Mesopotamie, Mesopotamia 746

Messageth, the Massagetae, a nation east of the Caspian Sea 899

Messie, Moesia 1017

Messimbria, μεσημβρία, Southern quarter of sky 2280

Moabite, the Moabites 779

Molvent, a name for Zephirus 1704

Monoceros, an animal of India 689

Montrine, a name for Sicily (Trinacria) 1315

Moretaigne, Mauritania 1235

Morte Mer, the Dead Sea 1644

Moyses, Moses 776

Mutun, Aries, first sign of the zodiac 2345, 2352

Nabaioth, Nebajoth, son of Ishmael (Gen. 25, 13) 854

Nabathé, the Nabathaei a nation of Arabia 853

Nazareth 834

Nembroc, Nimrod, son of Cush (Gen. 10, 8) 756, 1653

Nerbone, city of Narbonne 1149 *CDG*

Nerboneys (France), Gallia Narbonensis 1148 *CDG*, 1150 *CDG*

Nicee, Nicaea, a city of Asia Minor 939

Nil, the Nile 509, 873, 877, 1371

Ninivé, Nineveh 749

Ninois, King Ninus 751

Noé, Noah 815, 925

Norich, Noricum, a name for Bavaria 1003

Norweie, Norway 1013

Numide, Numidia 1334

Orcoban, the Oscobares Mountains 506n

Orestes, a nation of India 566

Orkenie, the Orkney Islands 1177, 1187

Ovides, the poet Ovid 968

Padus, the Po 1121

Palestin, a name for the city of Ascalon in Palestine 804

Palestine 803, 829, 833

Pamphilie, Pamphylia 964

Pannonie, Pannonia 1075

Parchie 722, 728; **Parthie** 767n R: Parthia

Parithone, Paratonia (Paraetonium), a city of Libya 1204

Pelope, King Pelops 1062

Pelopenens, the Peloponnesus 1061n

Pennine, Pannónia 1019n

(1) **Pentapolis,** a country between Arabia and Palestine 837n

(2) **Pentapolis,** a name for Cyrenaica in Northern Africa 1211

Perdue v. Ydle
(1) **Perse,** Persia 735
(2) **Perse,** King Perseus or Persus 736
Persipolin, city of Persepolis 737
Pessuns, Pisces, twelfth sign of the zodiac 2401
Phenon, a name for the planet Jupiter 1892n
Pheton, a name for the planet Saturn 1896
Philene (mer), a name for the Libyan Sea 1206
Phison, the Ganges 505
Pigneos (munt), error for Pygmaeos, the Pygmies 569n
Pirro, Pyrrhus 1036
Platun, Plato 1366
Pliades, the Pleiades 2409
Pol (seint) Saint Paul 962, 2787
Pontil (mer) 967, **Pontin** 1001; the Black Sea
Pontus, a region of Asia Minor 965
Protomeu 1278, **Prothomeu** 1279; Prometheus
Ptolomaide, Ptolemais, a city of Cyrenaica 1214
Puille, Apulia 1113 (cf. Schwan-Behrens, sec. 11R)
Pyroys, a name for the planet Mars 1888

Ratisbon 1006n
Reblate, Reblata, a former name of Antioch 791n
Rifei (munz), Riphaean Mountains 978
Rin 1129, 1131, 1140; **Ren** 994: the Rhine
Rome 823, Appendix 26, 31, 34, 40; **Rume** 1091, 1097

Romul 1092, **Romulus** 1099; Romulus
Ronne, the Rhone 1154
Dane, Danaus, brother of Aegyptus 871n
Ruge Mer 512, 867, 1575; **Mer Ruge** 536: the Red Sea
Rumein, the Romans 1225

Saba, Seba, son of Cush (Gen. 10, 7) 770, 771
Sagitrarie, Sagittarius, ninth sign of the zodiac 2395n
Salamun 105, **Salomon** 109, 1601; **Salemon** 819 C: King Solomon
Salem, Jerusalem 812
(1) **Samarie,** the district of Samaria 829
(2) **Samarie,** city of Samaria 831
Sarazin, the Saraceni, a nomad tribe of Arabia 781, 847
Sardin, King Sardinus 1332, 1333
Sardine, Sardinia 1331
Sare, Sarah, wife of Abraham 848
Sarmareth, the Sarmatae 900
(1) **Saturne,** the god Saturn 1080, 1082, 1083
(2) **Saturne,** the planet Saturn 1895, 1948, 1965, 2022, 2023
Sauver, the Saviour, Appendix 14
Scilbon, Stilpon the sage 95n
Scille v. **Stille**
Scorpiun, Scorpio, eighth sign of the zodiac 2387
Sebaste, Sebastia, a name for the city of Samaria 832
Sechin, Cethim, the ancient name of Greece 1030
Sem, Shem, son of Noah 812, 815
Semiramis, Queen Semiramis 757
Septemtriun, the North Wind 1685
Seres, the capital of Serica 903